INSIGHTS FROM
THE *RISALE-I NUR*

Said Nursi's Advice for Modern Believers

INSIGHTS FROM THE *RISALE-I NUR*

Said Nursi's Advice for Modern Believers

Thomas Michel

New Jersey

16 15 14 13   1 2 3 4

Published by Tughra Books
345 Clifton Ave., Clifton,
NJ, 07011, USA

www.tughrabooks.com

Library of Congress Cataloging-in-Publication Data Available

ISBN: 978-1-59784-289-1

Printed by
Görsel Dizayn Ofset Matbaacılık Tic.Ltd.Şti., Istanbul - Turkey

Contents

Said Nursi: The Most Influential Muslim in Modern Turkey 1

My Encounter with the *Risale-i Nur* 7

"Be United Also with the Truly Pious and Spiritual Christians"...........11

Pardon and Peace according to Pope John Paul II and Said Nursi 35

Grappling with Modern Civilization...51

War and Peace..73

The Damascus Sermon: a Spiritual Physician's Prescription for
the Sicknesses of Our Age 85

God's Justice in Relation to Natural Disasters 97

"For You, Illness Is Good Health": Advice in Time of Illness 107

The God-centered Life: an Antidote to a Culture of Violence............125

Dialogue among Believers 139

The Mystery of Human Responsibility...149

The Resurrection of the Dead and Final Judgment 163

Dialogue, Tolerance and Engagement with the Other........................181

Sincerity and Wisdom in the Fully Human Person.............................195

The Prophets: a Blessing for Humankind..207

Democracy and Societal Values: an Evaluation of Social Ethics 219

Theology of Hope and the State of Societies Today............................225

The Supreme Sign: an Invitation to Wonder.......................................239

Index...251

Said Nursi: The Most Influential Muslim in Modern Turkey

S aid Nursi is probably the most influential Muslim thinker in Turkey in the 20th Century. It has been estimated that between 8 and 13 million Muslims regularly study his 6000-page commentary on the Qur'an entitled the *Risale-i Nur*, or "Message of Light," on which Nursi worked for more than 40 years. People don't just read the Message of Light once and go on to something else; the book forms the basis of an ongoing program of spiritual growth.

In the city of Ankara, where I was living until a short time ago, there are about 90 groups who gather every week in faith-sharing sessions to study and discuss Nursi's "Message of Light." In my experience, these sessions appear to be especially attractive to professionals in medicine and engineering and, in Ankara, the capital, to civil servants in various government ministries. They come together in the evening and read a passage from the *Risale-i Nur*; the reading is followed by a discussion guided by one of the experts in the book in order to apply the insights found in this enormous book to their personal and social lives. These experts are often people who have dedicated their whole lives to the study of the Qur'an as elucidated in Said Nursi's commentary.

I first came to know about Nursi and his Qur'an commentary from my students. In 1985, the Pontifical Gregorian University in Rome, where I was teaching, signed an academic agreement with Ankara University's Theology Faculty which entailed an exchange of professors. Until today, every year, a Turkish professor goes to Rome to teach Islamic studies, and I or another professor from Rome teaches Christian theology in Turkey. So, in 1986, after I began teaching in Ankara, some of my students introduced me to the writings of Said Nursi. In those days, very little of the "Message of Light" had been translated into English, so with my students in the evenings I began to read those parts that had been translated and published as small pamphlets.

Several aspects of his thought attracted me immediately. Long before others were speaking of it, Nursi urged unity between his followers, students of the *Risale-i Nur*, and true Christians who were striving to follow the teachings and example of Jesus. He didn't write about "dialogue," because the word wasn't yet in current usage; but he used an even stronger term, *unity*, encouraging true Muslims and Christians to achieve a kind of unity of purpose. Writing before World War I and again after World War II, amidst tensions and enmity between Muslims and Christians, Nursi proposed that the two communities should avoid disagreements and polemics and give a united witness of faith to a world that was suffering from the growth of aggressive atheism. These were the years when the Soviet communist system was advancing through Eastern Europe and even threatening Western European nations like Greece, Italy, and France.

Nursi called for unity and cooperation between the two communities already fifty years before the Vatican II called upon Christians and Muslims to recognize that they should move beyond the conflicts of the past and work together for the common good to build peace, establish social justice, defend moral values, and promote true human freedom. As a Christian whose theological attitudes toward Muslims were formed by the teachings of the Second Vatican Council, I was attracted to learn more about Said Nursi as someone who shared a similar vision to that later proposed by the Catholic Church.

Another aspect of Nursi's thought I find attractive is his strong rejection of violence. Although as a youth he fought in the Ottoman army to repulse the Russian invasion of Turkey in World War I, he later came to the conclusion that the days of the "jihad of the sword" are over. The only appropriate way for Muslims to struggle for their beliefs was the "jihad of the word" or the "jihad of the pen," that is, through personal witness, persuasion, and rational argument.

Nursi was convinced of the primacy of love in Islam. "That which is most worthy of love," he wrote, "is love, and that most deserving of our enmity is enmity. It is love and loving," he went on, "that render people's social life secure and lead to happiness. The time for enmity and hostility is finished," he concluded. Nursi wrote these words 100 years ago this year, in 1911, in a Friday sermon he delivered to several thousand worshipers at the Umayyad Mosque in Damascus. That sermon, which has been translated and published in many languages, has become one of the classics of modern Islamic spirituality.

I can't do justice to all the topics treated in the 6000 pages of the *Risale-i Nur*. Nursi has included treatises directed at the youth, the aged, the sick, prisoners, and victims of disasters. He has a special concern to defend belief in the afterlife, to reconcile the teachings of Islam with science and technology. Some of the most beautiful parts of the *Risale-i Nur* are his contemplative reflections on God's attributes of power, mercy, and love as they are evident in nature and the created universe.

For most of the 20th Century, the Turkish Republic was governed by leaders influenced by the European Enlightenment who regarded religious faith as backward, suitable for simple people and primitive societies but incompatible with modern science and an obstacle to be overcome if the nation is to progress. A dictum often repeated in the intellectual atmosphere of the day held that religion was doomed to wither away as modern people came to accept a scientific understanding of life and society. In this, the thinking of Atatürk, İnönü and their Turkish associates was not much different from that of Garibaldi, Cavour and the other leaders of the Italian Risorgimento, and those whose ideas shaped the Mexican and Russian revolutions.

Faced with this climate of suspicion, many Muslim leaders in Turkey reacted by condemning the political and military authorities as godless agents of Satan. Some went so far as to revolt, which in turn drove the authorities to persecute the religious scholars as enemies of the state. In this conflictual situation, Nursi relied on rational argument. He criticized the government authorities on religious grounds but did not foment rebellion. The legacy of European modernity, he said, has a positive aspect and a negative one. He had no argument with the fruits of science and technology; these he saw as beneficial to humanity. But he felt that by cutting people off from their religious heritage, the leaders were spiritually impoverishing the people. Through its policy of radical secularism, the government was depriving Turkish society of the guidance, the solace, and the hope that comes from faith, so that religious adherence was reduced to a private collection of beliefs and rituals.

One of the insights of Nursi that has had much influence on his followers is his view that the real enemies of Muslims are not one or another group of people. Rather, he said, the real enemies of human-kind are three: *ignorance, poverty,* and *disunity*, and it is against such enemies that Muslims must do jihad with the weapons of knowledge, science, and hard work.

Nursi was not an armchair philosopher offering the world com-fortable platitudes. The lessons he learned and taught were hard won, and many of his experiences read like the scenario of an adventure film. In 1915, Nursi formed and led a volunteer militia against the Russian troops invading Anatolia from the Caucasus. He is credited with being responsible for saving the lives of several thousand Arme-nians at that time by escorting them across battle lines to safety. Nursi was captured by the Russian troops and detained in a prisoner-of-war camp in northern Russia at the time of the October Revolution in 1917. After the war, Nursi was active politically in trying to set the direction that modern Turkey would take after the dissolution of the Ottoman Empire. He had plans for a new type of university, which he called the Madrasah az-Zahra ("The School of Brilliance"), that would combine scientific excellence with moral and religious values, but these hopes never came to fruition due to government opposition.

As time went on, Nursi became convinced that real social change would never occur simply by changing social and political structures. He began to withdraw from public life and urged his disciples to spend their time studying and meditating on the Qur'an. Despite this, Nursi was seen as a threat by the Turkish government. He was sen-tenced to many years in prison and house arrest, and his writings were banned and forbidden to be published or even read in Turkey.

The way the *Risale-i Nur* was written and distributed is itself a story of courage and conviction. Nursi was forbidden paper and pen while he was under arrest, and he was consequently forced to write with smuggled pencil or crayon on scraps of paper, discarded envelopes, in the margins of newspapers, on the backs of labels and soap-wrappers. These fragments were then smuggled out of prison by visitors, mail-men, and sympathetic guards. Forbidden access to printing presses, his followers—many of the scribes were women, and many were students—painstakingly transcribed the "Message of Light" by hand and distributed it secretly. I have personally seen many of these original fragments of the *Risale-i Nur* that circulated as a kind of *samizdat* in Republican Turkey.

Through such primitive methods, Nursi's following continued to grow so that today they number in the millions. In the last years of his life, the Turkish government allowed Nursi a measure of freedom, although he was constantly under surveillance by the military and harassed by a hostile judiciary and bureaucracy. Only in 1956, four years before his death, was Nursi finally exonerated by the courts and his students given permission to print and publish the *Risale-i Nur*. Nursi sent one of the first printed versions of the *Risale-i Nur* to Pope Pius XII about ten years before the opening of the Second Vatican Council. Although I did not succeed in discovering that early copy in the archives of the Vatican Library, I have seen the courteous acknowledgement of the reception of the work sent to Nursi signed by the Papal secretary.

Nursi died in 1960 at the age of 82. He was buried in the city of Urfa, very near the reputed birthplace of Abraham. However, the dramatic events surrounding his life were not yet over. A short time after his death his body was stolen from the tomb in the middle of the night and until today its location has never been disclosed. The presumption is that this was done by the military to keep the tomb from becoming a focal point for anti-government criticism.

Nursi believed that the Islamic community would only be renewed as an instrument for combating the enemies of ignorance, poverty, and disunity once enough Muslims had been personally transformed by the study of his Qur'an commentary.

My Encounter with the *Risale-i Nur*

The essays in this volume are a collection of talks that I have delivered on various occasions, at successive "International Symposia on Bediüzzaman Said Nursi" and in other situations. They are the results of the efforts of one reader of the *Risale-i Nur* to glean some of the wisdom found in this comprehensive commentary on the Qur'an. I do not claim to have a very deep or thorough knowledge of the thought of Said Nursi, but maybe that in itself will recommend this collection to others. This volume is not the elaboration of a specialist, but merely some insights of a dedicated beginner that might be of use to fellow students. For those who have been reading and studying the *Risale-i Nur* for many years, often in the original Turkish, I hope that these essays might occasionally provide fresh perspectives.

I myself am a Christian, in fact, a Catholic priest. One might ask why a Christian is spending his time studying and writing about the thought of a Muslim scholar. Does Said Nursi have anything to say to Christians or others who do not follow the religion of Islam? Are there any points of convergence or agreement between the views expressed in the *Risale-i Nur* and my own deeply held faith convictions?

Actually, I first approached the *Risale-i Nur* with some of these questions. I wanted to see how Said Nursi regarded Christians and whether he felt that there was any hope for mutual understanding and respect between the followers of the two religions. This research resulted in the earliest of the essays included in this book, the one entitled, "Muslim–Christian Dialogue and Cooperation in the Thought of Bediüzzaman Said Nursi."

As time when on, and I continued to study the *Risale-i Nur* further, I realized that this early notion of "Muslim–Christian dialogue" was too timid a concept to comprehend Nursi's more daring proposal. He never uses the word "dialogue," which implies that what Muslims and Christians ought to be doing is *talking* to one another. Instead, he speaks boldly of "Muslims being *united*, or coming into *unity*, with true Christians." This was a daring concept when Said Nursi first enunciated it a century ago, around 1911. However, he never wavered in his view, and down through the years Nursi continued to call for a cessation of hostilities and theological disputes—at least for the time being—so that Muslims and Christians might together confront the challenges of the modern world.

As my studies continued, I was struck by many similarities and parallel lines of thought between the approach of Said Nursi and that of my own fellow Christians. As a Catholic, I was impressed by the frequent convergence of ideas and approaches between Said Nursi and recent Popes such as Paul VI and John Paul II. In "The Ethics of Pardon and Peace: a Dialogue of Ideas between the Thought of Pope John Paul II and the *Risale-i Nur*," I explore how Bediüzzaman and the late Pope regarded the essential preconditions for building a true peace. In "Nursi's View of Tolerance, Engagement with the Other, and the Future of Dialogue," I tried to juxtapose Nursi's positions with those expressed by Pope Paul VI in his encyclical *Ecclesiam Suam*.

Thus, one thing led to another and I found myself gaining many new insights from the *Risale-i Nur* that enriched my faith life as a committed Christian. There is a universal aspect to true wisdom, whatever its origin and by whomever it is expressed. There is not a Muslim wisdom intended exclusively for Muslims and a Christian wisdom of value only for Christians. It is the one and same God who generously uses holy and insightful persons to guide and inspire us all. When a man like Said Nursi devotes so many years of his life—from the activism and idealism of youth, through the imprisonment and persecution of his middle years, to the pains and illnesses of old age—to the reading, study, and prayerful contemplation of the Qur'an, he has much to teach all of us. He becomes an instrument by which God implants His guidance in the hearts of men and women.

In all this, there need not be any sense of rivalry or aggressive competition. Those who seek to be faithful to God message and obedient to God's will should not hesitate learn from one another, even when their religious convictions are different. Said Nursi himself states in his beautiful "Treatise on Sincerity" that rivalry and disagreement also arise even among good people who are sincerely seeking the truth. This is not so much the result of their lack of zeal and good intentions but is due, rather, to their very eagerness to guide and instruct others.

Said Nursi explains how a spiritual guide can get seduced by jealousy and a sense of rivalry: "Thinking to oneself, 'Let me gain this reward, let me guide these people, let them listen to me,' he takes up a position of rivalry towards a true brother who faces him and who stands in real need of his love, assistance, brotherhood and aid. Saying to oneself, 'Why are my pupils going to him? Why don't I have as many pupils as he has?' he falls prey to egoism, inclines to the chronic disease of ambition, loses sincerity, and opens the door to hypocrisy."[1]

Thus, our good intentions can themselves become distorted by pride and end in personal ambition, dishonesty and hypocrisy. Those whom we should see as fellow pilgrims on the path of doing God's will, we regard as competitors or rivals or, in the worst case, even enemies. According to Said Nursi, the only way to prevent this corruption of ideals is to strive for pure sincerity. "'God's pleasure is won by sincerity alone,' and not by a large following or great success," he states. "Quantity should not receive too much attention, for sometimes to guide one man to the truth may be as pleasing to God as guiding a thousand. Moreover, sincerity and adherence to the truth require that one should desire Muslims to benefit from anyone and in any place they can. To think 'Let them take lessons from me so that I gain the reward' is a trick of the lower soul and the ego."

There is much to be learned in these words and in this attitude toward the truth. I thank God that I have been able to learn much from Said Nursi's writings. It is my hope that Muslims, Christians, and others might also find benefit in the simple reflections on the *Risale-i Nur* to be found in these essays.

---

[1]   Said Nursi, *The Flashes*, The Twentieth Flash, "On Sincerity," İstanbul: Sözler Neşriyat, 2000, p. 204.

"Be United Also with the Truly Pious and Spiritual Christians"[2]

1. Nursi and interreligious dialogue

Already in the early part of the 20th Century, Said Nursi proposed to his students that they should "unite also with the truly pious and spiritual Christians." Nursi never spoke of "dialogue with Christians," for the term did not come into current usage until after his death in 1960. Consequently, one would search in vain in the *Risale-i Nur* for references to Said Nursi's views about dialogue with Christians or the followers of any other religion. Instead, Nursi used a stronger word: Muslims should strive for *unity* with faithful, God-fearing Christians. Nursi's advocacy of Muslim–Christian unity was based on a conviction that Muslims and Christians had a God-given task in society that could only be achieved by working together. His awareness of the need for cooperation and friendship between the two communities of faith mark him as one of the pioneers of dialogue in the 20th Century.

For Nursi, the days of the "jihad of the sword" are over, so there is no question of any obligation to engage in warfare against the People of the Book. But questions regarding the proper way for Muslims to relate to the followers of the earlier religions remain. Was it determined by God that Muslims and Christians should live in enmity and rivalry, or that one community would be in full possession of the truth while the other was irredeemably in error? Are there any grounds on which Muslims might propose that the two communities of believers

---

2   The original version of this essay was prepared for the *Brill Companion of Said Nursi Studies*.

could live in a mutually beneficial way and together make a contribution to society and work for the good of all? What can be said concerning Qur'anic verses such as the following: *"O you who believe! Take not the Jews and Christians for friends and allies"* (al-Maedah 5:51). Nursi addressed such questions in the *Risale-i Nur*, not in the form of a systematic treatise on the Islamic theology of religion, but variously, as events in his life and questions from students raised the issues.

If Nursi had held that Christians and Muslims were irreconcilable enemies, to be opposed by pen or sword, any real dialogue between the members of the communities would have been impossible. Similarly, if Nursi had believed that the teachings of the "heavenly" religions, as he called them, were so different and contradictory that no meaningful encounter was conceivable, or if he considered Christianity as being wholly corrupt and devoid of any holiness, truth, and goodness, he could not be said to advocate a dialogue of religions. However, what is clear from the *Risale-i Nur* is that Nursi regarded the other religions as possessing elements of holiness, truth, and goodness. These elements can be considered as legitimate bases for a real conversation and cooperation among the followers of the three religions.

This chapter will be limited to Nursi's views about relations with Christians and the possibility of dialogue and unity with the true followers of Christ. Living most of his life in Eastern and Central Anatolia, Nursi wrote relatively little about relations with Jews, with whom he had few dealings. The reasons for his silence concerning the religions of Buddhism, Hinduism, and other "Asian" religions is still more obvious, for such were not encountered in Anatolia in his day. The *Risale* was written as practical information and advice aimed at forming devout Muslims and answering their questions, not as a theoretical treatise on religions. The great majority of non-Muslims who the students of the *Risale-i Nur* encountered in their daily lives were Christians, so it was on the relationship of Muslims to these that Nursi focused.

2. The universality of worship of God

Nursi affirms that not only Muslims, but also the followers of other religions worship God, each in their own way. Not only does the inanimate world worship the one God by performing the natural functions commanded by God, but also the various religious communities seek to do God's will as they understand it. This is an argument, according to Nursi, for the existence of the One God. If the followers of the earlier religions perform a certain type of genuine worship of God, it follows that there is a kind of spirituality and holiness present in them. Nursi asserts:

> The absorption of each class of men in a mode of worship dictated by their innate dispositions, the species of worship engaged in by other animate beings, as well as inanimate beings, through the performance of their essential functions, the way in which all material and immaterial bounties and gifts in the cosmos become means inciting men to worship and thanks, to praise and gratitude; the fashion in which all the manifestations of the unseen and epiphanies of the spirit, revelation and inspiration, unanimously proclaim the exclusive fitness of one God to receive worship—all of this in most evidential fashion, proves the reality and dominance of a single and absolute Divinity.[3]

In holding that "the fashion in which all the manifestations of the unseen and epiphanies of the spirit, revelation and inspiration unanimously proclaim the exclusive fitness of one God to receive worship," Nursi is inviting Muslims to acknowledge some of the ways in which the One God might be active also in other religions. When taken up by later Muslim scholars, such theological investigations could form the basis of an "Islamic theology of religions." Moreover, if evidence of spiritual, inspired, and revelatory experiences is to be found among the followers of other religions, as well as demonstrations of the unseen Divine activity, or grace, a basis for religious communication between Muslims and adherents to the earlier religions is posited. While not developing this theme of grace-filled Divine activity in other religions in a systematic way, Nursi establishes the possibility of God's being at work in and through other religions.

---

[3] Said Nursi, *The Rays*, The Supreme Sign, Second Chapter, First Truth, İstanbul: Sözler Neşriyat, 2002, p. 172.

3. The possibility of friendship

If there are genuine elements of holiness and goodness in the other religions, it follows that is proper for Muslims to befriend and love their neighbors of the People of the Book. Challenged that this was against the teaching of the Qur'an (5:51), Nursi demonstrated that the Qur'anic verse in question was not a general (*'amm*) injunction to be applied to all times and places where Muslims cohabit with Jews or Christians, but rather a limited or specific (*mutlaq*) judgment whose application is determined by the concrete situation. Muslims can befriend Jews and Christians on the basis of the "Islamic" qualities that many individual Jews and Christians possess. Nursi illustrates his case by citing the human example of a Muslim man married to a woman from one of these communities. "Of course he should love her,"[4] states Nursi.

Nursi affirms, even in the most tragic of circumstances, that he had Christian friends. When Nursi visited Van after the destruction of the city as a result of the Russian invasion, he wept without distinction for both the Christian and Muslim victims, who had been his "friends and acquaintances." "Most of the people of those houses had been my friends and acquaintances. The majority of them had died in the migrations, may God have mercy on them, or had gone into wretched exile. Only the Armenian quarter remained, all the Muslim houses of Van had been leveled."[5]

4. The two sides of Europe

Nursi accepts that because of the elements of goodness and truth in the earlier heavenly religions, Muslims can make friends with their adher-

---

[4] Said Nursi, *Münazarat*, İstanbul: Yeni Asya Yayınları, 1996, pp. 70–71. The *Münazarat* [*Dialogues*] is a part of the *Risale-i Nur* that has not been translated in full into English. First published in 1913, it relates the "dialogues" or question-and-answer sessions that Nursi held with tribesmen in Eastern Anatolia. I have used the partial translations made by Zeki Sarıtoprak in "Said Nursi's Teaching on the People of the Book; a Case Study of Islamic Social Policy in the Early Twentieth Century, in Islam and Christian-Muslim Relations," *Islam and Christian–Muslim Relations* (Birmingham), II/3, 2000, pp. 325–328.

[5] *The Flashes*, The Twenty-Sixth Flash, For the Elderly, p. 315.

ents. Moreover, the challenges of modern life provide a positive impetus that should lead Muslims and Christians into dialogue and cooperation. Nursi adopts a nuanced approached to what he calls "Western" or "European" civilization. He acknowledges that modern civilization is not all bad and affirms that there are many good qualities evident in Western civilization. The positive qualities to be found in European civilization derive "especially from the guidance of the Qur'an, *and from the preceding revealed religions.*"[6]

Historically, the greatest influence on the development of European culture has been from the Christian tradition. The European heritage from true Christianity is to be found in two areas: in those fields of study that promote justice and goodness and in the sciences that are oriented toward social happiness. Nursi states: "There are two 'Europes.' I am not criticizing the Europe of scientific works, of justice and equity, of useful and beneficial artwork for humanity and the welfare of people, with all its inspiration and enlightenment learned from true Christianity and Islam."[7] Nursi has no argument with the achievements of European civilization in the fields of technological progress, good government, and the extension of educational and economic opportunity, but he questions the philosophical assumptions that laid the groundwork for irreligious secularism.

Nursi considers that the positive virtues beneficial for humankind handed on by European civilization are outweighed by a number of negative values that modern civilization has adopted from non-religious and anti-religious philosophies. The result is a two-sided Europe. One current, inspired by the teachings of true Christianity, has worked to establish justice and to develop scientific thought for the benefit of society. The second current, rejecting Europe's Christian heritage, has pursued a variety of atheistic and materialistic philosophies to produce a selfish, impoverished, self-destructive civilization.

With the first current, that is, the Europe of faith, Nursi has no argument, but the second Europe he considers a danger, not only to

---

[6] Said Nursi, *The Words*, The Twenty-Fifth Word, First Light, Third Ray, İstanbul: Sözler Neşriyat, 2002, p. 421.

[7] *The Flashes*, The Seventeenth Flash, Fifth Note, p. 160.

Islam, but to all the revealed religions.[8] "I am addressing the second corrupt Europe which, through the darkness of the philosophy of naturalism and supposing the evils of civilization to be its virtues, has driven mankind to vice and misguidance."[9] In opposing themselves to "the bases of all heavenly laws," those who promote the atheistic current of European civilization produce more harm than good and actually give false guidance to humanity.[10]

Since the Divine and humane values beneficial to humanity are taught not only by the Qur'an, but also by the earlier religions, such values form the basis for dialogue and cooperation between the followers of the "revealed religions" of Judaism, Christianity, and Islam. One can conclude from the *Risale-i Nur* that dialogue among Jews, Christians, and Muslims is a legitimate and vital tool for the religions to carry out their mission to embody and bear witness in contemporary society to the spiritual values found in God's Word.

5. Critique of actual Christians

Although he believed that true Christianity had made a valuable contribution to the development of European civilization, Nursi sharply criticized the actual behavior of Christians and even some of the theological presuppositions of Christian faith. He felt that Christians were led astray by excessive love of the Prophet Jesus, just as, in his view, the Shi'a deviated from the true path through their excessive devotion to Ali.[11] He cites a *hadith* in which Muhammad is reported to have said to Ali: "As was true of Jesus, two groups of people will perish on your account: one because of excessive love, the other because of exces-

---

[8] Said Nursi, *Emirdağ Lahikası*, İstanbul: Sözler Neşriyat, 1959, I / 270. The *Emirdağ Lahikası* is a collection of letters written by Nursi during his period of house arrest in Emirdağ between 1944 and 1951. The collection has not yet been translated into English.

[9] *The Flashes*, The Seventeenth Flash, Fifth Note, p. 160.

[10] *Emirdağ Lahikası*, İstanbul: Sözler Neşriyat, 1959, II / 99–100.

[11] *The Words*, The Thirty-Second Word, Third Stopping-Place, p. 673. Nursi makes a similar observation in regard to the way many Sufis are excessively devoted to their sheikhs and saints. Said Nursi, The Twenty-Ninth Letter, Ninth Section, pp. 531–532.

sive enmity. Christians, on account of their deep love for Jesus, transgressed the limits and called him—God forbid!—'the son of God,' while the Jews, because of their hostility, went to the other extreme by denying his message and virtue."[12]

This disproportionate love for Jesus is, according to Nursi, dangerous for Christians[13] because it leads them to overstep the bounds. Dissatisfied to accept him as a Prophet of God, they affirm a belief in Jesus as Son of God. Nursi denies that Jesus was responsible for such an institutionalized personality cult,[14] for most of the dogmas, regulations and religious practices that focused on Jesus as Son of God were, according to Nursi, developments of a later age.

> In the religion of Jesus, only the fundamentals of religion were taken from Jesus (upon whom be peace). Most of the injunctions concerning social life and the secondary matters of the Law were formulated by disciples and other spiritual leaders. The greater part was taken from former Holy Scriptures. Since Jesus (upon whom be peace) was not a worldly ruler and sovereign, and since he was not the source of general social laws, the fundamentals of his religion were as though clothed in a garment of common laws and civil rules taken from outside, then given a different form and called the Christian law. If this form is changed and the garment transformed, the fundamental religion of Jesus (upon whom be peace) may persist.[15]

It is worth noting that, according to Nursi, although the basic elements of Jesus' teaching ("the fundamentals of his religion") came to be dressed in man-made, earthly practices that were eventually known as "the Christian law", i.e., religion, it is still possible for the followers of Jesus to transform the evolved structures and restore the primordial Prophetic faith brought by Jesus. Nursi describes this by analogy to the various wardrobes (the externals of religion) a person may wear, while the person (that which is fundamental) remains the same.

---

[12] Said Nursi, *The Letters*, "The Miracles of Muhammad," Sixth Sign, İstanbul: Sözler Neşriyat, 2001, p.137.

[13] *The Flashes*, The Fourth Flash, p. 41.

[14] *The Letters*, The Twenty-Ninth Letter, Seventh Section, p. 510.

[15] Ibid., p. 508.

Thus, he believes that Christians can discard the historically conditioned practices and dogmas that evolved after the time of Christ and dress themselves anew in the original teachings of the Prophet Jesus.

In regard to Scripture, Nursi claims that the Biblical texts have undergone change. The Divine Speech brought by the Prophets has been adulterated by translations, additions, and human interpretations and, as a result, the Biblical passages do not display the unique extraordinary power of the Qur'anic text. This charge of *tahrif*, or corruption of Scripture, is not new with Nursi, but was a perennial feature of Islamic polemic in regard to the People of the Book. However, Nursi does not raise the issue in a polemical context so much as to underline the splendor of the Qur'an.

> The words of the Torah, the Bible, and the Psalms do not have the miraculous quality of those of the Qur'an. They have also been translated again and again, and a great many alien words have become intermingled with them. Also, the words of commentators and their false interpretations have been confused with their verses. In addition, the distortions of the ignorant and the hostile have been incorporated into them. In these ways, the corruptions and alterations have multiplied in those Books.[16]

It was not the fundamentals of faith but the later developments that occurred in Christian history that caused Islam and Christianity to diverge in many respects.[17] Nursi holds that the original, true Christianity has been corrupted by the writings of materialist philosophers, which have engendered self-centered and egoistic tendencies among Christians.[18] Under the influence of philosophical thought, Christians today understand others than God as being the actual causes of things, in contrast to the Islamic view (at least, of the Ash'arite orthodoxy followed by Nursi) of God as the only true cause of all that occurs.

At the popular level, the Christian acceptance of causality translates into a belief that their clergy and saints can independently inter-

---

[16] *The Letters*, "The Miracles of Muhammad," Sixteenth Sign, Second Proof, p. 201.

[17] *The Letters*, The Twenty-Ninth Letter, Seventh Section, p. 510.

[18] Said Nursi, *The Damascus Sermon*, Second Addendum, Second Part, İstanbul: Sözler Neşriyat, 1989, p. 119.

cede and bestow help and favors on devotees. To this popular perception he contrasts the Islamic position in which Prophets and holy persons are but manifestations of the power and qualities of the One God, unable to assist others or achieve anything without the unique enabling power of God. It can be observed that Nursi's formulation coincides better with the Christian theological position, that the saints can achieve nothing on their own and that all grace and power come from God, than does the popular perception of many Christians.

> Because it has been corrupted, present-day Christianity considers causes and intermediaries to have an effect, and looks on them as signifying themselves. Their belief in Jesus as the son of God and in the priesthood demands and urges this. They regard their saints for their own sakes as though they do not signify another ... We [Muslims] look on the saints as signifying the meaning of another, that is, as a place of reflection and manifestation, like a mirror spreads the sunlight.[19]

This observation provides the basis for Nursi's view, which runs throughout the *Risale-i Nur*, that there is a "true Christianity" brought by the Prophet Jesus and still followed by a certain number of his disciples, and a "false, corrupted Christianity" that is the result of human interventions and innovations. When Nursi addresses "Europe," he is usually referring to those elements and currents of European civilization that have rejected the sound Christian teaching and inspiration that comes from the person and message of Jesus.[20]

Nursi admits that Muslims as well have not been immune from corrupting developments. Both through the introduction of "Masihiyyat" from early Christian converts to Islam[21] and of "Isra'iliyyat" intro-

---

[19] *The Damascus Sermon*, Second Addendum, Second Part, p. 118. Cf. also, *The Letters*, The Twenty-Sixth Letter, Third Topic, p. 384.

[20] "O Europe corrupted with vice and misguidance and drawn far from the religion of Jesus!" *The Flashes*, The Seventeenth Flash, Fifth Note, p. 161.

[21] Said Nursi, "In the time of the Companions of the Prophet (peace and blessings be upon him) most of the Jewish and Christian scholars entered Islam, and their former knowledge became Muslim along with them. Some of their former knowledge which was contrary to the truth was imagined to be a part of Islam." *The Words*, The Twenty-Fourth Word, Third Branch, Third Principle, p. 351.

duced by converts from Judaism, as well as borrowings from Greek philosophy[22], Muslims adopted views incompatible with Qur'anic teaching which sowed confusion in their ranks. In a criticism of the popular misperceptions concerning Islam that were prevalent in his day, Nursi wrote: "Abandoning the essence and kernel of Islam, we fixed our gaze on its exterior shell. Through misapprehension and ill-manners, we did not afford Islam its right nor pay it its due respect. ... We mixed Isra'iliyyat with the fundamentals of belief, and stories with the tenets of faith, and metaphors with the truths of belief, and did not appreciate its value."[23]

Nursi saw lessons for Muslims in Turkey that could be derived from the unhappy religious history of Europe. In obvious references to Inquisition trials and the Galileo affair, he criticizes the Catholic Church for having silenced its scholars and having demanded blind adherence to authority.[24] In the political sphere, the Catholic Church came to be instrumentalized by the ruling classes in order to maintain their power and control the poor. When the poor rose up against unjust rule, they rejected the Church as well.

> For a long time in France, the Christian religion, and particularly the Catholic Church, had been a means of domination and despotism in the hands of the upper and ruling classes. By that means the upper class perpetuated its influence over the ordinary people. It was a tool for oppressing the patriots, those who were awakened among the common people and were called Jacobins, and a tool for oppressing the freedom-seeking thinkers, who attacked the despotism of the upper class tyrants. Since for nearly 400 years it had been considered to be a cause, through revolutions in Europe, of overturning the stability of social life, the Catholic Church was attacked, not in the name of irreligion, but by the other Christian sects.[25]

---

[22] *Münazarat*, p. 7. Cited by Şükran Vahide, *Islam in Modern Turkey: An Intellectual Biography of Bediüzzaman Said Nursi*, Albany: SUNY Press, 2005, pp. 162.

[23] *Münazarat*, pp. 16-18. Cited by Vahide, *Islam in Modern Turkey*, pp. 161–162.

[24] *The Letters*, The Twenty-Ninth Letter, Seventh Section, p. 510.

[25] Ibid., p. 509.

6. Possibility of virtue among Christians

Despite his critique of the actual practice of Christianity, Nursi notes that Christians, even though they do not accept Muhammad as Prophet, are not abandoned by God. They can experience a kind of Divine grace (light, *nur*) that pervades their lives, giving rise to a type of religious faith and producing ethical behavior and good character. He wrote: "Even if they cast out from their hearts the light of the Prophet Muhammad (peace and blessings be upon him), lights of a sort may remain. They may continue to have a sort of belief in their Creator and in Moses and Jesus (peace be upon them), which will allow them to attain good morals and character."[26] Thus, it is in their faith in God as Creator and their obedience to God's commands as they know them through the Biblical Testaments of Moses and Jesus that Christians and Jews can arrive at pious and ethically upright lives.

To the pious and obedient Christian or Jew, Nursi contrasts the unbelieving Muslim who has rejected his Islamic faith and Prophet and consequently has nothing to sustain and enrich his spiritual life. Such a person will not accept another Prophet and will find himself lost and alone in a secular wasteland. However, the Christian, who has never known Muhammad as Prophet, is still able to rely on his Christian faith and national heritage and in this way can continue to grow in virtue and hope. Nursi asks: "Do you not see that a Westerner who rejects the Prophet Muhammad (peace and blessings be upon him) can still console himself with his Christianity and his Western civilization, which contains elements of his nation's customs? It is possible for him to preserve in his spirit some laudable virtues and make praiseworthy efforts to improve his worldly life."[27]

Nursi's concern is obviously with those Muslims who have abandoned Islam and follow a secular, non-religious way of life. He acknowledges that, by comparison, the lives of Christians who conscientiously follow their religion are more characterized by praiseworthy qualities

---

[26] *The Words*, The Twenty-Fourth Word, Fifth Branch, p. 373.

[27] Said Nursi, *Mathnawi al-Nuriya [Epitomes of Light]*, İzmir: Kaynak A.Ş., 1999, pp. 466–467.

and efforts to progress in virtue. It is not only the deeply devout believer who can display sensitivity to religious matters. Even a Christian who does not regularly follow the practice of his religion can provide positive input to social life and respond faithfully to God in many religious demands. "A Christian may still contribute to society, even if he is irreligious. He may accept some sacred matters and may believe in some of the Prophets, and may assent to Almighty God in some respects."[28]

It is obvious that Nursi does not consider all Christians to be living distant from Divine truth and ethical norms. Some have "good morals and character," display "laudable virtues," make "praiseworthy efforts to improve," and "accept some sacred matters, believe in some of the Prophets, and assent to God in some respects." These realities form the basis for the kind of unity and cooperation to which Nursi calls conscientious Muslims and Christians.

7. The battle against the forces of evil

Although his judgment could be harsh on what he regarded as theological corruptions and innovations, on the religious wars and forms of oppression found in Christian history, and on the sad realities of life and practice among many Christians, Nursi repeatedly expressed a hope that Christians would undergo a purification to live the true message of Christ more faithfully. He was convinced that as Christians come closer to practicing the faith they received from Jesus, they will in the process also come closer to the teaching of Islam.

The starting point for this hopeful expectation is a *hadith* report from Muhammad that states that at the end of time a purified Christianity will be transformed into a kind of Islam.[29] At that point, the renewed Christian community will overcome irreligious and atheistic ideas and behavior to live as faithful followers of Jesus.[30] They will oppose and overcome an antireligious and hedonist way of life repre-

---

[28] *The Letters*, The Twenty-Ninth Letter, Seventh Section, p. 512.

[29] *The Letters*, The First Letter, p. 22.

[30] "On the coming of Jesus (peace be upon him) and emergence of the true Christian religion, the Antichrist's irreligious way will be wiped out and will cease." Said Nursi, *The Rays*, The Fifth Ray, p. 101.

sented by the figure of the Dajjal, the Islamic equivalent of the Antichrist in Christian tradition.

An appreciation of Nursi's expectation of future times demands an understanding of the concept of corporate or collective personality. Unlike most Muslim scholars, who regard the Dajjal as an individual who will be confronted by the man Jesus upon his return to earth, Nursi understands both "Jesus" and "Dajjal" as collectives. According to this reading, "Dajjal" represents not an evil individual but all those materialist, atheistic forces, human and demonic, that oppose faith and obedience to God's will on earth, whereas "Jesus" indicates the collectivity of all those who follow a purified, incorrupt Christian faith and remain faithful to Christ's sound teaching. Nursi expects to see a power struggle between these two human forces, with the eventual victory of the purified Christian community, represented by the collective personality of Jesus, over the powers of irreligion and immorality.

> At the point when the current [of Dajjal] appears to be very strong, the religion of true Christianity, which comprises the collective personality of Jesus (upon whom be peace), will emerge. It will descend from the skies of Divine Mercy. Present-day Christianity will be purified in the face of that reality; it will cast off superstition and distortion, and unite with the truths of Islam. Christianity will in effect be transformed into a sort of Islam.[31]

Also within the Islamic community there will be a struggle. Among Muslims there will appear a Dajjal-like figure called Sufyan, who will seek to turn the Islamic community from its path of truth and uprightness and will try to sow discord, wrongdoing, and disobedience.

> Sufyan, the Islamic Dajjal, ... will try to abrogate some of the eternal injunctions of the shari'a of Muhammad (peace and blessings be upon him). Destroying the material and spiritual bonds of human life, and leaving headstrong, drunken, out-of-control souls, he will unfasten the luminous chains of respect and compassion. By giving people a freedom which is pure despotism so they fall on one another in a swamp of lust, he will open the way to terrible anarchy.[32]

---

[31] *The Letters*, The Fifteenth Letter, p. 78.
[32] *The Rays*, The Fifth Ray, Second Station, p. 114.

Like the Dajjal, Sufyan is not to be interpreted as an individual personality, but as a collectivity of all those within the Islamic *umma* who want to turn the community away from the Straight Path. It includes thinkers, movements, and governments that encourage Muslims to abandon and renounce Islamic teachings. Just as the true Christians will rise up to defeat the Dajjal outside the Islamic community, so will the collective personality of "Mahdi" lead the faithful Muslims to defeat the forces of unbelief in their midst.

In Nursi's understanding of the future, the true Christians and pious Muslims who are struggling against antireligious tendencies in society will not, on their own, be strong enough to defeat the forces of unbelief. But once the two communities unite and work together—which Nursi sees as happening under Muslim initiative—they will achieve a victory for true religion. Jesus, the representative of the unique perennial Prophetic religion, having descended from his place in the heavens, will lead the religious current.

> True religion will become a mighty force. Although defeated before the atheistic current while separate, Christianity and Islam will have the capability to defeat and rout it as a result of their union. Then the person of Jesus (upon whom be peace), who is present with his human body in the world of the heavens, will come to lead the current of true religion.[33]

8. Must Christians convert to Islam?

Nursi's anticipates that in the future true Christianity will re-emerge and "stripping off superstition and corrupted belief, will be transformed into Islam.[34] This view gives rise to further questions. Firstly, does Nursi expect Christianity to go out of existence as a separate religious community at some future time when Christians, in individual or communitarian conversion, adopt Islam? The second question regards Nursi's time line. Is Nursi referring to a far-off eschaton in close proximity to Judgment Day, or is he envisioning Jesus' return and the bat-

---

[33] *The Letters*, The Fifteenth Letter, p. 78.
[34] *The Damascus Sermon*, p. 36.

tle against the Dajjals as occurring during his lifetime or shortly after his death?

Concerning the question of the form that the union between purified Christianity and Islam will take, the ambiguity of Nursi's answer underlines the inevitable ambiguities connected with speaking about the future. Nursi appears to have a complex scenario in mind. He is looking forward to a community of Christians coming to live in a faithful manner according to the message and example of Jesus. They will discard any superstitions that had crept into Christian faith and will reject the unhealthy influences originating in naturalist philosophy.[35] When they engage in this purification, they will become a powerful force, in fact, the only spiritual force strong enough to be able to overcome the attacks of Dajjal, or organized irreligion. Nursi writes:

> He [Dajjal] will be so powerful and long-lived that only Jesus (upon whom be peace) will be able to kill him; nothing else will be able. That is, it will only be a revealed, elevated, pure religion that will be able to overturn his way and rapacious regime, and eliminate them. Such a religion will emerge among the true followers of Jesus (upon whom be peace), and it will follow the Qur'an and become united with it.[36]

Nursi uses various phrases to express the kind of union that he expects between Muslims and Christians. Some expressions give the impression that the Christian community will simply enter Islam and follow the Qur'an.[37] Others imply that as Christians become more faithful in following the teaching and example of Jesus they will "blend the essence of true Christianity with the essence of Islam,"[38] thereby becoming similar to and living near in friendship to Muslims. Elsewhere, he speaks of Christianity "accepting truths of Islam" and evolving into "a *sort* of Islam,"[39] with the implication of their retaining a distinctive Christian identity. Elsewhere, Nursi speaks simply of close

---

[35] *The Letters*, The First Letter, p. 22.

[36] *The Rays*, The Fifth Ray, p. 101.

[37] *The Letters*, The First Letter, p. 22; cf. also The Fifteenth Letter, p. 80.

[38] *The Rays*, The Fifth Ray, Second Station, p. 108.

[39] *The Letters*, The Fifteenth Letter, p. 78.

cooperation between the two purified communities,[40] and of Jesus' returning to bring his religion to its proper conclusion.[41]

Perhaps Nursi's most intriguing insight is his expectation of the emergence of a unique community that maintains its Christian identity but whose faith and practice will be no different from the reality of Islamic faith. It is this purified Christian community that Nursi expects to be instrumental in defeating the Dajjal. He writes: "A zealous and self-sacrificing community known as a Christian community but worthy of being called 'Muslim Christians' [the Muslim representatives of Jesus' mission] will be united with the reality of Islam, and will kill and rout that society of the Dajjal, thus saving humanity from [transgression]."[42]

A second question regards when all this is to happen. Here Nursi is wisely vague. Nursi appears to hold that after true Christianity emerges and unites with Islam there will appear another period of nearly universal apostasy which will last almost until the approach of Judgment Day.

> With the emergence of the true religion of Christianity and its being transformed into Islam, it will spread its light to the great majority of people in the world, but when the end of the world is near, an atheistic current will again appear and become dominant. ... "Allah! Allah!" will not be uttered by a significant group which holds an important position on the earth. The people of truth will form a minority or will be defeated, but they will remain permanently till the end of the world. At the moment Judgment Day occurs, as a sign of Divine mercy, the spirits of the believers will be seized first so that they do not see the terrors of the Last Day, but it will break forth over the unbelievers.[43]

When Jesus returns, it is not necessarily the case that everyone will recognize him. Only those who have remained faithful to his teach-

---

[40] *The Flashes*, The Twentieth Flash, "On Sincerity," p. 203. Cf. also, "In the continents of the future ... there will be only Islam and the real religion of the followers of Jesus, which will transform into Islam and get rid of superstitions and alterations. It will follow the Qur'an and ally (*ittifak eder*) with Islam." *The Damascus Sermon*, p. 36.

[41] *The Letters*, The Fifteenth Letter, p. 78.

[42] *The Letters*, The Twenty-Ninth Letter, Seventh Section, p. 515.

[43] *The Letters*, The Fifteenth Letter, p. 80.

ings will "through the light of belief"[44] identify him. These views have led some contemporary students of the *Risale-i Nur* to the opinion that Jesus has already returned and that the struggle against the Dajjal and Sufyan is not to be construed as occurring at some point in the distant future, but is taking place at the present time.

Some passages of the Risale would seem to support such a "contemporary" interpretation of Nursi's eschatology. Nursi appears to refer to the conflicts taking place in his own Turkey between the proponents of secular society and politics and the more religiously oriented groups, as instances of the conflict between the collective forces of faith and godlessness.

> Because both Dajjals will win the assistance of a secret ... society which nurtures a terrible desire for revenge on Islam and Christianity, and that of another secret society which uses women's liberation as a screen, and because the Islamic Dajjal will deceive even [certain secret] lodges and win their support, they will be supposed to possess tremendous power. Also, it is understood from the divinations of some of the saints that the Dajjal called Sufyan who will come to lead the Islamic world will be a leading politician who is extremely capable, intelligent, and active, who does not like ostentation and gives no importance to personal rank and glory. He will be a military leader who is extremely bold, forceful, energetic, and resolute and does not condescend to fame-seeking; and he will captivate the Muslims.[45]

9. Getting at the root of the problem

Nursi's advocacy of Muslim–Christian unity was not abstracted from the difficult realities of tense and even wartime relations. His formulations of peaceful co-existence arose from challenges posed by angry or worried interlocutors. In the early years of the Turkish Republic, subsequent to the First World War, some Kurdish tribesmen in Eastern Anatolia found the idea of freedom for Greeks and Armenians offensive. Memories of the massacres, betrayals, and retaliations that occurred on all sides were still fresh in their minds, and they asked Nursi's advice

---

[44] Ibid., pp. 78–79.

[45] *The Rays*, The Fifth Ray, Second Station, p. 115.

on the new republican government that was being formed to replace the defunct Ottoman state.

Nursi challenged the tribesmen to see the freedom of Christians as a constitutive element of the Muslims' own freedom.[46] He defended the right of a Christian to be a member of the constitutional assembly, and affirmed that, according to the *shari'a* a Christian could also be appointed governor or military commander. He not only affirmed the right to liberty of these Christian peoples as something commanded by the *shari'a* but went farther to turn the question back on the tribesmen, challenging them to recognize the deeper problem as one that lay at the heart of their own ignorance and hard-heartedness. "Their [the Christians'] freedom consists in leaving them in peace and not oppressing them," he said, "for this is what the *shari'a* enjoins. More than this is their aggression in the face of your bad points and craziness, their benefitting from your ignorance."[47]

Nursi went on to state that the real enemy is not this or that group of Christians, but rather the situation of degradation into which all had fallen. He stated: "Our enemy, that which is destroying us, is Lord Ignorance, his son Poverty Effendi, and grandson, Enmity Bey. If the Armenians have opposed us in hatred, they have done so under the leadership of these three corrupters."[48] This identification of the triple enemy facing not only Muslims, but the conscientious followers of all religions, is one of the most oft-quoted lines from the *Risale*. The value Nursi placed on peaceful *convivenza* can be summarized in his words to the tribesmen: "I am telling you with a certainty that the happiness and salvation of this nation lies only in a friendly relationship with the Armenians. Relations with them are not to be forged in

---

[46] *Münazarat*, pp. 20-21.

[47] Ibid., p. 20. Much later in his life Nursi would contrast the freedom granted to the Christians by the Caliph Umar with the oppression and harassment he received from Republican authorities. *The Rays*, The Fourteenth Ray, pp. 373, 380, 398, 444.

[48] *Münazarat*, (Ottoman edition) in *Asar-ı Bediyye*, n.p, n.d., p. 433. Cited in Şükran Vahide, *Bediüzzaman Said Nursi: The Author of the Risale-i Nur*, İstanbul: Sözler Neşriyat, 1992, p. 95.

a despicable way, but by extending the hand of peace... Enmity is completely the wrong approach."[49]

10. Christians as martyrs

Nursi lived through some of the most disastrous times of the 20th Century. World War I alone resulted in a population loss of more than 30% in Anatolia. Many years later, writing from his period of house arrest in Kastamonu, Nursi learned of the carnage that accompanied the invasion of Russia by the army of Nazi Germany. He felt compassion for his erstwhile Russian captors and regarded them as a kind of martyrs. "Even if those innocent people were unbelievers," he wrote, "in return for the tribulations they suffered due to that worldly disaster, they will receive such a reward from the treasury of Divine mercy that if the veil of the Unseen were to open, a great manifestation of mercy would be apparent in relation to them and they would declare, 'O Lord, thanks be to You! All praise belongs to God.'"[50]

Nursi wrote that he was moved to intense compassion and pity when he saw the sufferings of innocent people, and he was "touched strongly by the affliction, poverty and hunger visited on unfortunates as a result of mankind's disaster and the winter cold, as well as by a harsh non-physical, spiritual cold." He held that those innocent people who died in such circumstances "were martyrs of a sort, whatever religion they belonged to," and that "their reward would be great and save them from Hell." "Therefore," he concluded, "it may be said with certainty that the calamity which those oppressed Christians suffer, those connected to Jesus (upon whom be peace), is a sort of martyrdom for them."[51]

Not all those who died in the war were innocent of wrongdoing. Those who oppressed others and did evil against their neighbors, declared Nursi, will be punished by God. By contrast, he said, "If those

---

[49] *Münazarat*, p. 68. Cited by Sarıtoprak, "Said Nursi's Teaching," p. 326.
[50] Said Nursi, *Kastamonu Lahikası*, İstanbul: Sözler Neşriyat, 1959, p. 45. Nursi was criticized by the state authorities for his view: cf. *The Rays*, The Thirteenth Ray, p. 369.
[51] *Kastamonu Lahikası*, p. 75.

who suffered the calamity hastened to assist the oppressed, strove for the welfare of humanity, and struggled to preserve the principles of religion, revealed truths and human rights," their reward will be so great from God as to completely transcend their earthly suffering.

11. Sincere religion and Muslim–Christian relations

One of the passages of the *Risale-i Nur* to which Nursi attached special importance was his "Treatise on Sincerity." So central is this passage to his thought that Nursi recommended that his students read it at least once every two weeks. The essay, which could alternately be called the "Treatise on Pure Intention," consists of nine counsels by which Nursi's students could build and maintain a loving unity within their group.

Nursi perceived at times an element of rivalry and competition among his disciples. He recognized that such rivalry could easily lead, if left unattended and unchecked, to hard feelings, envy, resentment, and divisive factions in the community. Moreover, Nursi saw that although these tendencies are found among the students of the *Risale-i Nur*, they are even more evident in the broader Islamic community. These divisive inclinations must be taken seriously for, in Nursi's view, disunity—along with ignorance and poverty—amounts to the most serious enemy to be faced by modern society. Combating these destructive tendencies presents pious Muslims with their most pressing social challenges. Nursi's advises his students that the way to combat tendencies toward factionalism and personal aggrandizement is through the practice of "sincerity" or, as I would prefer to translate it, "purity of intention." His advice can be summarized in the form of nine rules:

1. Act positively with love for one's own point of view, but avoid enmity for other views; do not criticize the views of others nor interfere in their beliefs and practices.
2. Build unity within the fold of Islam by recalling the numerous bonds of unity that evoke love, brotherhood, and harmony.
3. Adopt the rule of conduct that the follower of any sound position has the right to say, "My outlook is true, or very good," but not "My outlook alone is true," or "My outlook alone is good," implying the falsity or repugnance of other views.

4. Consider that union with pious friends brings Divine aid and supports one's faith.
5. Remember that error and falsehood will be defeated through unity among pious believers, which depends upon their ability to create a united and collective force to preserve justice and right.
6. Defend truth from the attacks of falsehood.
7. Abandon self-centered egoism.
8. Give up the mistaken notion of self-pride.
9. Reject all trivial feelings aroused by rivalry.[52]

Nursi's point is that differing opinions and views need not cause factions and enmity within the community. If a Muslim is willing to admit that others also have part of the truth, even when they disagree with one's personal view, unity can be maintained despite differences of opinion. However, one will only succeed in this if one does everything solely with the sole intention of worshiping God. To this end Nursi cites the Qur'an: *"Truly We sent the Book down to you in truth, so worship God in sincerity, for God's is sincerely practiced religion"* (Qur'an 39:2).

It is significant that Nursi adds a footnote to his Rules for Sincerity. He cites a *hadith* from Prophet Muhammad: "It is recorded in authentic traditions of the Prophet that at the end of time the truly pious among the Christians will unite with the People of the Qur'an and fight their common enemy, irreligion. In our day, too, the people of religion and truth need to *unite sincerely not only with their own brothers and fellow believers, but also with the truly pious and spiritual among the Christians*, refraining temporarily from the discussion and debate of points of difference in order to combat their joint enemy, aggressive atheism."[53]

By linking the rules for sincerity with the Prophetic expectation of Muslim–Christian unity, Nursi ties the principles of sincerity not only to the way that Muslims should relate to one another, but also applies this advice to the way that Muslims should act towards sincere and pious Christians. Read in the context of Muslim–Christian relations, Nursi's rules for sincerity provide sound guidelines for dialogue between the

---

[52] *The Flashes*, The Twentieth Flash, "On Sincerity," p. 203.
[53] Ibid.

two communities of faith. He urges all to refrain from interfering in the beliefs and practices of others; to build unity by emphasizing those features of shared history that evoke love, brotherhood and harmony; to affirm one's own belief without implying the falsity or inadequacy of others'; to recognize the value of associating with God-centered individuals; to work together with others for justice and right; to strive for humility in one's faith and life. These counsels, applied to relations between Muslims and Christians, offer a sound starting point for the two communities to live together in harmony and cooperation.

12. Discussing faith with Christians

Nursi approved of his students making contact and discussing religious topics with Christians. He felt that the dangers arising from atheistic communism were a common threat that should draw the two religious communities together. Through their contacts and discussions, Nursi felt that Muslims and Christians could better defend religious faith from intellectual attack and could build a greater unity that would foil attempts to drive a wedge among religious believers.

One of Nursi's students, Selahaddin Çelebi, was friends with some Christian missionaries in İstanbul, with whom he read parts of the *Risale-i Nur* and to whom he distributed copies of some passages.[54] Nursi was asked whether this was acceptable and gave the answer: "In connection with Selahaddin giving the American *The Staff of Moses*, we say that it is essential that missionaries, Christian spiritual leaders, and Nurcus [students of the *Risale-i Nur*] be extremely careful. Sooner or later the Northern movement will try to break down the alliance of Muslims and missionaries, in order to defend itself from attacks by Islam and Christianity..."[55]

Conclusion

Nursi's views on living in peace with Christians and cooperating with them to defend religious values such as faith, justice, and moral upright-

---

[54] *Emirdağ Lahikası*, p. 154, 179.
[55] Ibid., p. 156.

ness were ahead of his time. He often had to defend his position as well as to challenge his Muslim interlocutors. He took practical initiatives, considered daring at the time, to promote greater understanding between the two communities. In 1951, he sent a copy of the *Risale-i Nur* to Pope Pius XII in Rome, and received a letter of thanks from the Vatican dated 22 February 1951. Two years later he visited H.B. Athenagoras, the Greek Orthodox Patriarch in İstanbul. Five years before his death, he supported the Baghdad Pact, noting that by it not only would Turks gain 400 million brothers and sisters among Muslim peoples, but that the international accord would also gain for Muslim Turks "the friendship of 800 million Christians"[56] and be a step toward a much-needed peace and general reconciliation between the two communities of faith.

Knowledge of Nursi's views of Muslim–Christian relations will grow in international scholarship as the remaining parts of the *Risale-i Nur*—particularly the all-important collections of letters[57]—are translated into English and other European languages. His writings on the importance of unity between the pious followers of Islam and Christians who are seeking to follow faithfully the religion of Christ has inspired many to a greater openness toward the other religion. Nursi's exhortation to his followers to "be united also with the truly pious and spiritual Christians" to oppose together humankind's perennial enemies of ignorance, poverty, and disunity will remain a lasting legacy of his thought.

---

[56] *Emirdağ Lahikası*, II: 24, 56, cited in Vahide, p. 354.

[57] The *Barla Lahikası*, *Emirdağ Lahikası*, and *Kastamonu Lahikası* are collections of letters sent by Nursi to colleagues and students written during his periods of house arrest in those cities. These portions of the *Risale-i Nur* have not yet been translated into English.

Pardon and Peace according to Pope John Paul II and Said Nursi

At international congresses around the world, there are always many papers and speeches about peace. We hear the speakers of each religious group profess that their religion wants peace, teaches peace, and builds peace. The leaders of various nations say how they are committed to peace among nations, peace in their regions, and civil peace within their societies. There is a human paradox here that we must face. It seems like everyone is in favor of peace, no one ever admits to being against peace, and yet there is very little peace in the world. The problem, I believe, lies in the fact that we are all in favor of peace in the abstract, but without saying in what peace consists, and without examining what is involved in building peace.

Of those religious thinkers in modern times who have attempted to study the concept of peace to explore what is involved in establishing and maintaining peace, I want to compare the thought of two religious scholars of blessed memory who have made a remarkable contribution to the topic. One is a Christian, Pope John Paul II, leader of the Catholic Church, and the other a Muslim, Said Nursi, the author of the *Risale-i Nur*. In this paper I hope to bring together the thinking of these thinkers into a kind of dialogue on the theme: "the ethics of peace." I will do this by summarizing the position of the Pope as the basis or point of view from which I will then read and explain the views of Said Nursi as found in the *Risale-i Nur*.

1. John Paul II: Peace rests on two pillars: justice and forgiveness

As he does every year on 1 January, also this year, 2002, Pope John Paul II sent a message for the World Day of Peace at the beginning of the new year. In this message, the Pope proposes that true peace must rest on two pillars: *justice* and *forgiveness*. Without these, you cannot have real peace. Both justice and pardon are necessary. One element without the other is not enough.

The Pope's reasoning goes like this. Any real peace, if it is to be more than simply a cease-fire or temporary cessation of hostilities, has to get to the heart of the conflict and try to heal the breach in human relations that was ruptured. When peoples are at war, when individuals are estranged and alienated from one another, they are angry, suspicious, and resentful of one another. They see the other as an enemy to be overcome, defeated, the object of retaliation, rather than a fellow-human with whom one ought to be reconciled. Thus, no talk about peace can proceed effectively without addressing the issue of broken relationships and without taking positive steps to repair those relations.

If any group or individual is being oppressed or treated unjustly by another, one cannot hope for peace between the two until there is justice. The Pope sees justice in two ways: firstly, as a "moral virtue," that is, as a human quality which a person can acquire and develop with God's powerful assistance (which Christians call *grace*), and secondly as a "legal guarantee," that is, part of the functioning of the national and international rule of law.[58] The aim of justice, both as a personal quality and as an element of the international system of relations among peoples, is to insure "full respect for rights and responsibilities" and to carry out a "just distribution of benefits and burdens."

Justice is thus a first, indispensable condition for peace. Unless someone treats another justly, that is, with respect for the other's rights and duties and by giving them their proper share of what is due to them, there will be no peace between them. The same holds true between social groups, ethnic groups, peoples and nations. Where there is aggression, oppression, occupation, transgression, there can be no peace. First, justice has to be established, and only then can peace be built.

---

[58] John Paul II, "No Peace without Justice, No Justice without Forgiveness," *Message of His Holiness Pope John Paul II for the World Day of Peace*, 1 January 2002, p. 5.

All of this the Pope has said before. However, in his Day of Prayer for Peace message, he adds another element that he sees as intrinsic to the peace-making process. This is *forgiveness*, which goes beyond strict justice to strive to heal the historical burdens brought about by one individual's or one group's injustice and wrongdoing towards another.

Every nation, every religious or ethnic group, can draw up a long list of grievances that they have against each other, of wrongs that their group has suffered at the hands of the others. This is the human burden of past misdeeds experienced that we all bring into our relations with others and that complicate the way we relate to individual members of the other group. This burden of the past can poison all efforts at cooperation and reconciliation and can flare up into renewed violence at the slightest provocation.

Justice alone is not sufficient to heal these wounds; we need to exercise forgiveness. Forgiveness is, as the Pope states, "a personal choice, a decision to go against the natural instinct to pay back evil with evil." In doing so, it always involves an *apparent* short-term loss, but brings about the possibility of achieving a *real* long-term gain. "Violence," the Pope notes, works exactly the opposite: "opting for an apparent short-term gain, but involving a real and permanent loss."[59] "Forgiveness," the Pope notes, "may seem like weakness, but it demands great spiritual strength and moral courage."

It should not be surprising to discover that both Christianity and Islam lay great importance on the notions of justice and forgiveness, if these are to be the indispensable pre-conditions of peace. In the Gospel, Jesus taught his disciples: "You have heard it said, 'Love your neighbor and hate your enemy,' but I say to you 'Love your enemies and pray for those who persecute you.'" In a similar vein, the Qur'an permits vengeance up to the limits of strict justice but no farther, and always adds: "But it is better to forgive."

---

[59] Ibid., p. 12.

2. Social Ethics in the *Risale-i Nur*

When we turn to the *Risale-i Nur*, we find that for Said Nursi, as for Pope John Paul II, ethics, as the study of what is good and bad, is primarily oriented toward the social sphere. In the thought of both men, a religiously based ethical system above all must treat questions of right and wrong in society, and only secondarily regards the good-ness or evil of acts of private morality. Moreover, both root this pri-macy of social ethics in the Scriptural teaching of their respective faiths. For Said Nursi, ethical systems drawn up by philosophers and put into practice by public and private welfare associations fail to reach the levels of social commitment demanded by the teaching of the Qur'an. He states: "Together with all its associations for good works, all its establishments for the teaching of ethics, all its severe discipline and reg-ulations, [society] has not been able to reconcile these two classes of mankind [the rich and the poor], nor heal the two fearsome wounds in human life."

The evils of which he is speaking here are *social complacency* on the part of the wealthy who feel no responsibility to share what they have with the poor and needy, and *class struggle* on the part of the poor who seek to take by force from the rich what they will not give freely. "The Qur'an, however," Said Nursi continues, "eradicates the first [social irresponsibility] with its injunction to pay *zakat*, and heals it, and uproots the second [class struggle] by prohibiting usury and interest, and cures that. Indeed, the Qur'an stands at the door of the world and declares usury and interest to be forbidden. It reads out its decree to mankind, saying: 'In order to close the door of strife, close the door of usury and interest!' and forbids its students to enter it."[60]

In contrast to the ethics of the jungle where the rich and power-ful take what they can and defend what they have by use of force, or that of class struggle in which the poor and oppressed seek to obtain their rights by force, Said Nursi sees the Divinely-guided ethic pro-posed by Islam as one in which truth, justice and harmony are para-mount. "The civilization the *shari'a* of Muhammad (peace and bless-

---

[60] *The Words*, The Twenty-Fifth Word, First Light, Third Ray, p. 422.

ings be upon him) comprises and commands is this: its point of support is truth instead of force, the marks of which are justice and harmony. Its goal is virtue in place of [selfish] benefit, and its characteristic marks are love and attraction. Its bonds of unity are the ties of religion, country, and class, in place of racialism and nationalism, and the mark of these are sincere brotherhood, peace, and only defense against external aggression. Its life is the principle of mutual assistance instead of that of conflict, and its mark is accord and solidarity."[61]

Said Nursi holds that philosophically-based ethical systems fail to reach the heights of moral teaching proclaimed by the Qur'an because they fail to take into account an essential element of the human reality, that is, human weakness. If an ethical system presumes that people know what they want and will always work to achieve their desired goal, it will miss the point, for in fact people often act against their best interests out of anger, timidity etc. For reasons of selfishness, laziness, ignorance, and the like they fail to achieve what they desire.

However, a religious outlook, exemplified in Qur'anic teaching, takes into consideration and allows for the reality of human weakness and failure by urging believers to return to God in repentance, seeking forgiveness, and starting over. Thus, he calls on believers to be shaped by a "God-given ethics," which he holds to be an essential element in the message of all the Prophets. "Be distinguished by *God-given morals* and turn towards God Almighty with humility, recognizing your impotence, poverty, and defectiveness, and so be a slave in His presence."

Philosophically-based ethical systems, Nursi holds, tend to ignore this element of human nature and arrogantly aim at perfection through human efforts alone. This basically amounts to self-deception. "The essence of humanity," he states, has been kneaded with infinite impotence, weakness, poverty, and need, while the essence of the Necessarily Existent One is infinitely omnipotent, powerful, self-sufficient, and without need."[62] He concludes: "The aim of humanity and duty

---

[61] *The Damascus Sermon*, Seeds of Reality, p. 106.
[62] *The Words*, The Thirtieth Word, First Aim, p. 564.

of human beings is to be molded by God-given ethics and good character: by knowing their [own] impotence to seek refuge with Divine power, by seeing their weakness to rely on Divine strength, by realizing their poverty to trust in Divine mercy, by perceiving their need to seek help from Divine riches, by seeing their faults to ask for pardon through Divine forgiveness, and by realizing their deficiency to be glorifiers of Divine perfection."[63] Thus, if they are to act in an ethical way people need to be informed and guided by God's revelation and to be supported by God's strength or grace. These two elements (Divine guidance and Divine strength) are often ignored in philosophically-based ethical systems that do not take into account elements of God's revealed word.

3. Inner peace

a. How does the concept of peace fit into Said Nursi's ethical thought? In the *Risale-i Nur*, he treats various aspects and elements of peace, not from a theoretical perspective, but as a practical guide for those who seek to pursue peace. In the first place, he treats of *eternal* peace as the ultimate goal of human life, almost synonymous with salvation. Specifically, it is the final destination of the collective personality of those who study the *Risale-i Nur*. He sees the *Risale-i Nur* students, through their efforts carried out in solidarity and sincerity, as contributing in their diverse activities to the building of an eternal realm of peace and happiness.

> O Risale-i Nur students and servants of the Qur'an! You and I are members of a collective personality... like the components of a factory's machinery which produces eternal happiness within eternal life. We are hands working on a dominical boat which will disembark the community of Muhammad (peace and blessings be upon him) at the Realm of Peace, the shore of salvation. So we are surely in need of solidarity and true union, obtained through gaining sincerity.[64]

---

[63] Ibid., p. 563.
[64] *The Flashes*, The Twenty-First Flash, "On Sincerity," p. 214.

This concept not only gives meaning and direction to individual acts, but in this way the believer also achieves a kind of conquest over death. "Through the mystery of true brotherhood on the way of Divine pleasure... there are spirits corresponding to the number of brothers. If one of them dies, he meets death happily, saying: 'My other spirits remain alive, for they in effect make life continue for me by constantly gaining reward for me, so I am not dying. By means of their spirits, I live in respect of merit; I am only dying in respect of sin.' And he lies down in peace."[65]

b. A second way in which the *Risale-i Nur* looks at peace might be called the *psychological* sense, as tranquility and peace of mind, an inner confidence born of faith that enables the religious believer to face adversity without anxiety or despair. Particularly when one is facing the approach of death, the believer can attain a peace of mind that will enable the person to overcome spiritual turmoil and fear.[66] Reflecting on his long periods of incarceration, he notes that his close companions, students of the *Risale-i Nur*, who were imprisoned with him did not waste their time giving in to selfish expressions of worry, complaint, or pride, or trying to change what cannot be altered, but they achieved a peace of mind and steadfastness that bore witness to the spiritual values and dignity that they had achieved.[67]

This interior peace, not only of individuals but of whole societies, he sees as one of the marks of Islamic civilization. Along with justice, harmony, brotherhood, solidarity, human progress and spiritual advancement, peace should characterize the Islamic community.[68] It is peace as the basis of societal relations which should be the force that attracts others to Islam.

c. A third aspect of peace studied by Said Nursi is *universal* peace. Particularly in his rewriting of *The Damascus Sermon* in the years immediately following the Second World War, he reflects the widespread conviction of the time that humankind can sink no lower in criminal-

---

[65] Ibid., p. 215.
[66] *The Rays*, The Ninth Ray, p. 203.
[67] *The Rays*, The Thirteenth Ray, p. 343.
[68] *The Letters*, Seeds of Reality, p. 548; *The Damascus Sermon*, p. 106.

ity towards its own kind[69] and expresses the longing for a time of peace and prosperity for all.[70] This Nursi sees as the specific mission of Islam, that "God willing, through the strength of Islam in the future, the virtues of civilization will prevail, the face of the earth cleaned of filth, and universal peace be secured."[71] Muslims have therefore, as part of their mission in the world, the building of universal peace. Nursi is optimistic that this hope for peace through Islam is no vain desire, but that people may confidently "expect from Divine mercy to see true civilization with universal peace brought about through the sun of the truth of Islam."[72]

It is in his analysis of peace, based on truth, as the only viable alternative to the use of brute force that the thought of Said Nursi prefigures that of Pope John Paul II. Said Nursi notes that wars and violence can never resolve ethical conflicts or establish who is in the right. All that wars and violent actions can accomplish is to show which party has access to greater reserves of force which can be used to coerce obedience from others and to punish the recalcitrant.[73] Truth, on the other hand, is characterized by justice and harmony and seeks goodness and virtue instead of selfish gain.[74]

He sees a tendency in modern governments and rulers which is relevant for the discussion of war and peace. Modern governments, and the communications media they directly or indirectly control, foment a kind of false nationalism, which in reality amounts to a type of racism, by picturing those of another nationality or religion as the enemy against whom war must be waged. The enemy is "dehumanized" and caricatured as evil and without redeeming human qualities. This process of demonization is a common strategy of the propaganda departments of some governments to lay a basis for justifying their warlike and genocidal policies.

---

[69] *The Damascus Sermon*, p. 29.

[70] Ibid., p. 43.

[71] Ibid., p. 38.

[72] Ibid., p. 39.

[73] *The Words*, The Twenty-Fifth Word, First Light, Third Ray, p. 422.

[74] *The Letters*, Seeds of Reality, p. 548.

At the same time they are waging a propaganda war against the alleged "enemy," the governments undertake to provide amusements to gratify the senses and favor consumerist policies to "create needs." The result, he states, is "a sort of superficial happiness for about 20% of mankind and cast 80% into distress and poverty."[75] By contrast, the Qur'an, he states, takes truth rather than force as its starting point. Hence the Qur'an proposes an alternative to the use of force in resolving conflicts, and advocates negotiation, compromise and uprightness as key elements of conflict resolution, rather than the employment of brute force with the very limited and short-sighted aim of "winning" the contest.

Said Nursi's opposition to war as an inhumane and ultimately useless endeavor was highly controversial in his time, for in any nation all citizens are expected to support whatever wars are decided and carried out by their governments, and anyone opposing war is accused of being disloyal. In fact, ruling parties and cliques have been known to *foment* conflict and war in an attempt to increase their popularity and rally support for an unpopular or incompetent government. Nursi notes that he was often disparaged and even accused of disloyalty because of his commitment to peace. Critics claimed that war against British and Italian incursions provided an opportunity to revive Islamic zeal and to assert the moral strength of the nation. They claimed that Said Nursi, who proposed prayers for peace and negotiated settlement, was indirectly supporting the invaders' aims.[76]

In response, Said Nursi averred that he wanted release from the attacks of aggressors, but not by using the same methods which the attackers were employing. In other words, he rejected the practice of opposing force by force. Religion teaches people to seek truth and uprightness, not to try to achieve their aims by use of force. In consequence, he felt that the students of the *Risale-i Nur* could better use their time studying the Qur'an than by engaging in military service. Later in his life he was asked whether freely relinquishing one's rights

---

[75] *The Words*, The Twenty-Fifth Word, First Light, Third Ray, p. 422.
[76] *The Flashes*, The Sixteenth Flash, p. 144.

for the sake of peace could not be considered a form of compromise with wrongdoing. Again reflecting on his prison experiences, he responded: "A person who is in the right is fair. He will sacrifice his one *dirhem*'s worth of being in the right for the general peace, which is worth a hundred."[77]

In the long run, he concludes, the preoccupation with current events and international crises is of secondary importance to seeking the personal, interior transformation of peace that comes through the study of Scripture. Said Nursi carried this principal to an extreme degree, as he recounts:

> For a full two years in Kastamonu and seven years in other places I knew nothing of the conflicts and wars in the world, and whether or not peace had been declared, or who else was involved in the fighting. I was not curious about it and did not ask, and for nearly three years did not listen to the radio that was playing close by me. But with the Risale-i Nur I triumphantly confronted absolute unbelief, which destroys eternal life, and transforms the life of this world even into compounded pain and suffering.[78]

This attitude, which places a higher value on an interior peace that is based on the study of God's Word than on current events, presents a challenge to modern people for whom the daily newspapers and evening news on television are fixed appointments in their daily schedules. However, when one reflects on the degree to which the news media is slanted by the prejudices, policies and propaganda, not only of individual journalists but also of those who own and direct the communications industry, one can see in Said Nursi's practice the freedom of the honest individual who renounces an obsession with transitory events which will be forgotten in a few years in favor of the search for eternal, unchangeable truth presented in the Word of God.

The irony is that Said Nursi was often accused of being a troublemaker guilty of disturbing the peace and inciting his followers to revolt. He was accused of "working secretly in Emirdağ. He poisoned the minds of some people giving them the idea of disturbing the

---

[77] *The Rays*, The Thirteenth Ray, p. 345; *The Flashes*, The Twenty-Eighth Flash, p. 362.
[78] *The Rays*, The Fourteenth Ray, p. 373.

peace."[79] In defending himself against false accusations of fomenting public disorder, he also defends the students of the *Risale-i Nur* against similar charges. "In twenty years, six courts of law and the police of ten provinces... have not recorded any incident involving the disturbance of public order and breaching of security in connection with the 20,000 or perhaps 100,000 people who enthusiastically read copies of the *Risale-i Nur*." In fact, in the more than 50 years since Nursi's death, there are no instances of the students of the *Risale-i Nur* engaging in rebellious activity.

Nursi asserts that his reputation of being a troublemaker and rabble-rouser was based on the fear of non-religious people in regard to those who take religious faith seriously.

> 'The worldly' are exceptionally and excessively suspicious of me. Quite simply, they are frightened of me, imagining non-existent things in me, which even if they existed would not constitute a political crime and could not be the basis of accusation, like being a shaykh, or of significant rank or family, or being a tribal leader, and influential, and having numerous followers, or meeting with people from my native region, or being connected with the affairs of the world, or even entering politics, or even the opposition. Imagining these things in me, they have been carried away by groundless fears.[80]

He makes it clear that his silence must not be interpreted as agreement with all decisions made by public officials, but should be understood rather in terms of passive resistance. He states:

> I support neither intellectually nor on scholarly grounds the arbitrary commands, called laws, of a commander, which have made Aya Sophia into a house of idols and the Shaykh al-Islam's Office into a girls' high school. And for myself I do not act in accordance with them. But although for twenty years I have been severely oppressed during my tortuous captivity, I have not become involved in politics, nor provoked the authorities, nor disturbed public order. And although I have hundreds of thousands of Risale-i Nur friends,

---

[79] Ibid., p. 447.
[80] *The Letters*, Addendum to the Sixteenth Letter, p. 96.

not a single incident has been recorded involving the disturbance of the peace.[81]

Along with Gandhi and Martin Luther King, Said Nursi must be seen as one of the Twentieth Century's great exponents of non-violent resistance.

4. Peace and forgiveness

When we turn to the question of the relationship between peace and forgiveness, the similarity of thought between Said Nursi and the later views of Pope John Paul becomes even more striking. He analyzes the nature of wrongdoing. In the case of a crime such as murder, the killer might derive a momentary satisfaction by having taken revenge on his enemy, but he pays for it over and over by suffering the consequences, not only of imprisonment, but also of fear of retaliation by the relatives of the murdered person. The result is fear, anger, and anxiety. "There is only one solution for this," states Said Nursi, "and that is reconciliation, which the Qur'an commands, and which truth, reality, benefit, humanity, and Islam require and encourage."[82] He notes that Islam commands that "one believer should not be vexed with another believer for more than three days," and that so long as there is no reconciliation, both sides perpetually suffer the torments of fear and revenge." His conclusion is that "it is essential to make peace quickly."

Often a person's unwillingness to forgive arises, according to Said Nursi, from a lack of self-knowledge, a resistance to finding in oneself many of the same qualities that one condemns in the other. If someone is unwilling to confront the defects in one's own attitudes and actions, it is much easier to demonize the other and regard them as an enemy. Said Nursi's advice is to "Look at the defect in your own soul that you do not see or do not wish to see. Deduct a share for that too. As for the small share which then remains, if you respond with forgiveness, pardon, and magnanimity, in such a way as to conquer

---

[81] *The Rays*, The Fourteenth Ray, p. 417.
[82] Ibid., p. 484.

your enemy swiftly and safely, then you will have escaped all sin and harm."[83] Thus, self-awareness should lead to repentance, repentance to forgiveness, forgiveness to reconciliation and the seeds for a lasting peace are laid.

So long as no reconciliation takes place, the wounds to the human relations fester and grow and turn into resentment. Discord produces more discord, violence engenders even greater violence, and the state of conflict is perpetuated. The only way out of a spiraling succession of violent reactions and counter-reactions is for one party to take the initiative to reconcile. Reconciliation heals what force can never heal, the suspicion and resentment caused by wrongdoing one against another. As Said Nursi puts it, "A minor disaster becomes a large one, and continues. But if they make peace, and the murderer repents and prays continuously for the man he killed, then both sides will gain much and become like brothers. In place of one departed brother, he will gain several religious brothers."

Said Nursi's analysis of peace and reconciliation is very similar to the words of Pope John Paul with which I began: "Forgiveness is a personal choice, a decision to go against the natural instinct to pay back evil with evil. In doing so, it always involves an *apparent* short-term loss, but brings about the possibility of achieving a *real* long-term gain. Violence works exactly the opposite: opting for an apparent short-term gain, but involving a real and permanent loss. Forgiveness may seem like weakness, but it demands great spiritual strength and moral courage." Here we find a strong convergence between these two great religious teachers.

So important is the element of forgiveness in human relations that Said Nursi commands the students of the *Risale-i Nur* to pardon each other's faults speedily. In fact, mutual forgiveness should be a characteristic mark that identifies students of the *Risale-i Nur*. He states:

> It is absolutely essential that you completely forgive each other.
> You are brothers closer to each other than the most devoted blood
> brother, and a brother conceals his brother's faults, and forgives

---

[83] *The Letters*, Twenty-Second Letter, First Topic, p. 316.

and forgets. I do not attribute your uncustomary differences and
egotism here to your evil-commanding souls, and I cannot reconcile it with the Risale-i Nur students. I rather consider it to be a
sort of temporary egotism found even in saints who have given up
their souls. So on your part, do not spoil my good opinion through
obstinacy, and make peace with each other.[84]

Since the study of the *Risale-i Nur* creates a relationship even closer than that of blood brothers, there is no offence so serious that it
should go unforgiven among its students. Said Nursi goes so far as to
state, "I swear that if one of you were to insult me most terribly and
entirely trample my honor but not give up serving the Qur'an, belief,
and the *Risale-i Nur*, I would forgive him and make peace with him
and try not to be offended."[85]

Said Nursi sees a relationship between God's abundant forgiveness of the faults of humans and the need for believers to forgive one
another. Just as God is generous in forgiving anyone who repents, so
Said Nursi encourages the students of the *Risale-i Nur* to imitate these
Divine qualities by acting with love and forgiveness toward those
who wronged them.

> Your sincerity, loyalty, and steadfastness are sufficient reason to
> disregard one another's faults... For the powerful brotherhood
> within the Risale-i Nur is such a good thing it causes one to for-
> give a thousand evils. Since at the Last Judgment when good
> deeds will preponderate over evils, Divine justice will forgive, you
> too, seeing that good deeds preponderate, should act with love
> and forgiveness.[86]

One must even forgive one's enemies and those who have done
them wrong. Said Nursi repeatedly expressed his forgiveness for his
prison wardens,[87] judges[88], government officials,[89] law officers[90], and

---

[84] *The Rays*, The Thirteenth Ray, p. 369.
[85] *The Rays*, The Fourteenth Ray, p. 510.
[86] Ibid., p. 355.
[87] Ibid., p. 487
[88] Ibid., p. 416.
[89] Ibid., p. 460.
[90] Ibid., p. 416.

civil authorities,[91] who had treated him unjustly during his period of courtroom trials and subsequent imprisonments. His point in forgiving others is that the relationship of enmity created by the wrong done by one person to another can only be overcome and superseded by forgiveness. Otherwise, one becomes a prisoner of circumstances, events, and the deeds of others, and history becomes a string of injustices and retaliations. This chain of evil and violence can only be broken by one who is willing to take the initiative to forgive.

In conclusion, I might mention that according to Said Nursi forgiveness and peace-making should not be limited only to students of the *Risale-i Nur* or, more generally, to fellow Muslims. He argues that members of the People of the Book, Jews and Christians, if they want to make peace, should be allowed to do so. "A Christian may," he states, "accept some sacred matters and may believe in some of the Prophets, and may assent to Almighty God in some respects."[92]

5. A convergence of ideas

When I examine the thought of Pope John Paul and that of Said Nursi, I am stuck by the many similarities. Both understand peace to be not only a universal human longing, but also a cornerstone of the Message that God has revealed to humans. It is not only that humans long for peace, but God desires and intends that all people live in peace. Both thinkers are convinced that the use of violence and force can never be the truth path to peace. Both hold that societies can succeed only if they are founded on the principles of justice and harmony. Both agree that the cycle of injury and revenge, wrongdoing and retaliation, violence and counter-violence can be broken when people take recourse to forgiveness and pardon. This act, which seems to be a sign of weakness and to result in a short-term loss, is in fact a courageous effort to move beyond past conflicts and establish reconciliation. Both agree that true forgiveness is beyond humankind's unaided resources and is made pos-

---

[91] Ibid., p. 395.
[92] *The Letters*, The Twenty-Ninth Letter, Seventh Section, p. 512; *The Flashes*, The Seventeenth Flash, Seventh Note, p. 168.

sible only by the guidance and strength that come from God. The human race would certainly be facing a better future if people would heed the advice of these two great moral teachers.

Grappling with Modern Civilization

1. The need to discern

One of the most difficult challenges which our age presents to every believer in God is to assess critically the modern civilization in which we live. The life in which we find ourselves today is a confusing, even bewildering, mix of contradictions. There is much in modern civilization that is attractive, much that is useful and that makes life easier, more comfortable, and more enjoyable. At the same time, everyone who takes seriously the gift of faith with which God has blessed him or her is aware that modern civilization is not always in agreement with that faith and, in fact, it often seems to oppose the life of faith and obedience to which we are called.

To many people, religion seems unnecessary, for many of the reasons that in former times led people to turn to religion are today handled by science. When modern people are sick, they go to the doctor. When depressed, they see a psychiatrist or counselor. When they need water for their crops, they don't pray for rain, but install an irrigation system. From that, it is a short step for modern people to say that they no longer need God, for science can provide adequate solutions to the problems that arise in regard to survival, health, and well-being.

For believers, it is not simply that modern civilization tends to banish God to the margins of daily consciousness and activity. Modern civilization also offers a value system that is at odds with that of religion. It defines happiness differently from religious thought. Success and failure are counted in different terms. Self-fulfillment is regarded as a basic human motivation, and possession of consumer goods is considered a mark of personal achievement. From this it follows that competition becomes the motive force of modern life, and the world comes to be divided into the winners and the losers.

For those of us, Muslims, Christians, and others for whom God is the beginning, the center, and the end of our existence, and for whom God's will is the criterion of good and evil, we need a way to sort out what is truly valuable in modern civilization from what is ephemeral and destructive. We need intellectual tools to be able to analyze the civilization in which we live so that we do not buy rotten fruit along with the fresh, so that we do not throw out the baby with the bath water.

In my opinion, the lifetime achievement of Said Nursi lies in his ability in the *Risale-i Nur* to provide modern Muslims with the interpretative tools they need to analyze modern civilization, so that they can discern what is of genuine and lasting value in modern life from the harmful and self-destructive tendencies that lie beneath its glittering surface. Nursi's analysis of modern civilization is complex and subtle, and I can do no more than mention several aspects that appear to me as especially worthy of our reflections today. I will approach this topic in two parts, firstly, by summarizing Said Nursi's critique of modern civilization in the *Risale-i Nur* and, secondly, by looking at his efforts to reconcile what is good in this civilization with the demands of religious faith.

NURSI'S CRITIQUE OF MODERN CIVILIZATION

2. Modern civilization is two

What we are accustomed to call "modern civilization" or "Western civilization" Said Nursi usually referred to as "European civilization," or simply as "Europe." This is logical, since modernity, not only in the sense of scientific and technological advances, but also in its philosophical underpinnings, first took root in Europe and from there was brought to every corner of the world. Today much of the leadership in propagating the modern world-view and life-style has been taken up by the U.S.A., which employs its extensive financial, military, organizational, and communication resources to this end. The globalization trends which Nursi foresaw almost a century ago have now made what he was accustomed to refer to collectively as "Europe" into a truly worldwide phenomenon, with cities like Tokyo, Seoul, Singapore, and Sao Paolo taking their place as focal points of disseminating modernist ideas alongside earlier centers such as Paris, London, Berlin and Washington.

So when Nursi makes his famous statement, "Europe is two," he is really writing about the modern world in which we are all living today. Looking at our world at the start of the 21st Century, religious believers could well apply Nursi's basic insight and say "Modern civilization is two" [i.e., "two-faced" or "two-sided."] From this starting point concerning the duality of modern civilization, Nursi posits the need to discern and distinguish among the contradictory phenomena that go to make up globalized modernity. He states:

> Europe is two. One follows the sciences which serve justice and right and the industries beneficial for the life of society through the inspiration it has received from true Christianity; this first Europe I am not addressing. I am rather addressing the second, corrupt Europe which, through the darkness of the philosophy of naturalism, supposing the evils of civilization to be its virtues, has driven mankind to vice and misguidance.[93]

If Nursi's evaluation of European civilization can sometimes appear to focus on the negative, it is because he has no quarrel with the "first Europe," which retains the values of faith, justice, and social harmony. He is concerned rather with warning people about the destructive elements in modern civilization so they can take the necessary measures to withstand its dangerous charms. He is seeking to refute the corrupt Europe's false claims and lay bare its harmful philosophical infrastructure. He notes:

> On my journey of the spirit at that time I said to Europe's collective personality, which apart from beneficial science and the virtues of civilization, holds in its hand meaningless, harmful philosophy and noxious, dissolute civilization: "Know this, O second

---

[93] *The Flashes*, The Seventeenth Flash, Fifth Note, p. 160.

Europe! You hold a diseased and misguided philosophy in your right hand, and a harmful and corrupt civilization in your left, and claim, 'Mankind's happiness is with these two!'"[94]

Nursi sees modern man at a crossroads. What direction is he going to go? What path will he take? Will he accept and live according to the whole package that modern life offers, or will he take the time and effort to stop to analyze and distinguish? What intellectual and spiritual tools will he employ to sort out the grain from the mass of dirt and stones with which it is gathered? For Nursi, it is the Qur'an that offers the criteria for what is to be saved and what is to be discarded.

> Of two brothers, one is a believing spirit and a righteous heart. The other is an unbelieving spirit with a depraved heart. Of the two roads, the one to the right is the way of the Qur'an and belief in God, while the left one is the road of rebellion and denial. The garden on the road is man's fleeting life in human society and civilization, where good and evil, and things good and bad and clean and dirty are found side by side. The sensible person is he who acts according to the rule: 'Take what is pleasant and clear, and leave what is distressing and turbid,' and goes on his way with tranquility of heart.[95]

3. A civilization built on materialist values

In numerous places, Nursi points up the contrast between the societal values proposed by modern civilization and the vision of society presented by the Qur'an. To Nursi the Qur'anic vision differs only in details from what had been proposed by all the Prophets before Muhammad, hence it is a vision that Muslims share with "true Christians" who genuinely follow the teachings of the Prophet Jesus. Jesus' Christian followers sought to build Europe on these Prophetic values, but this effort was sabotaged from the beginning by their reliance on Greco-Roman philosophy.[96]

---

[94] Ibid.

[95] *The Words*, The Eighth Word, p. 45.

[96] *Muhakemat*, 37–38; *Sünuhat*, 43–46; *Sözler* 119–120, 379–382, 664–666. For these references in Turkish I am indebted to Şükran Vahide's paper, "Jihad in the Modern

In the 18th and 19th Centuries, by way of the naturalist and materialist philosophies propounded by the scholars of the Enlightenment, even the vestiges of Prophetic teaching which remained in European civilization were attacked and abandoned. Thus, the Enlightenment philosophers set about building "modern Europe" on principles of their own making, and modern Western civilization is the fruit of their labors. Since the principles on which they based the new civilization were the result of their human rationalist speculations that rejected the teaching of the Prophets, modern civilization offers a very different set of values which should characterize social relations.

Nursi saw the same process that had previously occurred in Europe taking place in Turkey in his own day. Working on the notion that religion was an obstacle to progress, many in the Turkish Republic were attempting to replace religious values and way of life with ways of acting derived from modern Europe, and consequently they opposed the dissemination and study of the *Risale-i Nur*. In his defense in the Afyon court, Nursi pointed out the futility of the campaign to replace a religious outlook with one of secular modernity.

> An irreligious Muslim does not resemble any other person without religion. No sort of progress or civilization can take the place of religion, or righteousness, or the learning of the truths of belief in particular, which are the innate need of the people of this country, who for a thousand years have illumined the world with their religion and heroically preserved their firmness of faith in the face of the assaults of the whole world.[97]

Those promoting modern values claim that they are simply interested in providing a good life for the majority of the people. Upon examining this concept of the good life, Nursi concludes that it is one of the "deceptive, opiate fantasies of civilization."[98] What the concept involves is limited to responding to bodily needs, on the supposition that if people have food in their stomachs, a roof over their heads,

---

Age: Bediüzzaman Said Nursi's Interpretation of Jihad," in the Third International Symposium of Bediüzzaman Said Nursi, 24–26 September 1995, İstanbul.

[97] *The Rays*, The Fourteenth Ray, Defense to the Afyon Court, p. 379.
[98] *The Words*, The Thirteenth Word, Addendum to the Second Station, p. 167.

and access to medical treatment when needed, they have achieved "the good life." To Nursi, this is a short-sighted understanding of the true needs of humankind. A person also has spiritual needs, which cannot be met by the facilities of modernity.

> O foolish friend! Do you suppose your life's duty is restricted to following the good life according to the requisites of civilization and to gratifying the physical appetites? Do you suppose the sole aim of the delicate and subtle senses, the sensitive faculties and members, the well-ordered limbs and systems, the inquisitive feelings and senses that make up your life are restricted to satisfying the low desires of the base soul in this fleeting life?[99]

The basic problem, according to Nursi, is that modern civilization has clouded people's minds so that they are unable to see the value of the life of the spirit. Modern life focuses on the immediate, the temporal, the ephemeral, and finds it difficult to see beyond to questions of eternal importance. "At this time, due to the domination of European civilization and the supremacy of natural philosophy and the preponderance of the conditions of worldly life, minds and hearts have become scattered, and endeavor and favor divided. Minds have become strangers to non-material matters."[100] Instead of seeking the truly good life intended by God for people, men and women are caught up in a rat race of seeking wealth, prestige, pleasure, and political power in the mistaken fantasy that these things will bring them happiness.

The psychological toll of modernity is high, and people can become frozen into inactivity. Modern man, "since his thought is submerged in philosophy, his mind plunged in politics, and his heart is giddy at the life of this world,"[101]is unable to evaluate seriously questions of eternal weight. His mind becomes dulled to reality and he becomes unable to take serious decision and to exert his creativity in a positive direction.

---

[99] *The Words*, The Eleventh Word, p. 139.
[100] *The Words*, The Twenty-Seventh Word, Third Obstacle, p. 496.
[101] Ibid.

Through philosophical investigation and natural science, and the seductive amusements of dissolute civilization and its intoxicated passions, sick philosophy has both increased the world's frozen state and inaction, and made denser heedlessness, and increased its opaqueness and turbidity, and caused the Maker and the hereafter to be forgotten.[102] By contrast, the teaching of the Qur'an "gives the world a transparency and removes its turbidity.

4. Contrast between European and Qur'anic civilization

In the aphorisms that make up the *Seeds of Reality*, Nursi succinctly summarizes some elements of difference between the two visions. "Modern civilization, he states, has been founded on five negative principles."

1. Its point of support is force, the mark of which is aggression.
2. Its aim and goal is self-interest, the mark of which is competitive jostling.
3. Its principle in life is conflict, the mark of which is strife.
4. The bond holding the masses together is racism and negative nationalism, which is nourished through devouring others; its mark is collision.
5. Its enticement is inciting lust and passion and gratifying the desires.[103]

The five principles might be stated succinctly as follows:

1) Might makes right,
2) Self-interest and competition,
3) The law of the jungle, everyone for himself,
4) My race and nation are superior,
5) I have a right to whatever I want.

To these principles, which Nursi sees as both destructive and self-destructive, he contrasts the teaching of the Qur'an:

The civilization the shari'a of Muhammad (peace and blessings be upon him) comprises and commands is this: its point of support

---

[102] *The Words*, The Twenty-Fifth Word, Third Light, Second Gleam, p. 451.
[103] *The Letters*, Seeds of Reality, aphorism 61. Cf. also, *The Words*, The Twelfth Word, Third Principle, where he elaborates the same points of contrast. Cf. also, *The Letters*, "Flowers from the Seeds of Reality: A Dream Assembly".

is truth instead of force, the mark of which is justice and harmony. Its goal is virtue in place of self-benefit, the mark of which is love and attraction. Its means of unity are the ties of religion, country, and class, in place of racism and nationalism, and the mark of these is sincere brotherhood, peace, and only defense against external aggression. In life is the principle of mutual assistance instead of the principle of conflict, the mark of which is accord and solidarity. It offers guidance instead of lust, the mark of which is human progress and spiritual advancement.[104]

The contrast is clear; the Qur'an proposes very different principles. In the civilization envisioned by the Qur'an (and the teachings of the earlier Prophets):

1) It is *truth*, not might, which makes right.
2) *Virtue*, non self-interest, is the proper motivation for human acts.
3) *Unity* rather than conflict should be the basis for social relations, and
4) *Mutual assistance* instead of cutthroat competition,
5) Divine *guidance* rather than human whims as the norm for ethical behavior.

A society built on such principles will be characterized by values like justice, harmony, love, peace, brotherhood, and solidarity. It will attract others by virtue of its own good qualities, rather than by imposing its views or by dominating and looking down on others.

When a civilization accepts the principle of "might makes right," the result is injustice. When civilization operates on the principle of immediate gratification of desires, the result is laziness, inactivity, and torpor. Nursi accuses Muslim societies of having too often adopted these negative principles of modern civilization and the result is "hunger, financial loss, and physical trials." The Qur'an teaches hard work and industry and to share one's wealth with the poor. But Muslims have not lived according to this teaching and followed instead the principles of modern civilization. He says, "When comparing modern civilization with the principles of the Qur'an, all immorality and instabil-

---

[104] Ibid.

ity in the social life of man proceeds from two sources: 1) 'Once my stomach is full, what do I care if others die of hunger?' and 2) 'You work, and I'll eat.'"[105]

5. Destructive social, political, and spiritual consequences

The effects of trying to recreate society on the basis of a materialist outlook are not found only in the cultural field, but also in the economic and political realm. Nursi saw a clear ideological development from the principles of the French Revolution which led eventually to dehumanizing values of Soviet Communism. In rejecting and even oppressing the sacred, man removes all limits to class and national conflict and ends in anarchy. Applying the Qur'anic teaching about Gog and Magog to modern history, Nursi traces a direct development from French libertarianism to communism to anarchy.

> Socialism sprang up in the French Revolution from the seed of libertarianism. Since socialism destroyed certain sacred matters, the ideas it inculcated turned into bolshevism. Because bolshevism corrupted even more sacred moral and human values and those of the human heart, of course the seeds it sowed will produce anarchy, which recognizes no restrictions whatsoever and has respect for nothing. For if respect and compassion quit the human heart, those with such hearts become exceedingly cruel beasts and can no longer be governed through politics.[106]

Nursi sees the almost continual warfare that has occurred in the modern age as the most tragic effect of ordering society on materialist principles. He views the two World Wars as "a manifestation of Divine Wrath in punishment for the vice and misguidance of civilization."[107] This need not be understood as God unleashing Divine wrath to bring about wars as punishment for humankind's misdeeds, but rather in God allowing the natural effects of human error and arrogance to run their destructive course. If people build civilization on the principles of conflict, competition, and enmity, the result will inevitably be war and

---

[105] *The Letters*, The Twenty-Second Letter, Second Topic, p. 324.
[106] *The Rays*, The Fifth Ray, Second Station, Fifteenth Matter, p. 105.
[107] *Kastamonu Lahikası*, pp. 80–81.

mutual destruction. He comments on the Qur'anic passage about "the blowers on knots" in the context of 20th Century history.

> The sentence the blowers on knots 'coincides' with the dates when due to their ambition and greed the Europeans tyrants who caused the two World Wars, instigated a change of Sultan and the Balkan and Italian Wars with the idea of spoiling the consequences of the Constitutional Revolution which favored the Qur'an. Then with the outbreak of the First World War, through the political diplomats blowing their evils, material and immaterial, and their sorcery and poison into everyone's heads through the tongue of the radio, and inculcating their covert plans into the heart of human destiny, they prepared the evils that would savagely destroy a thousand years of the progress of civilization, which corresponds exactly with the meaning of the blowers on knots.[108]

It is clear from the *Risale-i Nur* that for Said Nursi, the "spiritual darkness arising from science and philosophy" was not merely an intellectual problem. It was a burden that affected him personally. In his "Treatise for the Elderly," he records that the struggle brought him great inner pain and struggle. He states: "relying on what they had learnt from the people of misguidance and philosophers, my soul and Satan attacked my reason and my heart."[109] He thanks God for the victory over the despair and confusion against which he was struggling and shared his experience of spiritual crisis in the hope that it might help others who had been led astray in their youth "by matters which though called Western philosophy or the sciences of civilization, are in part misguidance and in part trivia." Through meditation on the Qur'an, Nursi was able to arrive at an understanding of Divine unity that recognized in all creatures the artwork of a loving Creator. As he says,

> And so, through this most subtle, powerful, profound, and clear proof, my soul, which had been a temporary student of Satan and the spokesman for the people of misguidance and the philosophers, was silenced, and, all praise be to God, came to believe completely. It said: "Yes, what I need is a Creator and Sustainer who possesses

---

[108] *The Rays*, The Eleventh Ray, Eleventh Topic, p. 287.
[109] *The Flashes*, The Twenty-Sixth Flash, Eleventh Hope, p. 306.

the power to know the least thoughts of my heart and my most secret wishes, who will answer the most hidden needs of my spirit and will transform the mighty earth into the Hereafter in order to give me eternal happiness."[110]

6. Demonic influences

In the previous section, we noted that Nursi observed Satan's utilizing, even in his own thinking, the intellectual underpinnings of Western civilization to tempt him to disbelief. He saw demonic influences responsible for much of the evil in modern society.

Modern civilization is ambiguous because its sources of inspiration are varied. From the truths of revealed religion, modern civilization retains basic notions of the importance of love, harmony and justice. However, the destructive elements of modernity come from anti-religious philosophical ideologies and perhaps also from evil spirits. "Modern civilization, which is the product of the thought of all mankind and perhaps the jinn as well, has taken up a position opposed to the Qur'an. With its sorcery it impugns the miraculous nature of the Qur'an."[111]

He sees a satanic strategy in false nationalist ideologies that seek to impose a way of life based on European civilization. It promises much, but it offers nothing of value, particularly to pious believers and to those who suffer. Nursi states:

> Is the greatest benefit of the believers and the pious to be found in a European-type civilization? Or is it to be found in thinking of eternal happiness by means of the truths of belief, in traveling the way of truth and finding true solace? The way that the misguided and bogus patriots have taken extinguishes the spiritual lights of the pious people of belief, destroys their true consolation, and shows death to be eternal nothingness and the grave to be the door to everlasting separation. Are the benefits of disaster victims, the sick, and those who have despaired of life, to be found in the way of a European-type, irreligious civilization?[112]

---

[110] Ibid.
[111] *The Words*, The Twenty-Fifth Word, First Light, Third Ray, p. 420.
[112] *The Letters*, The Twenty-Ninth Letter, Fourth Satanic Strategy, p. 493.

Nursi sees a diabolical element in the tendencies to material luxury and self-satisfaction, a conscious effort to replace the Paradise intended by God for those who believe with an earthly paradise. This is the work of Dajjal, whom Nursi finds in the collective personality of the "second Europe."

> The Dajjal is superficially like a human being. He is arrogant and Pharaoh-like and has forgotten God, a foolish satan and intriguing person who calls his superficial, tyrannical rule godhead. His huge current of [transgression], his collective personality, is truly vast... The Dajjal's false paradise are the alluring amusements and enticements of civilization. [He] brings a false paradise for the dissolute and the worldly, while for the people of religion and Islam, like the angels of Hell it brings dangers in the hand of civilization, and casts them into captivity and poverty.[113]

Nursi is not pessimistic, however. He feels that a union of Muslims and Christians will in the future succeed in defeating the Dajjal and its false promises. The need for unity in combating the attacks of atheistic philosophy and behavior Nursi sees as one of the strongest motivations for true Christians and Muslims to come to an understanding between themselves.

> At that point, when the [atheistic] current appears to be very strong, the religion of true Christianity, which comprises the collective personality of Jesus (upon whom be peace), will emerge. It will descend from the skies of Divine Mercy. Present-day Christianity will be purified in the face of that reality; it will cast off superstition and distortion, and unite with the truths of Islam. Christianity will in effect be transformed into a sort of Islam. Following the Qur'an, the collective personality of Christianity will be in the rank of follower, and Islam, in that of leader. True religion will become a mighty force as a result of this union. Although defeated before the atheistic current while separate, Christianity and Islam will have the capability to defeat and rout it as a result of their union.[114]

---

[113] *The Letters*, The Fifteenth Letter, Answer to the Fourth Question, p. 79.
[114] Ibid.

7. The dangers of consumerism

One of the most pernicious aspects of modern civilization is the proliferation of material goods and the consequent urge to convince people that they need such goods to obtain happiness. This does not happen by accident. Nursi sees this preoccupation with the material as a direct result of the abandonment of the spiritual side of life. Having rejected the value of loving obedience to God in daily behavior and given up the hope of everlasting life with God, modern people become obsessed with the acquisition of material goods and comforts in order to give meaning to their lives. In a letter written near the end of his life after visits to İstanbul, Said Nursi wrote:

> Since modern Western civilization acts contrary to the fundamental laws of the revealed religions, its evils have come to outweigh its good aspects, its errors and harmful aspects its benefits. General tranquility and a happy worldly life, the true aims of civilization, have been destroyed. Since wastefulness and extravagance have taken the place of frugality and contentment, and laziness and the desire for ease have overcome endeavor and the sense of service, it has made unfortunate mankind both extremely poor and extremely lazy. In explaining the fundamental law of the revealed Qur'an: Eat and drink, but waste not in excess, and Man possesses naught save that which he strives, the Risale-i Nur says: Man's happiness in this life lies in frugality and endeavor, and it is through them that the rich and poor will be reconciled.[115]

Nursi explains that in former times, people only needed a few material things to make them content and they were willing to work hard to obtain those basic needs. In modern life, however, "through wastefulness, misuse, stimulation of the appetites, and such things as custom and addiction, present-day civilization has made inessential needs seem essential, and in place of the four things which someone used to need, modern civilized man is now in need of twenty."[116]

To Nursi, consumerism is directly linked to the abandonment of religion. It is at once an impoverishment and a source of depravity and

---

[115] *Emirdağ Lahikası*, ii, 97–99
[116] Ibid.

aggression. If in former times, wars were fought for reasons of religion and justice, today they are fought for possession of oil fields, water rights, and control of markets. Said Nursi states:

> Since modern Western civilization has not truly heeded the revealed religions, it has both impoverished man and increased his needs. It has destroyed the principle of frugality and contentment, and increased wastefulness, greed, and covetousness. It has opened the way to tyranny and what is unlawful... It has encouraged depravity and dissipation, and wasted lives on useless things.[117]

RECONCILING RELIGION AND MODERN CIVILIZATION

8. Thanking God for human progress

If one were to read only Nursi's critique of modern civilization, one might conclude that he is fixated on the past, intent on promoting a nostalgic return to a romanticized past age when life was in better shape. Such a conclusion would, I feel, be a misreading of the *Risale-i Nur*. To view Nursi as unalterably opposed to all forms of progress and to all aspects of modernity is to forget his basic premise: that modern civilization is by its nature dualistic. "Europe [that is, modern civilization] is two." Against the first he has no complaint; it is the "second Europe" of irreligious philosophers, scientists, and politicians that he directed his criticisms.

Said Nursi was not an obstinate traditionalist who sought to turn back the clock. He affirmed that "there are numerous virtues in [modern] civilization," and went on to hold that the positive values of modern life were not solely the products of Europe, but are the property of all and arise from "the combined thought of humankind, the laws of the revealed religions, innate need, and in particular from the Islamic revolution brought about by the *shari'a* of Muhammad."[118] With such elements of modern civilization, religious people have no quarrel, but

---

[117] Ibid.
[118] *Mesnevi-i Nuriye,* "Hubab," p. 81.

rather, they accept and rejoice in the benefits this civilization brings to humankind.

In fact, during his lifetime Nursi was often accused by his opponents of being totally opposed to progress and the advancement of civilization. Such accusations were regularly leveled against him in the frequent court proceedings at which he was forced to appear. In the charges brought against him in the Denizli Court, he was accused, for "having criticized the evils and faults of modern civilization," of rejecting the use of the radio, airplanes, and trains. In his defense speech, Nursi had to defend himself against what he regarded as preposterous accusations.[119] He stated that such technological achievements were actually blessings from God, but instead of thanking God wholeheartedly for guiding men to invent such modern wonders, men have used them to attack and destroy one another.

> Almighty God's great bounties of the airplane, railway, and radio should be responded to with great thanks, yet mankind had not done this and had rained down bombs on men's heads with the planes. While thanks for the vast bounty of the radio would be shown by making it a universal million-tongued reciter of the Qur'an, which would allow people all over the earth to listen to the Qur'an... Although I urged Muslims to work towards these wonders, I am accused of "opposing modern advances like the railway, airplane, and radio."[120]

In his court defense, Nursi repeatedly claims that he has been unjustly deprived of the very rights that the proponents of modernity claim to be championing. He states: "The way I have been treated these six years has been arbitrary and outside the law. They looked on me as though I had been stripped of all the rights of civilization and even of all worldly rights." In his righteous anger, he challenges those who have persecuted and imprisoned him on the basis of their own modernist philosophies to act according to the upright principles they proclaim. If they speak of human rights and justice, they should apply those also in his case.

---

[119] *The Rays*, The Twelfth Ray, Defense Speech in the Denizli Court, p. 300.
[120] Ibid.

> Through the strength of the All-Wise Qur'an, I challenge all Europe including your irreligious people. Through the lights of belief I have published, I have razed the sturdy bastions they call the physical sciences and Nature. I have cast down lower than animals their greatest irreligious philosophers. If all Europe, of which your irreligious people are a part, were to gather, through God's assistance, they could not make me recant a single matter of that way of mine. [121]

It is the false proponents of modern civilization who violate their own principles. "What right do you have to propose to me the principles of your civilization?" he asks.

> Casting me outside the laws of civilization, you have wrongfully forced me to reside in a village for five years prohibited from all social intercourse and correspondence. While you left all the exiles in the town with their friends and relations, then gave them the papers granting them an amnesty, without reason you isolated me and did not allow me to meet with anyone from my native region with one or two exceptions. You do not count me as a member of this nation and a citizen. How can you propose to me that I apply your civil code to myself? [122]

9. Reconciling religious and secular education: the Medresetü'z-Zehra

Nursi's great dream, which was never realized due to political circumstances, was to erect the university-level Madrasah az-Zahra (Medresetü'z-Zehra) in Eastern Turkey. This grand project, for which he planned and sought funds as late as 1951, was to have two main goals: 1) to promote Islamic unity by bringing together Kurds, Turks, Arabs, and students from the Caucasus and Central Asia, and 2) to "reconcile the sciences of philosophy and those of religion, and make peace between European civilization and the truths of Islam."[123]

For this school, Nursi envisioned a new type of education, one that would unite secular and religious education. He foresaw a truly

---

[121] *The Letters*, The Sixteenth Letter, Addendum, p. 95.

[122] Ibid., Fifth Point, p. 92.

[123] Şükran Vahide, *Bediüzzaman Said Nursi: The Author of the Risale-i Nur*, "The Third Said."

modern school in agreement with the teaching of the Qur'an. If, as he says, that the great enemies of humankind are "ignorance, poverty, and disunity,"[124] it is easy to understand Nursi's passionate desire for the *madrasah* in Eastern Turkey which would combat all three enemies in one single project.

It is clear from this lifetime project of Nursi's that he found much in modern civilization which was not contradictory to religious belief. He held that the study of science was essential for modern believers, a conviction which he proved in his own life by spending much time in scientific studies. He notes that the Qur'an does not prohibit Muslims from having "admiration for the civilization and progress"[125] of Europe, or from borrowing from what is good in their civilization.

10. Human progress in civilization should lead to the awareness of the Creator

It was often the context of Nursi's court trials that occasioned some of his strongest statements in favor of the positive elements of civilization. At his 1948 defense of Risale students in Afyon, he denied that he was encouraging the students of the *Risale-i Nur* to reject modernity. Rather, he claimed that by reading the *Risale-i Nur* his students were laying the foundation for a true modern civilization grounded in the teaching of the Qur'an and defending the nation against the communist threat. He concludes:

> The basis of all human society, and especially the Islamic nation, is earnest love between relatives, concerned relations between tribes and groups, brotherhood and moral assistance for fellow believers arising from Islamic nationhood, self-sacrificing concern for one's fellow-countrymen and the members of one's nation, and unshakeable attachment and devotion to and support for the truths of the Qur'an... It is only by denying these bonds, which secure the life of society, and by accepting the Red Peril—which is scattering the terrible seed of anarchy in the north, destroying nations and their

---

[124] *Münazarat*, (Ottoman edition), p. 433, cited in Şükran Vahide, *Bediüzzaman Said Nursi: The Author of the Risale-i Nur*, p. 95.

[125] *Münazarat*, pp. 26–27.

youth, and by drawing everyone's children to itself, annihilates kinship and nationhood, and opens the way to the total corruption of human civilization and society—that the Risale-i Nur students can be called a political society in the sense of its being a crime. The Risale-i Nur students therefore do not hesitate to display their attachment to the truths of the Qur'an and their firm relations with their brothers of the hereafter.[126]

It is not simply a case of believers tolerating and passively accepting the human progress embodied in modern civilization. Said Nursi believes that reflection on the fruits of civilization should actually lead people to God and to an understanding of the Divine plan of creation. He recounts this in the parable of a man from a primitive society who enters a palace but cannot understand its marks of civilization or where they came from. The palace represents the world, and its furnishings represent the "fruits of civilization." He compares the man in the parable to a modern atheist, who looks at the world and the accomplishments of human endeavor and yet fails to recognize the God who has created this and guided human progress and achievement. The naturalist philosopher thinks that all this came about by accident and that human progress is the effect of unguided human design. To this person Nursi says: "Study His decree, listen to the Qur'an! Be delivered from your delirious raving![127]

As Nursi looks to the future, he envisions a new civilization which will arise from the destructive international and national relations of the present day, which will be firmly rooted in the Islamic *shari'a* and will incorporate the positive features of modern civilization. This new civilization, which will overcome and move beyond the present dichotomy between religion and science, will be one that Muslims will be the first to accept.

> For wondrously this calamity has made unfold compassion, Islamic solidarity and brotherhood, the leaven of our lives, and has expedited the shaking, the destruction, of civilization. Present-day low civilization will change form and its system will fall apart. Then

---

[126] *The Rays*, The Fourteenth Ray, p. 415; cf. also, The Eleventh Ray, Eleventh Topic.
[127] *The Flashes*, The Twenty-Third Flash, p. 243.

Islamic civilization will emerge, and Muslims will certainly be the first to enter it voluntarily.[128]

11. Engagement in and withdrawal from civilization

I hesitate to raise this final aspect of Said Nursi's approach to civilization, for the topic deserves a serious paper to itself. It is the whole question of involvement of the religious believer in worldly society and withdrawal from that society. Civilization, as we have seen, not only encompasses advances in technology—in Said Nursi's day, cars, trains, and airplanes; in our day, computers, internet, and cellphones—but it includes the active engagement in worldly affairs.

A fundamental question which every believer must answer for oneself is whether it is God's will that they should live out their religious commitments in the context of the complexities and dangers of worldly life, or whether they are called to retire from the activities of civilization. Many of the Sufis felt that in order to pursue their goal of achieving a union of love and will with God that they must withdraw from the world that presented temptations and obstacles to reaching their goal. Similarly, in Christianity, many followers of Jesus down through the centuries have felt called to "renounce the world" in order to pursue a monastic life dedicated to the worship of God, good deeds, and hospitality.

It is inevitable that a spiritual master like Said Nursi would be asked about the issue. Some disciples noted that the great Sufi saints had abandoned the world, yet the Companions of the Prophet were usually very actively involved in worldly affairs of civilization at that time. Said Nursi was challenged to defend his view that the least of the Companions was greater than even the holiest saint.[129] Nursi responded that to the Companions, the world was an arable field that had to be sowed, plowed, and reaped. It is true that they were greatly

---

[128] *The Letters*, "Flowers from the Seeds of Reality: A Dream Assembly".
[129] *The Words*, The Twenty-Seventh Word, Addendum, Second question, p. 510.

involved in the concerns of the civilization of their time, but this did not alienate them from their commitment to follow the Qur'an.

The world, he teaches, has a face that looks toward the Hereafter, and for believers to love that face is a path to attaining perfection. Moreover, there is an aspect to all worldly life, including the civilization of the present time, that reflects the Divine Names, that is, that point to and show forth the various qualities of God. In other words, to involve oneself in civilized life with a view to carrying out God's work—the sowing and reaping—does not separate one from the life of faith, nor does the effort to discover the beautiful qualities of the Creator in all that He has provided. The Companions of Muhammad engaged themselves in worldly activities in this spirit, and as such attained a high degree of goodness and uprightness.

The error of misguided people is to love the world and civilization for its own sake, a love that can never be reciprocated. He paraphrases one who holds such a view: "I consider happiness in this world and life's pleasures, and the progress of civilization and perfection of arts as all lying in refusal to think of the hereafter and to know God, in love of this world, in absolute freedom and license and in relying exclusively on myself." The love that such people should direct to God, they waste in triviality and self-interest, and for this they suffer the consequences. In short, engagement in the life of civilization without recognizing or serving God is both self-defeating and self-destructive.

> In accordance with the principles that 'the consequence of an illicit love is suffering a merciless torment,' you are suffering a fully justified punishment, for you are unlawfully employing your innate capacity for love, knowledge, thanks and worship that relate properly to the essence, attributes and Names of God Almighty, on your own soul and the life of this world. You have lavished the love that belongs to God Almighty on yourself. Your own soul has become your beloved and will cause you endless suffering: you are not giving true peace to that beloved.[130]

However, there comes a time in the life of the believer when it is necessary to withdraw from the world, to meditate in solitude, to devote

---

[130] *The Words*, The Thirty-Second Word, Third Stopping Place, pp. 663–664.

oneself to pursuits of eternal import. Circumstances often dictate such times; sickness, old age, or imprisonment, all of which Said Nursi experienced in his own life led him to an attitude of retirement.[131] In the beautiful "Treatise for the Elderly," he notes that such times are not to be regarded as loss, but can be a source of spiritual riches, growth in understanding of God's will, and a preparation for death.

After one of his final visits to İstanbul, he wrote of his retreat to Sarıyer to study the teachings of the spiritual masters, and offers his experience as counsel to elderly disciples:

> After receiving this reminder of the Qur'an, the graveyard became more familiar to me than İstanbul. Solitude and retirement became more pleasurable to me than conversation and company. I found a place of seclusion for myself in Sarıyer on the Bosphorus. There, Ghawth al-A'zam (May God be pleased with him) became a master, doctor, and guide for me..., while Imam-i Rabbani (May God be pleased with him) became a companion, sympathetic friend, and teacher... I was extremely happy I had approached old age, withdrawn from civilization, and free of social life. I thanked God. And so, respected persons who have entered upon old age and who frequently recall death through its warnings! In accordance with the light of the teachings of belief taught by the Qur'an, we should look favorably on old age, death, and illness, and even love them in one respect. Since we have an infinitely precious bounty like belief, both old age is agreeable, and illness, and death.[132]

In short, for Said Nursi, it is not a question of which is better, engagement or retirement, but the attitude with which either is faced. If one is seeking to do God's will and to discover the Divine Names in one's circumstances, even imprisonment, old age, and death can be seen as blessings. Civilization becomes a destructive alternative to a life of faith when it is regarded as an end in itself, as a way of loving and serving oneself, rather than of loving and serving the Creator and Final Goal of life. Ultimately, there are aspects of modern life which reflect God's qualities. These can be accepted and one should thank God for them. But those aspects of modernity that deny or ignore

---

[131] *The Flashes*, The Twenty-Sixth Flash, Thirteenth Hope, p. 310.
[132] *The Flashes*, The Twenty-Sixth Flash, Tenth Hope, p. 304.

God or banish God to the margins of consciousness and activity make lying promises they cannot keep. It is Divine wisdom to recognize and reject these false promises, but to accomplish this, the modern believer must discern and distinguish the good from the bad in modern civilization according to the interpretative light of the teaching of the Qur'an.

War and Peace

The *Risale-i Nur* on war

We are gathered for this seminar[133] at a particularly tragic moment of modern history. Even as we speak and study about peace, bombs are falling in the neighboring country of Iraq, innocent people are being killed and maimed, their homes destroyed, and their lives shattered. The international rule of law has been violated, and the United Nations, which after the last great World War was created as a structure for the promotion of universal peace and fellowship, has been ignored. The advance of civil society has been dealt a serious blow, and the human family has taken a great step backwards into barbarity. The law of the jungle in which might makes right is at the moment prevailing over the Divinely-revealed values of brotherhood, human dignity, morality, and peace.

For this reason, it is fitting that we come together to study the thoughts of a man who made a positive contribution to the understanding of the implications of war and the path to peace in the 20th Century. Said Nursi did not write about war and peace from an ivory tower. He experienced personally the horrors of two World Wars. The "Old Said" took an active part in the First World War, commanding militia forces in the Caucasus in defending his homeland against the Russian invasion, for which he was awarded a War Medal. He showed courage by remaining on horseback during the shelling and refusing to take refuge in the trenches. He proved his religious faith

---

[133] A paper delivered at the seminar: "Peace and Islam, under the illumination of the ideas of the *Risale-i Nur*," İstanbul, 30 March 2003.

by dictating Qur'anic commentary to a scribe in the midst of battle.[134] He was taken prisoner and deported to distant regions of Russia.

Thirty years later, Said Nursi lived through the Second World War. In the meantime, the "New Said" had undergone a spiritual pilgrimage, and the worldly events clashing around him hardly penetrated his awareness. He devoted his days and months of confinement to the study of the Qur'an and, as he states, "In these last four years, I have known neither the stages of the war, nor its results, nor whether or not peace has been declared, and I have not asked, I have not knocked on the door of this sacred *surah* to learn how many allusions it contains to this century and its wars."[135] Nursi's transformation from social activist to contemplative student of the Qur'an has been studied by persons far more knowledgeable than I, but I think that no one will deny that his wartime experiences played a great role in that transformation.

It is clear from the *Risale-i Nur* that Said Nursi's direct experience of war and the long periods of imprisonment, first as a prisoner-of-war in distant Russia and later confinement in his own homeland, were formative in the development of his character and religious vision. The numerous references in the *Risale-i Nur* to his life as prisoner-of-war and prisoner of conscience show that these periods were for him were what he called the "School of Joseph," places of solitary confinement far superior to the mountain caves of ascetics and recluses, where his time would not be wasted in vain and selfish pursuits.[136]

In a beautiful passage from *The Flashes*, Nursi recounts one of the contemplative experiences that brought about his spiritual growth.

> In the First World War, as a prisoner, I was in the distant province of Kosturma in northeastern Russia. There was a small mosque there belonging to the Tatars beside the famous River Volga. I used to become wearied among my friends, the other officers. I craved solitude, yet I could not wander about outside without permission. Then they took me on bail to the Tatar quarter, to that small mosque

[134] *The Letters*, "Bediüzzaman's Life, the *Risale-i Nur*, and Letters 1928–32," p. 579; *The Flashes*, "A Look at Bediüzzaman's Life and the *Risale-i Nur*," p. 481.

[135] *The Rays*, The Fruits of Belief, Eleventh Topic, p. 287.

[136] *The Flashes*, The Twenty-Sixth Flash, p. 336.

on the banks of the Volga. I used to sleep in the mosque, alone. Spring was close. I used to be very wakeful during the long, long nights of that northern land; the sad plashing of the Volga and the mirthless patter of the rain and the melancholy sighing of the wind of those dark nights in that dark exile had temporarily roused me from a deep sleep of heedlessness. I did not yet consider myself old, but those who had experienced the Great War were old.[137]

Experiences of death and suffering in war also shaped Said Nursi's understanding of the truths of religion. Writing about how the martyrs and others benefit from life in the Intermediate Realm, he recounts the death of his nephew Ubeyd. "I myself had a nephew and student called Ubeyd. He was killed at my side and in my place and became a martyr. Later, when I was being held as a prisoner-of-war, in a true dream I entered his grave, which was in the form of a dwelling-place under the earth, although I did not know where he was buried. I saw him living the level of life of martyrs. He evidently thought that I was dead, and said that he had wept much for me. He thought that he was alive, but having retreated from the Russian invasion, had made himself a good home under the ground." He concludes that this dream, unimportant in itself, convinced him of the reality of life-after-death for true believers.[138]

Even though believers can learn important lessons from the brutal realities of war, a person who is devoted to God cannot blind himself to war's evil causes and ugly effects. He perceives that people and governments did not accept the lessons to be learned from the First World War and this heedlessness led them into a second, more terrible war.[139] Nursi's views would seem to confirm the old adage that "Those who refuse to learn from the errors of history are condemned to repeat them." He describes World War II as "having plunged the world into chaos,"[140] and bringing about "widespread hunger, destruc-

---

[137] Ibid., pp. 299–300.

[138] *The Letters*, The First Letter, p. 23.

[139] *The Words*, "Gleams," p. 742.

[140] *The Rays*, The Fruits of Belief, Fourth Topic, p. 223.

tion, and waste."[141] Among those responsible for the widespread suffering caused by the war were, in Nursi's view, were the politicians and the media representatives.

Commenting on the verse in Surah al-Falaq (Qur'an 113:4) on the mischief of those who blow on knots, Nursi relates the passage to the self-serving propaganda of and diplomatic machinations of warmongering politicians and the news media they control. It was such politicians and media barons, he states, who were responsible for the First World War which set humankind backward and stopped human progress. "Through the political diplomats blowing their evils, material and immaterial and their sorcery and poison into everyone's heads through the tongue of the radio and inculcating their secret plans into the heart of human destiny, they prepared the evils that would savagely destroy a thousand years of the progress of civilization. This corresponds exactly with the meaning of "the blowers on knots."[142] Unfortunately, leaders did not learn the lessons of World War I, but responded with egotism, racism, pitiless cruelty, military dictatorships, tyranny, and fanatic nationalism,[143] all of which paved the way, for human treachery in the form of "envy, rivalry and clashes"[144] for the Second World War.

What is the way out of this cycle of the evils of one war producing the pretexts and causes for the next war, a recurrent pattern of destruction, fear, resentment and despair handed on one generation to the next? Said Nursi responds to this perennial question with a reflection which occurred to him on the occasion of *Lailat al-Qadr*, "the Night of Power." It is only the Word of God, that cuts like a sharp sword through the chain of wrongdoing, anger and desire for revenge, that can enable humankind to move beyond destructive and self-destructive patterns of behavior to seek for the genuine, eternal life which is humankind's true goal. As this is Said Nursi's deepest answer

---

[141] *The Flashes*, The Nineteenth Flash, p. 199.

[142] *The Rays*, The Fruits of Belief, Eleventh Topic, p. 287.

[143] *The Rays*, The Twelfth Ray, p. 316.

[144] *The Rays*, The Fruits of Belief, Eleventh Topic, p. 287.

to the human temptation to solve conflicts by means of violence and war, I will quote the passage at length:

> Because of the extreme tyranny and despotism of this last World War and its merciless destruction, with hundreds of innocents being scattered and ruined on account of a single enemy, the awesome despair of the defeated, the fearsome alarm of the victors and their ghastly pangs of conscience arising from the supremacy they are unable to maintain and the destruction they are unable to repair, and the utterly transitory and ephemeral nature of the life of this world and the deceptive, opiate nature of the fantasies of civilization becoming apparent to all, and the exalted abilities lodged in human nature... being wounded in a universal and awesome manner, and heedlessness, misguidance and deaf, lifeless nature being smashed by the diamond sword of the Qur'an, and the exceedingly ugly, exceedingly cruel true face of world politics becoming apparent... man's true nature will search with all its strength for eternal life, which it truly loves and for which it yearns.[145]

Because of this conviction that in the depths of his heart, mankind really seeks and desires eternal life that comes from living according to God's Word, Nursi has hope for the future. Wars show the true face of politics, the limitations of military power, and the transient nature of human life. All-powerful God is more powerful than the deceptions with which men surround themselves and is able to enlighten and change the hearts of leaders and rulers.

> Like the One Powerful Over All Things sweeps and cleans in a minute the atmosphere filled with clouds and shows the shining sun in clear skies, so He may also dispel these black and merciless clouds and show the truths of the Shari'a like the sun, and give them without expense or trouble. We await it from His mercy that He will not sell them to us expensively. May He give intelligence to the minds of those at the top, and belief to their hearts; that would be enough. Then matters would put themselves to rights.[146]

Said Nursi is not discouraged by the apparent weakness of the people of faith, of those who seek to live according to God's Word,

---

[145] *The Words*, Thirteenth Word, Second Station, p. 167.
[146] *The Rays*, The Fourteenth Ray, p. 436.

to affect the changes in human society to overcome humankind's self-deception. Although it appears that the forces of violence, power, and economic gain are winning out over those who live and promote humane and Divine values, they will not prevail in the long run, because they are acting in a manner contrary to the will of God who is All-Powerful. Said Nursi's final word on the subject of war is thus an affirmation of the ultimate victory of those who stand for Divine values. He states: "Even if falsehood prevails in this world, it cannot win the war. *"The future belongs to the God-conscious."*[147]

The *Risale-i Nur* on peace

In September 2002 in İstanbul, I gave a talk at the International *Risale-i Nur* Symposium on the theme of the ethics of pardon and peace. In that paper I tried to present the understanding of the nature and preconditions of peace as found in the *Risale-i Nur* and to show its correspondence with the views of Pope John Paul II. I will not repeat here everything that I said in that paper, but will try to reflect with you on several key points of the path to peace as envisioned by the *Risale-i Nur* in the light of the current world situation.

The first task of those who want to build peace is to have a clear idea of the kind of civilization they want to construct. What are our goals? What are we aiming at? Where do we want our efforts at building society to lead? For Said Nursi, the Divinely-guided civilization proposed by Islam is a society not ruled by the ethics of the jungle where the rich and powerful take what they can and defend what they have obtained by use of force, but rather a civilization based on truth, justice, and harmony.

Instead of the ethics of the jungle where the rich and powerful take what they can and use their superiority in technology and wealth to force others to obey them, or the principle of class struggle by which the poor and oppressed seek to obtain their rights by force, Said Nursi sees the Divinely-guided ethic proposed by Islam as one in which truth, justice and harmony are paramount.

---

[147] *The Words,* "Gleams," p. 760.

> The civilization the shari'a of Muhammad (peace and blessings be upon him) comprises and commands is this: its point of support is truth instead of force, the marks of which are justice and harmony. Its goal is virtue in place of [selfish] benefit, and its characteristic marks are love and attraction. Its means of unity are the ties of religion, country, and class, in place of racism and nationalism, and the mark of these are sincere brotherhood, peace, and only defense against external aggression. Its life is the principle of mutual assistance instead of that of conflict, and its mark is accord and solidarity.[148]

Muslims, following Said Nursi, rightly call such a civilization an "Islamic civilization." However, I must tell you that when I as a Christian read Said Nursi's description of a Divinely-guided civilization, I do not find the qualities expressed to be significantly different from the kind of civilization that I and my fellow Christians seek to build. You do not have to take my word for this. All the speeches and leaders of Pope John Paul II, the spiritual leader of Catholic Christians around the world, point toward just such a civilization as that described above in the *Risale-i Nur*.

There is no clash of civilizations between real Christians and real Muslims. There is nothing surprising in this, because both communities are believers in the one and only God and both seek to construct society on the principles and values taught by that God. If there is a clash, it is between, on the one hand, the civilization envisioned by "people of faith," or in the words of Said Nursi, "the God-conscious" and, on the other, a civilization that tries to banish God from everyday life, from politics, economics, and social interaction, and to reduce religion to privately-held beliefs, to ineffective ritual, to colorful folklore.

Ethical systems based solely on human reason fail because they do not take into account God as the Maker, Teacher and Guide of human life. Philosophical reasoning presumes that people know what they want and will always work to achieve the desired goal, but the sad reality is that people often act against their best interests due to anger, fear, jealousy and the like, and for reasons of selfishness, igno-

---

[148] *The Damascus Sermon*, p. 106.

rance, and laziness, they do not achieve what they desire. However, a religious orientation, such as we are taught in the Bible and the Qur'an, allows for the reality of human failure by urging believers to return to God in repentance, to seek forgiveness, and begin anew. Said Nursi considers "God-given ethics" to be an essential element in the message of the Prophets. "Be distinguished by *God-given morals*," he states, "and turn towards God Almighty with humility, recognizing your impotence, poverty, and defectiveness, and so be a slave in His presence."[149]

Thus, the first step towards building a civilization characterized by peace and justice is to realize that we will not succeed if we rely on our own efforts or follow our own ideas. We need the strength and the guidance that only comes from God. True peace can only be achieved if people follow God's commands and turn to God in humble repentance.

Said Nursi expresses the longing of millions of people around the world in his desire for universal peace. He saw with his own eyes the suffering, anguish, and destruction brought about by the two World Wars and wants to see a time of peace and prosperity for all.[150] Said Nursi saw this as the mission of Islam on earth, the task that Muslims are called to carry out. He said: "God willing, through the strength of Islam, in the future the virtues of civilization will prevail, the face of the earth cleaned of filth, and universal peace be secured."[151] This is a noble task that he envisions for Muslims, one which, in my opinion, must be shared as well by Christians and all those who worship, love and obey the one God. Universal peace is not only a human desire, but a vocation given to all people of faith by God himself. Said Nursi's conviction that Islam must play a role of peacemaker in today's world is paralleled by the declaration of the Catholic Church's Second Vatican Council that Christians and Muslims together have a common

---

[149] *The Words*, The Thirtieth Word, First Aim, p. 564.
[150] *The Damascus Sermon*, p. 43.
[151] Ibid., p. 38.

task of working together for the benefit of all to build "peace, liberty, social justice, and moral values."[152]

One can object that this goal has often not been followed by Christian peoples and governments in the past. One remembers religious wars, the Crusades, colonialism, and even today, the actions of government and military leaders who bomb and invade and occupy other, weaker nations. However, we must all remember that Christianity must not be judged by the actions of every individual or group or government that identifies itself as "Christian," any more than Islam should be judged by the deeds of every individual or group or government that calls itself "Islamic."

In fact, what people call themselves or what they are called by others is itself often a function of propaganda, an attempt to convince people of something contrary to the reality. Said Nursi states that he himself was often falsely accused of being a trouble-maker and disturber of the peace. He holds that such accusations are rooted in the fears of non-religious people towards those who take their faith seriously. He stated: "'The worldly' are excessively suspicious of me. Quite simply, they are frightened of me, imagining non-existent things in me, which even if they existed would not constitute a political crime... Imagining these things in me, they have been carried away by groundless fears."[153]

This does not mean that Said Nursi ever allowed himself to act against his conscience or to obey commands with which he could not agree. He states: "I support neither intellectually nor on scholarly grounds the arbitrary commands, called laws, of a commander... and for myself I do not act in accordance with them. But although for twenty years I have been severely oppressed during my tortuous captivity, I have not become involved in politics, nor provoked the authorities, nor disturbed public order. And although I have hundreds of thou-

---

[152] Second Vatican Council, "In Our Time," paragraph 3, in A. Flannery, *Vatican Council II*, Dublin: Dominican Pubs., p. 572.

[153] *The Letters*, Addendum to the Sixteenth Letter, p. 96.

sands of *Risale-i Nur* friends, not a single incident has been recorded involving the disturbance of the peace."[154]

At the time I delivered this paper, in 2003, when thousands of my fellow Americans were carrying out forms of civil disobedience and passive and non-violent resistance to protest a war they considered to be both illegal and unjust, the example of Said Nursi was highly relevant. As Said Nursi showed in his own life, peace cannot be achieved simply by obeying every command issued by authorities. Both as religious believers, whose first allegiance is to God's will, and as thinking citizens, whose allegiance is to the rule of law and civil society, a critical approach to authorities, who are often correct but sometimes deeply in error, is essential is peace is to be achieved.

My final point is one that Said Nursi reiterated over and over. That is the necessity of true reconciliation for any lasting peace. When one has wronged another, when a nation has aggressed against another, the result is fear, anger, anxiety. On the part of the aggressor there is a feeling of guilt and a desire to justify one's cause. High-minded motivations are brought forward to conceal and deny the real motivations, which are often those of greed, power, and revenge. The media in the form of television, newspapers, and scholarly journals is employed to make a government's policies and actions acceptable and to shape public opinion, but the reality remains that human greed and selfishness are usually at the heart of aggression and violence towards others. "There is only one solution for this," says Said Nursi, "and that is reconciliation, which the Qur'an commands, and which truth, reality, benefit, humanity, and Islam require and encourage."[155]

This requires honesty, an admission that the misdeeds of persons and nations are often motivated by unworthy factors. Noting that Islam commands: "one believer should not be vexed with another believer for more than three days," Nursi teaches that so long as there is no reconciliation, both sides perpetually suffer the torments of fear and revenge. His conclusion is that "it is essential to make peace quick-

---

[154] *The Rays*, The Fourteenth Ray, p. 417.
[155] Ibid., p. 484.

ly." Thus, in the thought of Said Nursi, there can be no real peace unless there is genuine reconciliation.

So long as no reconciliation takes place, the wounds to the human relations fester and grow and turn into resentment. Discord produces more discord, violence engenders even greater violence, and the state of conflict is perpetuated. The only way out of a spiraling succession of violent reactions and counter-reactions is for one party to take the initiative to reconcile. Reconciliation heals what force can never heal, the suspicion and resentment caused by wrongdoing one against another. As Said Nursi puts it, "A minor disaster becomes a large one, and continues. But if they make peace, and the murderer repents and prays continuously for the man he killed, then both sides will gain much and become like brothers. In place of one departed brother, he will gain several religious brothers."

At this moment of great tension in human affairs, let us all who believe in God pray that the wise advice of the *Risale-i Nur* be heeded, especially by the leaders of nations, as the peoples of our world seek to find just and lasting peace for humankind.

The Damascus Sermon: a Spiritual Physician's Prescription for the Sicknesses of Our Age

I n this talk, I will attempt to present the main ideas of Said Nursi's famous *Damascus Sermon* and to respond to religious vision expressed in that sermon. This treatise was first delivered in early 1911 as the Friday sermon at the Umayyad Mosque in Damascus. Almost 10,000 persons are said to have filled the great mosque to overflowing. Today, after a passage of more than 100 years, the sermon has been often reprinted and is still being read and studied. It is clear that the Said Nursi's analysis of Muslim societies and his spiritual counsel have continued to speak to the needs of Muslims of this past century. My reflections are the thoughts of a Western Christian and, as such, my paper can be regarded as an exercise in interreligious dialogue.

Two preliminary questions

Two preliminary questions of interest to scholars must be addressed before we examine the content of the sermon. Scholars of history will be interested in the textual question. The sermon was originally delivered in Arabic and subsequently twice printed in that language. A later Arabic edition was made in 1922. Many years later, in the 1950s, Said Nursi himself translated the sermon into Turkish and in doing so introduced revisions which addressed the current state of world affairs and appended addenda in response to questions put to him by his disciples. The text I studied is the English translation of Said Nursi's amplified Turkish version.

The sermon, first delivered in the early years of the 20th Century, in the twilight period of the Ottoman state, looks forward to the questions of faith that would occupy religious believers in the tumultuous decades to come. The expanded Turkish version of the sermon can be regarded as the author's own commentary on the original, made 40 years later in light of developments in world history which had in the meantime intervened: the birth of the Turkish Republic, two disastrous world wars, the rise of communism incarnated in the Soviet Union, the barbarous threat to humanity of Nazi and Fascist ideologies, as well as events contemporaneous with Nursi's Turkish translation—the extension of the communist system to Eastern Europe, the Maoist revolution in China, and the emergence of post-colonial nations in Arab countries, Africa and Asia.

Now, 40 years after the Turkish version, at the start of a new century, we find equally dramatic changes in geopolitical conditions: the Soviet experiment concluded and the Soviet Union dismembered, China moving toward a market economy, Turkey as well as the former Eastern European satellites applying for membership in the European Union, and Asian and African nations grappling with the challenges and problems of neo-colonialism and the globalization of market economy. The contemporary reader today must inevitably ask: "What is the relevance of *The Damascus Sermon* for religious believers after almost a century of turbulent change?

Scholars of religion will ask another question. *The Damascus Sermon* was delivered by a Muslim preacher to Muslim worshipers in the context of Islamic congregational prayer. The reflections I am about to offer are those of a Christian. Christianity and Islam are sister religions which, together with Judaism, look back to Abraham as our common ancestor in faith. Both Christians and Muslims profess to worship God alone and seek to do God's will in all things. Yet our two communities have not always treated one another with the love and respect that God desires of those who worship Him. Errors have been committed on both sides and the deeds of some members of our communities toward the other can only be described as criminal. With this background, both of common bases in faith and a history that has all too often reflected enmity rather than love, we are led to pose a second question: "In *The Damascus Sermon*, does Said Nursi have anything to say to Christians? Are his words directed exclusively to Muslims, or do they have relevance for all those who profess active faith in the One God?

The structure of *The Damascus Sermon*

Keeping these two preliminary questions in mind, let us turn our attention directly to *The Damascus Sermon*. The structure of the sermon is simple. After beginning by praising God and seeking God's blessing, Said Nursi states what he sees to be the most agonizing question for believers of his time: Why are non-believers who have abandoned God and religious principles progressing so rapidly in material development, while those regions where religious faith is strong are stagnating and even regressing towards greater levels of backwardness and poverty? Said Nursi's basic query, at the beginning of the 20th Century, reflects a believer's formulation of the basic criticism of religion posed by philosophers such as Feuerbach, Comte, Marx, and Nietzsche and embodied in policies of the Italian *Risorgimento*, the Mexican and Russian revolutions, and the Liberal parties in various European countries: the conviction that religion is a characteristic of primitive sages of humanity, but has become in the modern world an opiate, an obstacle to human progress and nation-building.

Said Nursi does not respond to this critique of religion by hurling condemnations. Rather, he admits that some of the diagnosis is correct. Religious believers are themselves to blame for the malaise that afflicts them. He notes six "dire illnesses" that must be faced if religious believers are to make a positive contribution to human progress in the coming decades. While noting the failures of believers, he also rejects the godless and materialist solutions proposed by the critics, which he foresees will lead to disaster, a claim which the subsequent history of the century proved to be only too accurate.

The remainder of the sermon is an effort to respond to this basic question and to treat the six fundamental illnesses which he saw to be afflicting religious peoples. Said Nursi does this in the form of Six

Words which correspond to each of the spiritual sicknesses suffered by religious societies. One can say that Said Nursi's methodology is that of a physician who must: 1) examine the *symptoms* to discover what is wrong, 2) name the sickness in *diagnosis*, 3) encourage the patient with a positive *prognosis* that affirms that there is a cure, and 4) *prescribe* what must be done to promote healing. Let us examine these Six Words to see how Said Nursi acts as spiritual physician to treat the basic maladies of the age.[156]

1. The sickness: *despair*, the cure: *hope*

The first sickness faced by religious societies is despair. Looking at the material progress of others and the relative stagnation of their own societies, believers are tempted to hopelessness, to feeling that God has abandoned them, that the future belongs to proponents of godless materialism who have the power, wealth, and energy needed to dominate the world. To meet this spiritual illness, Said Nursi prescribes *hope*. There are real grounds for hope, he declares. Not only has God promised that "the future belongs to Islam" and "its ruler shall be the truths of the Qur'an and belief" (*DS*, p. 27), but solid bases for hope can be found in history and in analysis of contemporary situations. If Muslims review their history, they will see that Muslims increased in civilization and progress to the degree they lived in accord with Islamic truths. Conversely, they fell to savagery, decline, disaster, and defeat insofar as they abandoned those truths (*DS*, p. 28.)

Another basis for hope is rooted in human psychology. Both individuals and societies cannot live happily and successfully without religion. In times of crisis, even the most irreligious person will take refuge in religion. Similarly, societies might prosper materially without religious faith, but in doing so must fall continually into competition, greed, and warfare which ultimately overwhelm and destroy their achievements. Thus, although religion would appear to be in decline in the 20th Century, one can expect that basic human needs for God

---

[156] Said Nursi, *The Damascus Sermon*, İstanbul: Sözler Neşriyat, 1996. The six maladies are enumerated on pp. 26–27.

will ultimately prevail over materialist ways of thinking and acting. Another sign of hope can be found in increased education, in that as people move beyond a blind following of their leaders and begin to think for themselves, the intrinsic worth of the basic truths of religious faith can be better understood and valued.

Said Nursi sees grounds for hope that Muslim societies will attain material prosperity. There is a strength rooted in religious faith that no human ideology can replace. Values rooted in faith in God—an appreciation of human dignity, the strength that comes from a commitment to follow God's command to "compete in doing good," courage balanced by compassion, a transcendent vision which surpasses immediate prospects of short-term gains, and a sense of justice which neither oppresses nor tolerates oppressors—are strengths that give genuine hope for a more humane, just, civilized and prosperous future. If the fruits of despair are indifference, despondency, laziness and self-contempt (*DS*, p. 44), hope enables people to attain the perfection intended by God in creating humans as the summit of God's creative activity. The battle between good and evil is not an equal contest. Evil, ugliness, and futility are secondary and minor in God's creation (*DS*, p. 40), with none of the innate strength of truth, beauty, and goodness. Since the aim of God's creation has been goodness, beauty, and perfection, believers can legitimately hope that God is guiding humanity towards these ends.

If I have tended to belabor this first sickness of despair and the word of hope, it is because in his sermon Said Nursi devoted more space to despair and hope than all the other illnesses combined. It is clear that for him, the basic disease afflicting modern Muslims is *despair* and the most important word of encouragement that needs to be offered is *hope*.

Said Nursi is speaking of Islam and his sermon is addressed to Muslims. However, as a Christian I find myself in agreement with his analysis, with his diagnosis of the situation, and with his prescription for overcoming the spiritual illness of our time. Christians agree that there is no spiritual malaise that closes our minds to God's grace more deeply than despair. Despair is in itself a form of unbelief, for it questions the power, the mercy, and the goodness of God to overcome our weaknesses and make us into the persons, and our societies into the societies, that God wants us to become. Christians believe that of all God's gifts, the greatest are three: faith, hope, and love.

Hope is that quiet gift that enables us to trust in God's presence even in moments of greatest darkness and failure, that leads us to throw ourselves on God's mercy and seek forgiveness when we have fallen into sin, that inspires us to mobilize our spiritual and physical energies to accomplish great things for God even when the tasks can seem greater than our abilities and the obstacles seem impossible to overcome. Thus, I conclude, following Said Nursi, that the great fruit of a life of faith that Muslims and Christians can offer to the modern world is that of hope, a solid hope rooted in God's own nature, a hope that is affirmed and confirmed by reflecting on the realities of modern life.

2. The sickness: *deceit,* the cure: *honesty*

The second malady of the age of which Said Nursi speaks in his sermon is the lack of truthfulness in social and political life. Honesty and truthfulness must form the basis of an Islamic society, yet the reality is that their contraries are debilitating weaknesses endemic to Muslim societies of his time. The lack of truthfulness is not simply telling lies but takes on many forms (*DS*, p. 45). Hypocrisy is a form of dishonesty by publicly affirming one thing but privately doing the opposite. Flattery is cowardly and self-serving insincerity. Deception involves manipulation of the truth, distortion of facts and promotion of half-truths. Duplicity involves playing both sides against the other while pretending to befriend both. Slander and calumny are destructive forms of dishonesty that not only harm others but destroy communal solidarity. Religious leaders are not exempt from dishonesty, as seen in the production of self-interested *fatwas*. Politicians display dishonest behavior in campaigns of political propaganda, by rationalizing and justifying their behavior and by misusing their positions to pursue their own ends and abuse the power that accrues to their office.

To the malady of untruth, Said Nursi prescribes honesty and transparency in public life. Muslim societies will never be able to offer the modern world a viable alternative to lying and corruption unless they themselves embody the principles of truthfulness and responsibility. In the Turkish translation of his original sermon, he makes the point that this principle is as valid in the 1950s as it was when he delivered the original sermon: "O my brothers in the Umayyad mosque! And O my brothers, 40 to 50 years later who form the 400 million believers in the vast mosque of the world of Islam! Salvation is only to be found through truthfulness and honesty... the strongest chain with which to be bound to salvation is *honesty* (DS, p. 48)."

3. The sickness: *enmity*, the cure: *love*

A third reason for the weakness of the Muslim world is that of enmity and hostility. The two world wars of the 20th Century, not to mention countless local and civil conflicts around the world have shown "how evil, destructive, and what an awesome wrong is enmity (DS, p. 50)." The roots of enmity and hatred lie in human arrogance and self-worship. They result in unjust hostility toward others without one's even being aware of it. Enmity can take on subtle forms, even among religious believers, and show itself as feigned approval, not interfering with wrongdoing, and insincere friendliness. People usually consider that the evils others do are proper grounds for hostility, but Said Nursi teaches that, unless others are aggressive, one should "not let the evils of our enemies attract your enmity. Hell and Divine punishment are enough for them (DS, p. 50)."

To the destructive sickness of considering others one's enemy, Said Nursi prescribes love. "The thing most deserving of love is love, and that most deserving of enmity is enmity (DS, p. 49)." It is love and loving others that make a person's social life secure and lead to happiness. He sees "love, brotherhood, and affection" as basic to Islam, its bond. Fairness and thinking favorably of others, giving others the benefit of the doubt, must mark the Islamic character (DS, p. 51).

4. The sickness: *disunity,* the cure: *unity*

The fourth sickness that Said Nursi finds in Muslim societies of his time is that of *disunity.* Ethnic and linguistic suspicions and tensions divide the worldwide Islamic *umma.* Even in a given nation the factors of language and ethnic identity can be a destructive factor in weakening Muslims. In raising this issue, Said Nursi was confronting real situations. He delivered his original sermon in Damascus, which in 1911 was a restive part of the Ottoman state. Within a decade, Syria would become a French protectorate. Said Nursi prepared his Turkish translation of the sermon 40 years later when Syria and its Arab neighbors were emerging as independent nations. Said Nursi's plea is that Muslims not allow ethnic and linguistic differences to divide and weaken the unity of their nations, nor that relations between Muslim nations be determined on national, ethnic and linguistic lines.

To the sickness of disunity, Said Nursi prescribes the *unity* of the Islamic *umma.* "The time for Islamic unity is beginning," he tells his hearers. "This necessitates not paying attention to one another's personal faults (*DS,* p. 54)." He tells the worshipers in the Umayyad mosque that they cannot claim that there is nothing they can do to promote Islamic unity and brotherhood. Such an attitude, he claims, is nothing but an excuse for laziness and idleness (*DS,* pp. 52-53). He appeals to Muslim leaders and preachers to work together in unity to rebuild the bonds of brotherhood among Muslims. He calls on the newly-emerging independent Arab nations to emulate the model of the United States of America who, by working together in unity, can in a short time achieve success and restore their people to their former glories.

5. The sickness: *despotism,* the cure: *Islamic dignity*

Said Nursi is well aware of the toll taken by colonial domination in Muslim regions. The foreigners have systematically plundered Muslim regions of their precious possessions and have paid them "a rotten price" in return (*DS,* p. 54). However, the material theft is the least destructive of the colonizers' legacy. Worse is that they have stolen from Muslims "our elevated morals" and "fine character in relation to social life." Here Said Nursi is pointing out the psychological damage inflicted by the colonial system—the corruption of morals in situations of oppression and servitude and the destruction of social character through a demeaning loss of dignity. The colonizers have left us, he states, with "dissipated morals and dissipated character."

Muslims must admit this sickness and exert their efforts to correct it. Otherwise the effects of colonial indignity and dissolution will continue to weaken Muslim peoples. The way for Muslims to treat this spiritual illness is by finding in Islamic teaching the path to restore their God-given human dignity. This is not, he insists, a call to involve themselves in politics, which of itself cannot rebuild shattered morals or social character. Nor must Muslims allow their Islamic faith to be manipulated and made a tool to serve any particular political interests. It is only by absorbing and integrating into their daily behavior the teachings of Islam that Muslims can rise from their lowly, dissolute state. He states: "Beware, my brothers! Do not imagine that I am urging you with these words to busy yourselves with politics. God forbid! The truth of Islam is above all politics. All politics may serve it, but no politics can make Islam a tool for itself."

6. The sickness: *individualism,* the cure: *consultation*

The final sickness in Islamic societies which Said Nursi addresses is that of "restricting one's endeavors to what is personally beneficial." Muslims cannot blame all their weaknesses on colonial rule. Belief means not humiliating others by oppressing them, nor bowing down before tyrants and acquiescing to their oppression. Such would be a form of *shirk* by allowing a human person to play God over one's life (*DS*, p. 57). If each person engages only in those projects which benefit him personally, the common good will be ignored and progress postponed indefinitely.

The Islamic answer to the sickness of individualism is consultation. He sees consultation as the Islamic alternative to individualistic despotism, just as it is the sound basis for true freedom and progress. Consultation "is the freedom that is in accord with the *shari'a*, born of the consultation enjoined by the *shari'a*, and the noble-mindedness and compassion of belief that will loosen and remove the fetters and chains of the various forms of tyranny" (*DS*, p. 56). By being willing to move beyond self-interest and personal ambition to consult and work together with others in sincerity and solidarity, "ten persons can perform the work of a thousand" (*DS*, p. 57).

Said Nursi acknowledges that there are no simple answers. The needs are endless. People can only hope to achieve lasting gains by consulting with one another, learning from each other, and working together to achieve common goals. He concludes his sermon with these words: "In the face of endless enemies and innumerable needs, man can continue his personal life only through the support and assistance proceeding from belief, and can maintain his social life only through the mutual consultation enjoined by the *shari'a* that proceeds from the truths of belief. Only thus can he halt his enemies and open up a way to secure his needs" (*DS*, p. 58).

Final reflections

Obviously, Said Nursi's concern in *The Damascus Sermon* was with Islamic societies. By analyzing these societies and offering directions on how they can treat the weaknesses and defects in these societies, his intention is clearly to set Muslims on the path to building effective, strong, and prosperous Muslim societies. As a Christian reading the sermon, I find no indication that his intention is to mobilize Muslims *against* Christians. It is obvious from his other writings in the *Risale-i Nur*[157] that Said Nursi has no quarrel with authentic Christians, whom he regards as co-believers in God who seek to live according to Divine values. He holds that the modern world needs the joint witness of true Muslims and Christians to the values that derive from faith in God.

---

[157] Cf. Thomas Michel, "Muslim–Christian Dialogue and Cooperation in the Thought of Bediüzzaman Said Nursi," *The Muslim World*, LXXXIX/3–4, July-October 1999, pp. 325–336.

In my opinion, the social analysis carried out by Said Nursi on the weaknesses of Muslim societies could be usefully employed by Christians to view critically their own societies. Christian societies in Latin America and Africa, while often rich in faith, are no less wounded by the effects of colonialism, no less prone to the sicknesses of despair, deceit, enmity, disunity, despotism, and individualism, and no less in need of hope, honesty, love, unity, human dignity, and consultation than are Muslim societies. Prosperous Christian and post-Christian societies of North America and Europe can profit from the sermon's warnings about the dangers of adopting a competitive, aggressive economic agenda which ignores the centrality of God and the human need for a spiritual vision.

At the end of this study, I can answer my preliminary questions in the affirmative. Yes, *The Damascus Sermon* continues to be relevant to the challenges of the 21st Century, and, yes, there is much in Said Nursi's analysis that should offer food for reflection by modern Christians. I believe that the Sixth Word, *consultation*, is one that needs to be carried out not only by Muslims within their own circles, but by all those who profess faith in God and seek to do God's will on earth. It is by following the call to mutual consultation between Muslims and Christians urged by Said Nursi that I have offered here my reflections on Said Nursi's *Damascus Sermon*.

God's Justice in Relation
to Natural Disasters

In the Name of God, the Merciful, the Compassionate
When the earth shall quake violently,
and the earth shall bring forth its burdens,
and man shall say: "What is happening to it?"
On that Day, it shall relate its tales,
as its Lord has inspired it. (Qur'an 99: 1–5)

At the time of the Indian Ocean tsunami on 26 December 2004, in which over 300,000 persons were killed, 168,000 in Indonesia alone, I was lecturing in Central Java in Indonesia. The island of Java was relatively unaffected by the tsunami, since it is sheltered from the Indian Ocean by the larger island of Sumatra. Nevertheless, everyone in Indonesia was shocked at the widespread destruction and loss of life, and there was much soul-searching in an effort to understand God's will in such a terrible disaster.

For Muslims, the questioning was especially acute, because Aceh, the North Sumatran province most severely affected, was well-known as being the most pious and faithful Islamic region of the country. Aceh is known in Indonesia as "the threshold of Mecca." Consequently, many Muslims were asking how God could permit such an event to occur in the most God-fearing region of Indonesia, and they wondered where God's justice could be found in an event in which good and bad perished indiscriminately.

The experience of discussing with Indonesian friends the mystery of God's will in relation to the tsunami provoked me to learn what Said Nursi had to say about natural disasters and how he reconciled such events with faith in God's justice and mercy. There is a passage in the *Risale-i Nur*[158] that specifically treats these questions. It was penned in response to many queries put to Said Nursi following upon a severe earthquake that occurred on 27 December 1939 in the Turkish province of Erzincan. The quake, which caused more than 30,000 deaths, was actually a series of seven powerful shocks (the most violent registering 7.9 on the Richter scale), that together went to produce the most lethal and destructive disaster to hit Anatolia in modern times. In his response, Said Nursi treats seven questions that people had put to him in regard to the earthquake.

First Question: What is the reason for the anxiety that people experience as a result of the earthquake? They are terrified that there will be another one. While admitting that the physical destruction and loss of life caused by earthquakes and other natural disasters are matters of great distress, Nursi notes that the spiritual and psychological crises that follow upon such calamities are often more severe than the material damage. The reason for this is that people who have experienced this type of disaster are traumatized; they are fearful that another quake will occur, and they live in despair since they do not know how to avoid this imminent danger or save themselves from it. The result of this fear and despair is that people lie awake nights worried about another earthquake, losing sleep and becoming depressed.

Said Nursi's answer is that licentious, blasphemous lifestyles lie at the heart of this fear and despair. He suggests that if people were truly engaged in pious behavior and faithfully living according to God's will, they would not be caught in the grip of torment, fear, and despair. They would see the hand of God even in the occurrence of natural calamities. "The reins of all those things that are hostile to you, from microbes to plagues, storms, famine, and earthquakes, are in the hands of the Compassionate, Wise One. Being wise, He does nothing in vain. Being compassionate, His mercy is superabundant. There is a form of grace and favour contained in everything He does."[159]

---

[158] *The Words*, The Fourteenth Word, Addendum, pp. 184–190.

[159] *The Words*, Thirty-Second Word, Third Stopping-Place, p. 665. Cf. also, *The Words*, The Eighteenth Word, p. 240: "Beneath the veil of events like storms, earthquakes, and plague, is the unfolding of numerous hidden immaterial flowers. The seeds of

If people were living in accord with God's will, they would not fear death because they would have a peaceful afterlife to look forward to. They would have the inner resources to confront disaster realistically and rationally and in this way find strength to overcome their fear as well as hope to overcome their despair. Nursi says elsewhere in the *Risale-i Nur* that if one views natural events with the eyes of faith, "he will realize that the storms and earthquakes and tempestuous events are all submissive officials, and understand that they are the means for instances of wisdom which though apparently harsh are in fact most gentle."[160]

It is noteworthy that Said Nursi's concern here is not to interpret the earthquake as a punishment for licentious living, but rather to note that the inner defects and inadequacies that people experience in confronting such disasters come from a lack of faithful, observant lives. However, the matter is complex. Elsewhere in the *Risale-i Nur*, he makes clear that at least some of the disasters that befall humanity are indeed the result of pride and obstinacy, of people thinking they know better than God. Certainly, this does not mean every individual is guilty, but it is the erroneous ideas and attitudes of the majority of people that bring down disasters upon the whole nation. Nursi states this view clearly in a dream debate with supporters of the secular state:

> The error of the majority is always the cause of general disasters. Mankind's misguided ideas, Nimrod-like obduracy, and Pharaoh-like pride swelled and swelled on the earth till it reached the skies. It upset the sensitive mystery of creation and it caused to descend from the heavens the plague and storm of the last war's quakes; it caused a heavenly blow to be visited on the infidel.[161]

In other words, there is a mysterious connection between the way that humans live, exemplified in the Qur'anic narratives of Prophets such as Noah, Hud, Salih, Lot, and Shuayb, the cosmic forces that sometimes "rebel" against human obstinacy and assail earthly society.

---

many potentialities which have not developed sprout and grow beautiful because of events which are apparently ugly."

[160] *The Words*, Twenty-Third Word, First Chapter, p. 322.

[161] *The Words*, "Gleams," p. 748. Cf. also, *The Letters*, Seeds of Reality, p. 548.

> **Second question:** Why don't these disasters happen in countries
> populated by non-believers? Why do they seem to occur very fre-
> quently in Muslim regions?

Said Nursi's answer is that chastisement for small sins and errors
is made quickly, on-the-spot, while the punishment for great matters
is deferred to a more august assembly. For example, one might be
forced to pay a trivial traffic fine immediately, but a serious case, such
as that of homicide or sedition, will be deferred to an important tribunal. In the same way, God punishes Muslims' less grievous sins in
this world immediately by disasters like earthquakes, while the more
serious sins of evildoers are deferred to the Final Judgment.

> **Third question:** If an earthquake is a punishment for sin, why are
> the innocent also punished for the sins of a few? Obviously, in any
> given region, not all people are evildoers, yet in a natural disaster,
> everyone suffers.

Said Nursi's answer is that it is not correct to say about any
human society that only a few people have sinned. In every society,
most people are in one way or another involved in the general wrongdoing. Whether it be the injustices visited upon the poor, the corruption of politicians and businessmen, public promiscuity, or general
disbelief, many people cooperate silently in such misdeeds in various
ways. Whether by complacently ignoring the wrong, by profiting from
the wrongdoing in one way or another, by passively putting up with
it and doing nothing to stop it, or by defending the rights of miscreants to carry out their offences, guilt is more widespread than that for
which a relatively small number of perpetrators is responsible. Nursi
here is raising the question of what might be called "social sin," the
general wrongdoing of a society for which no individual is responsible, but in which all are to a greater or lesser extent complicit.

> **Fourth question.** It could be argued that disasters like earthquakes
> atone for the sins that the people have committed. In other words,
> they are occasions by which people begin in this world to atone
> for the punishment due to their sinful deeds. But if this is so, it
> would seem unjust on the part of God to punish the innocent
> along with the guilty.

Said Nursi replies that the issue is bound up with the mystery of Divine determining, that is, God's omnipotent power over all things and the reality of human freedom to choose good or evil. He cites a Qur'anic verse to the effect: *"Fear tumult or oppression, which affects not only those of you who do wrong* (8:25)."* Nursi interprets this verse to mean this world is like a proving ground or examination hall in which each person's level of responsibility and accountability is being tested. If in the case of disaster the innocent were spared while the guilty were being punished, then evildoers would do what is right, not because they wanted to obey and believe in God, but simply out of self-interest, to avoid worldly destruction. The upright "Abu Bakrs" of this world would have no opportunity to show their positive, God-fearing qualities, nor would the self-serving, evildoing "Abu Jahls" be shown up for the cowardly, desperate people they had made out of themselves. Thus, it is necessary that in a disaster, both good and bad undergo the same misery, so that the spiritual stuff of which each is made will become evident.

Moreover, God does not forget His faithful, upright servants in time of disaster. God shows them mercy and treats their suffering as a type of martyrdom which will gain for them a great reward in the afterlife. Just as the deaths of innocent victims can be considered a kind of martyrdom, so also their property and livelihood which were destroyed in the disaster take on the status of alms, which will earn the faithful victims eternal benefit.

Nursi concludes that men have no right to complain in the case of disasters and illness, nor are they justified in accusing God of injustice. He gives three reasons for his view. Firstly, God as Creator and Provider has disposal over His creation to do as he wishes. Disasters provide an opportunity for God to display His beautiful Names by consoling and caring for the innocent victims. Secondly, "by means of disasters and sicknesses, life is refined, perfected, strengthened and advanced; it yields results, attains perfection and fulfils its own purpose. Life led monotonously on the couch of ease and comfort resembles not so much the pure good that is being, as the pure evil that is non-being."[162] Thirdly, this world is a testing-ground where patiently endured suffering purifies the person and becomes equivalent to an act of worship of God.

> **Fifth question:** Would it not be more in keeping with God's justice and mercy for Him to punish individual sins one-by-one, rather than by sending a general and indiscriminate punishment like an earthquake? Why doesn't God step in pre-emptively to prevent an earthquake or similar natural disaster from happening before such widespread destruction occurs?

Said Nursi answers that there are times when God allows the natural elements to rise up in anger against human sinfulness. The Qur'an recounts, for example, the flood visited on the people of Noah, the anger of the air at the denial of the peoples of 'Ad and Thamud peoples, the fury of the sea and water at the people of Pharaoh, the rage of the earth at Qarun, and the anger of Hell at the unbelievers in the Hereafter.[163] Obviously, Nursi is not claiming that the natural world has the capacity for an emotional response such as anger, but it is clear from the Qur'an that human sin is so disruptive of the cosmic order that on occasion the earth itself rebels against the corruption done by humans.

Even though God sometimes permits an element of the natural world to rise up in rebellion against human sin, if God were then to step in and prevent that element from following its set course, then in the long run, as many instances of good as of evil would have been prevented. Nursi recognizes that it is the function of some elements of nature to control and balance others. He expresses this view in the form of a prayer and says: "Just as the seas with their strange creatures recognize You and make You known, so do the mountains through the wise services they perform. They ensure that the earth is released from the effects of earthquakes and internal upheavals; they save it from being overrun by the seas, purify the air of poisonous gases, func-

---

[162] *The Flashes*, The Second Flash, p. 23.
[163] *The Flashes*, The Thirteenth Flash, pp. 118–119.

tion as tanks for the saving and storage of water, and act as treasuries for the minerals and metals necessary for living beings."[164]

The function of a natural element cannot be canceled in order to prevent a possible unwanted result. This would mean canceling as well all the good results tied to the intended action of that particular element. If an element were thus prevented from carrying out its given duty, it might avoid bad results, but at the same time, would cause the cancellation of an equal number of good results. Since God is good and without fault, such an action would not be in keeping with His Divine nature. In his mercy and wisdom, God selectively allows the occurrence of lesser evils for the greater good. For example, a disaster like an earthquake, while it causes serious destruction, also produces positive results in keeping with Divine providence, such as testing people's faith, rewarding faithful believers to the status of martyrs, and serving as a salutary warning to miscreants.[165]

> **Sixth Question:** Many modern people deny that Divine intervention is in any way involved in earthquakes, tsunamis, floods and similar disasters. They hold that such disasters can be explained by purely natural causes, such as an earthquake occurring because of a shift in the rock strata inside the earth or architectonic plates sliding against each other. They see no need for recourse to God, sin, punishment or any other religious reference to explain these events. For them, the universe consists entirely of matter, and disasters are entirely due to an unfortunate combination of material factors.

Said Nursi answers that the marvellous complexity of creation shows that not even the tiniest element of the cosmos can be outside the creation, control, and awareness of the Creator. God's providence, decision, and purpose are sovereign, and nothing occurs in the universe that is outside of God's determination. However, sometimes God in His wisdom conceals His power and acts through secondary causes. An earthquake is a case in point. It is in keeping with God's habitual way of acting that He will on occasion command the terrestrial strata to shift at a fault line, thus producing an earthquake.

---

[164] *The Rays*, The Third Ray, p. 60.
[165] I am grateful to Faris Kaya for this explanation.

Nursi offers an image to illustrate his point that God's ultimate agency must be affirmed for everything that happens in the universe. When a man is shot with a gun, it is not the gun that is blamed but rather the person who fired it. To presume the gun as uniquely at fault is ridiculous, for common sense tells us that one has to go beyond the material instrument to discover the true agent who employed that instrument. Similarly, to pretend that the earth is the ultimate cause of earthquakes and other natural events is to disregard the true actor, who is God the Creator. Nevertheless, those who do not believe in God are forced to relegate all natural events to the status of chance occurrences within the natural order, ignoring the One who set forth and directs the forces of nature.

> **Seventh Question:** What lessons can people learn from an earthquake occurring in a pious region of a predominantly Muslim country? It looks like God was intentionally aiming this earthquake directly at them. Why would God not choose some more irreligious part of the world to inflict with an earthquake?

Said Nursi's answer is that God sends such natural catastrophes in order to warn people that they should pray and avoid sinful behavior; moreover, God uses these occasions to punish wrongdoing and injustice. Nursi accuses the persecutors the students of the *Risale-i Nur* of being responsible for a series of earthquakes which occurred in Turkey:

> As is indicated by four severe earthquakes in four years coinciding exactly with the severe aggression against the Risale-i Nur students and their being persecuted, and on each occasion their occurring exactly at the time the students were attacked and their stopping when the attacks ceased, you are responsible for the heavenly and earthly disasters that have occurred on our being convicted![166]

This statement was misinterpreted, and Nursi was accused of claiming that the *Risale-i Nur* had some kind of magical power so that if it were attacked, natural disasters would occur in a kind of Divine retaliation. Nursi denied that he stated this and clarified his point as follows:

---

[166] *The Rays*, The Twelfth Ray, p. 312.

The wrong meaning has been given in the Indictment, for it has deemed an offence some instances of the Risale-i Nur's 'wonder-working' (keramet) which took the form of 'slaps.' As though disasters like earthquakes that occur when the Risale-i Nur is attacked are blows dealt by the Risale-i Nur. God forbid! We never said such a thing, nor wrote it. What we said in many places was that like acceptable almsgiving, the Risale-i Nur is a means of repulsing disasters. Whenever it is attacked, it hides itself; then calamities seize the opportunity and assault us... I have formed the conviction that those 'coincidences' are a Divine bestowal indicating the Risale-i Nur's acceptability and are a sort of wonder of the Risale-i Nur on account of the Qur'an.[167]

On the one hand, earthquakes occur in pious regions because in those places people have not sinned so seriously; consequently, through the natural disaster God is beginning to purify them from their sins. Here the question is connected with the mystery of human suffering, which Nursi views as a blessing and opportunity sent by God to grow in patience and trust. Elsewhere in the *Risale-i Nur* he offers twenty-five remedies for "the sick and those struck by disaster," by which he seeks to show how persevering in faith amidst illnesses and disasters can be a source of blessing and grace for the believer.[168] On the other hand, upright lives can sometimes prevent such disasters: "Through the blessings of the *Risale-i Nur*, Kastamonu was preserved from the disasters [earthquakes] more than any other province."[169]

However, Nursi hastens to admit that these are mere human speculations and the truth remains hidden with God. He cites a Qur'anic

---

[167] Ibid., p. 407.

[168] *The Flashes*, The Twenty-Fifth Flash, pp. 266–285. In my article, "For you, Illness is Good Health: Said Nursi's Spirituality in his Approach to Physical Illness," I try to outline the spiritual benefits that, in Nursi's view, can accrue to the believer in these moments of personal crisis. The paper is published in Turkish as "Hutbe-i Şamiye: Manevî Bir Doktorun, Çağımız Hastalıklarına Reçetesi," in *Bediüzzaman'a Göre Müslümanlık-Hıristiyanlık Münasebetleri*, (İstanbul: Etkileşim Yayınları, 2006), pp. 115-127.

[169] *The Rays*, The Twelfth Ray, p. 298. Cf. also, "So the exact coincidence of the two centres of the *Risale-i Nur*'s dissemination, Isparta and Kastamonu, being preserved from disaster relative to other places... is belief and good works." *The Rays*, The Thirteenth Ray, p. 348.

verse which states: *"All glory be to You! We have no knowledge except that which you have taught us"* (Qur'an 2: 32), thereby affirming that natural disasters are among those things about which humans can only conjecture, beyond the basic indications that God has revealed through the Prophets.

Conclusion

I have no doubt that many modern people will find Said Nursi's explanation of God's justice in natural disasters unacceptable. His understanding of God's sending or permitting disasters as a punishment for human sin they will consider simplistic and outdated. His view that God is accustomed to make use of these tragic events to test people and to bring blessings upon His faithful, patient servants they will regard as wishful thinking and an unfeeling response to the reality of human suffering.

However, Said Nursi could rightly respond to such criticisms of his faith-based perceptions by challenging non-believers to come up with their own more satisfactory explanation. Nursi has already pointed out the inadequacy of "blaming the instrument," and charts of architectonic plates, oceanic currents, and volcanic substrata will serve little to give hope to victims or make sense of the disasters that have afflicted human lives. Nursi, while admittedly trying to find the meaning contained in occurrences that surpass our human comprehension, at least provides people with a way to perceive the hand of a just and compassionate God in such events and offers guidance on the way to respond to the disaster so that it can be an occasion of growth and blessing, and not merely meaningless destruction. It is in such efforts to understand the workings of God that true human wisdom can be found.

"For You, Illness Is Good Health": Advice in Time of Illness

1. A need for spirituality

In a recent survey held in Europe, respondents showed a decreasing interest in "religion" but, surprisingly, a corresponding increasing interest in "spirituality." Although this would appear to be an inconsistency, I believe that there is an explanation. In expressing a lack of interest, the respondents were probably thinking of *religion* as connoting unattractive elements of religiosity such as dry ritual, external conformity to social expectations, legalistic obedience, and repetition of dogmatic formulae. Conversely, in their show of interest for *spirituality*, the respondents were expressing a need for something transcendent in their lives, for internalized ethical norms, for a discipline that would give structure and order to their behavior, for a way to discover the Divine in the midst of modern life, for an opening to encounter eternal values and wisdom.

Such felt needs underline the relevance of spirituality in modern life. A working definition might assert that spirituality is the way one internalizes the teaching and practice of religion so that it shapes, informs and transforms that person's behavior. Without a spirituality, one's religious practice remains at the level of repetition of dry ritual, external to one's interior life and incapable of contributing to spiritual growth. It is spirituality that gives depth and roots to one's experience of God, without which that experience remains ephemeral and superficial. Spirituality implies a discipline, a conviction of the rightness of what one is doing that inspires a strong motivation. In this way, spirituality provides a solid foundation on which one can build habits of behavior and persevere at times of discouragement, boredom, and doubt.

Finally, it is spirituality that enables the believer to apply the lessons he has learned from faith to the trials and challenges that inevitably arise in daily life. It is one's spirituality that comes to the fore at moments of crisis, when the normal patterns of activity, work and relaxation are disrupted, when relationships are strained, when things are not "the way they should be." At such times, a person without faith must fall back on his own resources, but those resources are too often inadequate to face the challenge; the person gives up, admits defeat, and falls into despair. However, through his spirituality, the believer is rooted in the Divine message and nourished by faithful practice and as a result has access to additional resources of God's guidance and grace which can strengthen him to face the critical moment.

2. Illness and spirituality

One moment of crisis that afflicts everyone at some point in their lives, and afflicts most people more than once, and some for lengthy periods, is physical illness. Even those fortunate few who manage to pass a whole lifetime in unbroken good health must still face the multiple crises which arise from illness as they accompany and care for spouses, parents, children, friends, and relatives who have been struck with poor health. A person's approach to this most common of human crises tells much about that person's spirituality. The way one approaches the disruptive reality of illness displays the attitudes and perspectives that have been produced inside individuals through their internalization of the message of their faith.

My decision to try to learn what might be revealed about the spirituality of Said Nursi in his approach to the question of illness did not originate solely from academic interest. A year ago I had a mild heart attack and my doctor sent me immediately to the hospital for emergency bypass surgery. While I was recovering, I was encouraged by the sympathy and kind words of various readers of the *Risale-i Nur*, who also shared with me some of the insights they had discovered in the writings of Bediüzzaman Said Nursi. This experience pushed me to read and study the *Risale-i Nur* more deeply in order to understand what Said Nursi's approach to sickness and human infirmity might disclose about his Qur'anic spirituality.

At one point in his treatise, "Message for the Sick," Nursi coins a startling paradox. "For you," he tells the readers of the *Risale-i Nur*, "illness is good health, while for some of your peers good health is a sickness."[170] In this paper, I would like to explore Said Nursi's thought on the question of illness, to see what he wants to teach by this apparently unreasonable assertion. I hope to show that Said Nursi has a serious point to make, a point that is consistent with the way his Qur'anic spirituality leads him to regard the common human reality of illness.

3. Sickness of the heart

First of all, it should be noted that Said Nursi is more concerned about what he calls "spiritual sickness" or "sickness of the spirit" than about physical illness; he is more interested in the causes of social ills than individual complaints.[171] He regards the identification of the weaknesses and incapacities of modern culture as one of the principal tasks of the community of his disciples, along with the presentation of Qur'anic teaching as a healing message for this world. As he stated in his defense in the Afyon court: "The collective personality of the *Risale-i Nur* has diagnosed the social, spiritual, and religious sicknesses of this age, and at a Divine command has offered to all humanity at this time the truths of the All-Wise Qur'an in a way that will cure its chronic social ills."[172]

The sickness of the heart that Nursi sees as afflicting modern men and women is one caused by a lack of faith. It is the sense of ennui, a feeling of being without direction or hope, the incapacity to love and a conviction of the absurdity of life that afflicts those whose life is not informed by faith. Positivist materialism, belief in nothing beyond what

---

[170] *The Flashes*, The Twenty-Fifth Flash, "Message for the Sick," p. 269.

[171] Nursi refers to "sicknesses of the spirit, mind, and heart" but often uses the terms interchangeably. In this paper, I will make no attempt to distinguish between these terms. Cf. *The Flashes*, Eleventh Flash, p. 87.

[172] *The Rays*, The Fourteenth Ray, p. 441.

one can see and touch, is thus a common spiritual sickness of our time.[173] This basic disorder arising from the lack of faith in God and a transcendent system of values precipitates multiple societal ills: İstanbul politics is a type of spiritual illness "like the Spanish flu"[174]; racism is a disease[175]; even frigidity in marriage can be said to be a type of spiritual sickness.[176]

It is not only unbelievers who suffer from spiritual sickness; there are other sicknesses of the spirit, such as innovation (unacceptable departure from the example of the Prophet),[177] scruples,[178] exclusivist and partisan mentalities,[179] or desire for acclaim,[180] which can afflict believers. Even saints and conscientious worshipers have lamented over the sickness of heart experienced in moments of tranquility.[181] One might ask whether in this last point Nursi is referring to the well-known state of soul described by the Sufi masters as *qabd*, the "dark night," when the believer is tested by God who, for a time, withholds from the *murid* all sensible delight in prayer and worship. Whether or not Nursi is referring to the Sufi state of *qabd*, there is no doubt that he regards Sufism as an effective remedy for treating the sickness of the heart.[182]

In this the Sufis have followed the example of the Prophet Jesus who was granted the twin blessing of being able to act as God's agent to heal physical and spiritual illnesses. However, Nursi saw this blessing not as a gift granted exclusively to Jesus; rather, it is one that the students of the *Risale-i Nur* can also obtain if they ask God and strive conscientiously for it. He states:

---

[173] *The Words*, "A Flower of Emirdağ," p. 474. Cf. Also, *The Rays*, Conclusion to Tenth Topic, p. 272.
[174] *The Letters*, Seeds of Reality, p. 549.
[175] *The Letters*, The Twenty-Ninth Letter, Sixth Section, p. 495.
[176] *The Rays*, The Fifteenth Ray, First Station, p. 587.
[177] *The Flashes*, The Sixth Flash, p. 44, The Eleventh Flash, p. 80.
[178] *The Words*, The Twenty-First Word, Second Station, pp. 281–283.
[179] *The Words*, "Gleams," p. 753; *The Letters*, The Twenty-Second Letter, First Topic, p. 317.
[180] *The Flashes*, The Twenty-First Flash "On Sincerity," p. 220.
[181] *The Letters*, The Twenty-Sixth Letter, Fourth Topic, p. 387.
[182] *The Letters*, The Fifth Letter, p. 41.

Just as the Qur'an explicitly urges man to follow Jesus' (peace be upon him) high morals, so it encourages him towards the elevated art and sovereign medicine of which Jesus was the master. "Remedies may be found for even the most chronic ills." ... Don't despair! Whatever the ill, its cure is possible. Search for it and you will find it... God is saying through the figurative tongue of this verse: "I gave two gifts to one of My servants who abandoned the world for Me. One was the remedy for spiritual ills, and the other the cure for physical sicknesses. Moribund hearts were raised to life through the light of guidance, and sick people who were as though dead found health through his breath and cure. You too may find the cure for every ill in the pharmacy of My wisdom. Work to find it! If you seek, you will certainly find."[183]

4. Praying for health and illness

There is much more that could be said about Said Nursi's approach to sicknesses of the spirit, but the above will have to suffice, for the main focus of this paper is not on spiritual sickness, but rather on physical illness. It is to this aspect of Said Nursi's spirituality that I will now turn.

The first point to be noted is that Said Nursi does not idealize sickness in the manner of some 19th Century Romantic poets. He is quite realistic in holding that good health is a blessing from God for which the believer should hope and pray, whereas illness is never to be sought for its own sake, nor brought about by one's own effort. It is a pious act to ask that if it be God's will, one may enjoy good health. In one of his prayers included in the *Risale-i Nur*, Nursi makes such an appeal: "Forgive me my sins, O God, bear with me, and heal my ills ... Pardon all my sins, and grant me health from all sicknesses, and be pleased with me for all eternity!"[184]

On the other hand, good health is not an absolute good. The believer can also find himself asking God to grant ills and their remedies, if that be God's will. Nursi alludes to a prayer made in the Shafi'i rite during the *tasbihat* following the Daily Prayers, in which the faith-

---

[183] *The Words*, The Twentieth Word, Second Station, p. 263.
[184] *The Words*, The Thirty-Second Word, p. 682.

ful ask God to bestow on the family of the Prophet both ills as well as the remedies for those ills.

> "O God! Grant blessings to our master Muhammad and to the family of Muhammad, to the number of ills and their remedies; bless him and them, and grant them unending peace." ... Just as illnesses are the most effective whip driving a person to the Divine Court, so also remedies, healing, and good health are the chief of the sweet bounties prompting him to give thanks earnestly and to truly offer praise. It is for this reason that this benediction is most meaningful and widely accepted. Sometimes when reciting the phrase "to the number of all ills and their remedies," I see the earth in the form of a hospital and sense the clearly obvious existence of the True Healer, Who supplies the remedies for all ills, physical and spiritual, and answers all needs, and His universal clemency and sacred all-embracing compassion.[185]

Nursi defends this unusual prayer by saying that just as illnesses are one of the surest means to drive someone to come before God in supplication and worship, so also release from illness is a privileged occasion for thanking and praising God. He notes that the prayer inspires him to see the world as a huge hospital, full of sick people, who come before God as the compassionate Healer who answers the needs of all. His spirituality leads him to understand that since both health and illness come from God, true faith consists of accepting willingly and patiently whatever God sends and placing one's trust in God who is the healer of bodies and souls.

5. Wisdom arising from experience

Said Nursi's understanding of physical illness is not the theoretical speculation of someone who has very seldom or never suffered from pain and infirmity. In the *Risale-i Nur* there are many references, too numerous for all of them to be cited, to the various illnesses that he experienced during his life. He experienced not only physical pain, but the lack of strength and stamina needed to accomplish the work he felt called to do. Because of his bad health and physical weakness,

---

[185] *The Rays*, The Second Ray, First Station, p. 16.

he had to refuse invitations to speak in the mosque,[186] and often felt too weak to teach and write.[187] At times he felt assailed by five or more illnesses at once.[188] Sometimes, the physical illness was compounded by the oppression and bad treatment he received during his periods of imprisonment, and he notes that several parts of the *Risale-i Nur* were written in such situations of psychological stress combined with physical pain and the discomfort of deprivations and mistreatment.[189] As he grew older, old age aggravated his illnesses[190] and made it more difficult to recover from them.

Beyond the purely physical effects of his illnesses, Nursi suffered the depression and anguish frequently experienced by those in poor health. He felt frustrated at being unable to continue his work. He tasted the powerlessness of ill persons who know that they can do nothing on their own to restore their health. He experienced the difficulty of concentrating and the mental exhaustion that often accompanies illness.[191] He was not a stranger to the common psychological effects of illness and a heightened awareness of the proximity of death, such as insomnia, nameless anguish, the feeling that one has wasted one's youth. He knew the loneliness, the feeling of being cut off from healthy friends and relatives that so often accompanies illness, a neediness that God alone can assuage. All this left him in a weakened, fragile condition that a tragedy such as the death of his nephew and spiritual son[192] could bring him almost to the point of despair.

In an intensely personal passage in the *Risale-i Nur*, Nursi shares his experiences of old age and sickness so that others might find in the teaching of the Qur'an the same hope that enabled him to endure and survive the spiritual crisis. He expresses beautifully the anguish

---

[186] *The Flashes*, The Twenty-Fourth Flash, p. 265.
[187] *The Rays*, The Fifteenth Ray, "The Shining Proof," p. 614.
[188] *The Flashes*, The Twenty-Fourth Flash, p. 260.
[189] *The Letters*, The Twenty-Eighth Letter, Seventh Matter, p. 440. Cf. also, *The Letters*, The Twenty-Eighth Letter, p. 423 and *The Rays*, Seventh Ray, p. 124.
[190] *The Flashes*, The Twenty-Sixth Flash, "For the Elderly," p. 289.
[191] *The Rays*, The Fifteenth Ray "The Shining Proof," Second Station, p. 622.
[192] *The Flashes*, The Twenty-Sixth Flash "For the Elderly," p. 310.

and loneliness that are frequently the felt reality experienced by the aged in poor health. Nursi articulates his misery, and alludes to the universal human reality experienced therein, by quoting the 17th Century Mawlawi poet Niyazi Misri. Because of its eloquence, I include the passage in full:

> Old age and illness attacked me in concert. Hitting me over the head, they chased away sleep. I had nothing binding me to the world like family, children, and possessions. Having wasted the fruits of my life's capital through the giddiness of youth, I saw those fruits to consist only of sins and mistakes. Crying out like Niyazi Misri, I said:
>
> > *I had concluded no trade; the capital of life was all lost;*
> > *I came to the road to find the caravan had moved on, unaware.*
> > *Lamenting, I continued down the road, all alone, a stranger;*
> > *My eyes weeping, my heart in anguish, my mind bewildered, unaware.*
>
> I was in exile at the time; I felt despairing sorrow, a regretful penitence, a longing for assistance. Suddenly, the All-Wise Qur'an came to my aid. It opened a door of hope so powerful and afforded a light of consolation so true that it could have dispelled despair and darknesses a hundred times more intense than mine.[193]

It is to Said Nursi's credit that he does not hide or gloss over such weaknesses and spiritual crises, but includes them in the *Risale-i Nur* in the hope that such trials will serve as guidance and comfort for others similarly oppressed by age and poor health. Even at moments of what he acknowledges to be "extreme weakness, wretchedness, and powerlessness,"[194] he never doubted the truth of the Divine favor and compassion he was receiving. It was this unshakeable conviction of God's power in his life which enabled Nursi to take consolation in God's presence, accept the illness, learn patience, and even "be content" with his situation of helplessness.

---

[193] Ibid., p. 289. Cf. a similar passage in *The Rays*: "Once, when a period of heedlessness coincided with my being shaken by various indispositions like old age, exile, illness, and defeat, I was overcome by a grievous anxiety that my very existence, to which I was intensely attached and by which I was captivated, would cease to be. Again I had recourse to the verse: *For us God suffices.*" *The Rays*, The Fourth Ray, p. 78.

[194] *The Flashes*, The Twenty-Fourth Flash, p. 260.

Divine favor pointed out the above fact to me while, during a few days of material and spiritual affliction, illness and trial the like of which I had never before experienced in my life, I was being crushed in particular by the despair and distress of the heart and spirit which resulted from my being unable to serve the Qur'an and belief with the *Risale-i Nur*. I was then content with my distressing illness and imprisonment.[195]

6. Lessons to be learned in time of sickness

Nursi's view is that even though sickness is never to be sought, much less brought about self-destructively by one's own misuse of the body, when God in Divine wisdom nevertheless allows illness to befall a person, there are some positive spiritual benefits which can be reaped and lessons to be learned. First of all, sickness is a salutary reminder of mortality without which people could go on for years in heedlessness and foolish complacency. "Since old-age, illness, disaster, and death open up frightful pain and are a reminder that even if the people who follow misguidance and vice enjoy a hundred thousand pleasures and delights, they most certainly experience a sort of hell in their hearts, although a profound stupor of heedlessness temporarily makes them insensible to it."[196] It is experiences like sickness, old age and natural disasters that can be an occasion for egoistic, misguided people to wake up and realize the hellish existence they have made for themselves.

Secondly, sickness makes one appreciate the blessing of health. Those who enjoy unbroken health can easily take this great gift of God for granted and presume that it is the normal state for all humankind. It is only when one undergoes a period of bad health that one is able to understand the great favor that is contained in good health. Nursi quotes the proverb: "Light is indebted to darkness; pleasure is indebted to pain; there is no health without illness."[197]

---

[195] *The Rays*, The Fourteenth Ray, p. 475.
[196] *The Words*, The Thirteenth Word, Second Station, p. 156. Cf. also, *The Damascus Sermon*, p. 130.
[197] *The Words*, "Gleams," p. 754.

In one passage of the *Risale-i Nur*, Nursi offers advice on why those who have been struck with sickness should not complain.[198] He offers three reasons. Firstly, sickness, like hunger, is necessary so that God can display His beautiful Names and Qualities. God is the Compassionate One who consoles the sick, the Healer who takes away illness, the Provider who gives food to the hungry. Secondly, illness is one of those events that show the value of life. Unbroken good health can become monotonous, flat, and empty; it resembles non-being more than the richness and fullness of life. Illness breaks the monotony and in doing so enriches, strengthens, and moves life forward. The third reason is that this world is a field of testing and service. Illness encourages the sick to become aware of their own powerlessness and their need for God, the compassionate Sustainer. Their helpless situation leads them to take refuge in God, to meditate on God, and to offer petitions.

For the believer, states Nursi, sickness is like a veil[199] that shields humans from the harsh reality of death. Were people to live constantly in good health, death would loom as an ever more terrible prospect, a horrifying reality which no one would be prepared to face. The fears and complaints about death would take over one's consciousness and destroy the pleasure of life. However, sickness veils the horrors of death and serves to prepare people psychologically for its eventual reality.

Should the sick pray that they be healed? Nursi sees great value in this and takes the Prophet Job as an example. Job prayed to be healed of his illness, not for selfish reasons of comfort and release from pain, but so that he would be able to worship and serve God better.[200] However, Nursi notes that the sick person should ask for healing with humility and trust, instead of accusing God and complaining about the unfairness of his situation. In contrast to complaining, which implies a criticism of God's nature as Sustainer of life, trust in God is a form of worship by placing confidence in God's goodness and willingness to heal.

---

[198] *The Flashes*, Second Flash, Points 2–5, pp. 23–26.
[199] *The Words*, The Twenty-Second Word, Second Station, p. 301.
[200] *The Flashes*, The Second Flash, Fifth Point, p. 26.

7. "Message for the Sick"

In addition to the many pieces of religious instruction found throughout the *Risale-i Nur* as regards the spirituality of illness, Nursi also devoted a lengthy treatise in the *Risale-i Nur* specifically aimed at offering guidance to those languishing in the throes of poor health and disease. This is his "Message for the Sick," found in the Twenty-Fifth Flash of *The Flashes* Collection. In this treatise, he brings together much of the teaching found dispersed in the *Risale-i Nur* and elaborates what he has said elsewhere at greater depth, and then adds new material and original observations.

In his introduction, Nursi confesses that he wrote this Flash more quickly than his other writings and he did not find the time to correct the treatise. In fact, he comments that he chose not to revise the text so that it would retain the "natural" and provisional quality of a rough draft rather than the polished character of a finished manuscript. As a result, one should not expect a logical, carefully organized thesis on remedies for illness; instead, it is a collection of 26 remedies from which a sick person might draw profit.[201] The term "remedy" could be misleading. The reflections which Nursi offers are not remedies in the sense of medicinal or physical cures which are meant to remove the illness, but are rather remedies for the types of despair and distress to which those in poor health are often inclined. As such they are spiritual remedies for the sickness of the soul that can sometimes follow upon that of the body.

Nursi recognizes that the two central problems for all those who suffer poor health are anxiety and impatience. Anxiety arises from a sense of helplessness, the inability to do anything to change the situation, the nagging fear that the illness will not be a transient state from which one will recover, but a permanent disability and ongoing affliction. Impatience comes from the sick person's feeling that time is passing too slowly and that he is wasting time that could be more profitably spent on other activities; consequently, the invalid harbors a desire to change the situation precipitately.

---

[201] The remedies are numbered 1–25, but there are two separate remedies under #6.

Most of the 26 remedies that Nursi offers are aimed at helping the sick person to overcome anxiety by accepting his afflicted state tranquilly and to find patience by placing his trust in God. By internalizing the implications of faith in God, the sick person can achieve peace of mind which, since it is conducive to physical well-being, can also help to bring about bodily recovery. The very personal nature of the remedies that he proposes indicates that these are reflections and insights that helped Nursi himself during his many periods of poor health. I will here briefly summarize each of the remedies.

1) Illness actually lengthens one's life. A life passed without trial or hardship is fleeting and insubstantial. The sick person should realize that God has given this opportunity to come to a deeper and richer appreciation of life.

2) The sick person who does not complain, but accepts illness patiently and takes refuge in God—that person is actually worshiping God. For worship is of two kinds: There is active worship, such as the Daily Prayers that one performs, or the Ramadan fast. Then there is what might be called passive worship, which consists of those periods of illness where the believer is simply aware of one's own weakness and powerlessness and of God's power and compassion. By submitting to God's will and trusting in God's power to heal, the invalid is performing a very pleasing form of worship to God.

3) Illness is an occasion for the believer to give witness that we are not on this earth to enjoy ourselves. We are here to work hard and prepare an everlasting life. Moreover, sickness is a reminder of death. Heedless people, whose attention is fixated on a trivial pursuit of pleasure and success, do not want to think about death. Illness forces one to reflect on more serious questions of what life is all about.

4) Your body, its members and functions, do not belong to you. It belongs to God who provides for it in God's own time and manner. Sickness is an occasion to learn that one's body is not a private possession to be disposed of according to one's whims, but is subject to the decrees of its true Owner and Provider.

5) Sickness can make people more mindful of their dissolute habits and of their duties to God. Illness is a time for waking up to what

life is really about. For many sick people, Nursi states, the time of sickness is a privileged occasion of God's grace leading to conversion; for them, *"illness is good health, while for some of their peers good health is a sickness."*

6) Sickness brings into sharp relief the previous times of good health and should lead one to thank God for such moments of happiness. Rather than giving in to bitterness and despair, the sick should reflect on the transient nature of their illness and place their hopes in God who will eventually restore the person to new times of good health and enjoyment.

6 bis) Sickness reminds one that our bodies are not indestructible; we have no claim to immortality. By shattering the "myth of invincibility," illness is an antidote to natural human pride and an invitation to recognize humbly one's powerlessness before God.

7) Illness makes a person appreciate the great blessing involved in good health. Those who enjoy good health constantly are not able to value properly what they have. Good health is a wonderful blessing of God, but in order that people appreciate it fully, God allows illness to afflict people from time to time.

8) Sick people tend to bemoan their fate, but the really serious diseases are those of the soul, those that arise from unbelief and disobedience. By patiently accepting one's illness and placing one's trust in God, the sick person is actually distancing himself from these greater and more eternally threatening diseases.

9) Much of the anxiety felt by the sick is based on a fear of death. The believer, however, can overcome this fear by reflecting on the good things that await a person at death: rejoining friends and relations, returning to one's true homeland, accepting the invitation to the gardens of Paradise extended to those who remain faithful to God. By concentrating on what faith teaches about the reward awaiting steadfast believers, the invalid can come to accept death as a reality that need not be feared.

10) Many sick people make their situation worse by worrying about it constantly. The only way to stop excessive worry is to hand over one's life and cares to God. God is wise and compassionate and pow-

erful. A believer can find no better solution to the self-destructive tendency to worry than that of placing one's trust in God, whereas obsessive anxiety is actually an accusation against God by implying that God is neither able nor willing to help.

11) This is an exhortation to remain patient and focused on the present moment. When the sick person thinks of the past, he should be grateful to God because he has been able to endure the illness up to this time. He should refrain from uselessly dwelling on future suffering, since that is something that does not exist and perhaps may never come to pass.

12) Sickness brings the benefit of knowing how much one is in need of God and how little one can count on one's own strength. The sick person discovers one's true significance and value in relation to the Creator. By pushing one to pray to God, sickness helps one to become aware that one's true glory is to be found, not in what one might have accomplished in life, but in one's very nature as creature of God.

13) Since no one knows one's appointed hour of death, sickness is beneficial in that it reminds a person to be heedful. Because of their suffering in this life, sick people are led to reflect on the life to come. Sickness thus increases their fear of God and leads them to be faithful and obedient, thus acting as a good preparation for eternity.

14) The loss of physical sight enables one to see spiritual realities more clearly. Physical sight can act as a veil that blinds one from a contemplation of Paradise. More broadly, whatever one lacks in the physical world can be used by God to teach and enlighten the sick person about deeper spiritual truths.

15) If illness were not good, God would not have granted it to God's most favored servants. Like the Prophet Job, those holy people who suffer their illness as a kind of worship of God become, in a certain sense, martyrs. "They result in a degree of sainthood like martyrdom." Moreover, by lessening one's attachment to the world, sickness eases the pain of one's departure from the world.

16) Illness makes one more compassionate. Constant good health can make one feel self-sufficient. Sickness shows people their own weak-

ness and need for others. They grow in respect and affection for those who help them and visit them. As a result of their own miseries, they experience greater fellow-feeling and are more ready to be compassionate toward other sick people and to disaster victims.

17) Some sick people complain that their illness deprives them from the opportunity of performing good deeds. However, in reality their illness makes them an occasion for others to do good works by assisting and visiting them and by praying for them. Especially in the case of close relatives, caring for the sick is an important act of worship. When the sick person prays for healing, that person's prayer is always heard and answered, but not always in the way the person seeks. However, the prayer, being sincere, is always acceptable to God.

18) Too often the sick person compares himself to those who are in good health and feels that his rights are being violated. However, the truth is that no one has the right to good health, which is a free gift from God. It is more advantageous to compare oneself to those who are worse off, so that one will be led to thank God that one's health situation is not worse.

19) Life spent in permanent good health becomes monotonous and boring. It is change and variety in conditions of life that one can realize life's value and come to appreciate its true pleasures.

20) People make their health worse by confusing real and imaginary illnesses and treating them in the same way. In the case of real sicknesses, one must follow the advice of conscientious, believing doctors. On the other hand, hypochondria should be given no importance for, if one dwells on it, one's morale is destroyed and one is in danger of actually damaging one's health through excessive concentration on the imagined illness.

21) The invalid should try to identify and enjoy the pleasures that come with illness, such as the signs of affection and human kindness that come from friends and relatives and the opportunity to rest from taxing duties. If one focuses on such pleasures, the pain of sickness will seem less burdensome.

22) Illness reminds people of the fleeting nature of human life in this world. Through belief and submission to God, one can reap spiritual benefit from even the most serious illness.

23) One who feels lonely and abandoned in time of sickness should contemplate the compassionate presence of the Creator. The loneliness felt by a faithful believer in time of illness is not true loneliness. True loneliness, which no human medicine can cure, is separation from God, but the believer who has faith in God's healing presence is never really alone.

24) This remedy is directed toward caregivers. Those who tend sick children and elderly should be aware that transient childhood illnesses are granted by God to build character in the child and are an integral part of the child's natural growth. Those who care for elderly parents will reap a special reward from God, both in this life and in the hereafter; care for aged parents is a form of worship especially pleasing to God.

25) Believers should take advantage of their illness to deepen their faith in God. Illness should be an occasion to cut down one's appetites, grow in heedfulness and reflection, and to deepen one's prayer life.

Nursi concludes his treatise by praying for the sick: "May God restore you to health and make your illnesses atonement for sins. Amen."[202]

8. Said Nursi's spirituality

Nursi's attitude toward physical illness should have become clear from this summary of the remedies proposed, and from them one can glean insights into his spirituality. For Nursi, sickness is a human reality that, like all human realities, should lead the believer to God. The frailty of the body is a forceful argument against all human tendencies toward self-sufficiency and complacent self-satisfaction. The sick person must confront a harsh but ultimately liberating reality, that one can do nothing to heal oneself, but must submit to what God ordains.

Nursi's appeals to the sick person to accept one's illness must not be construed as some kind of fatalism or defeatist passivity. He is very

---

[202] *The Flashes*, The Twenty-Fifth Flash, p. 285.

clear that when one is ill, that person must follow the prescriptions and advice of a well-trained doctor, must take proper care of oneself, and must pray for healing.[203] However, medical science cannot guarantee immediate cures and in many cases cannot bring about any improvement in fighting the disease. However, by working together with medical science, religious faith can often produce results that are impossible for the unbeliever. By accepting the fact that one is in the hands of a loving and compassionate God, the believer can overcome natural anxieties and attain peace of mind, which physicians agree to be the emotional and psychological state most conducive to bodily healing.

Moreover, Nursi is not guilty of romanticizing the sick person. In saying that "sickness makes one more compassionate," or "the sick person comes to a richer understanding of life," Nursi is not claiming that sickness gives people an inside track to virtue or that greater understanding and loving compassion are the automatic results of illness. What he is saying is that God can and does produce spiritual fruits such as compassion and understanding in the sick person who cooperates with God's grace, who submits to God's decrees, and who patiently accepts his condition without complaining or accusing the Creator. For such a person, God is able to use the time of illness to make that person more compassionate, for example, or to understand better what is really important in life.

Nursi sees that for someone without faith, the time of illness is often regarded as time wasted, an aberration from "normal" life when productive activity becomes impossible, an unhappy situation when pain, fear and anxiety threaten to eliminate joy from life, a bitter condition where frustration, anger and resentment can make a person irritable and disagreeable to others, a time of loneliness and alienation when one is tempted to despair and misery. However, faith in God provides the sick person with spiritual resources with which to transform the spiritual context of the illness. When the sick person is aware that he is worshiping God by his very act of submission and humility, this precludes his thinking of sickness as time wasted. By realizing that his life is in

---

[203] Ibid., p. 282.

the hands of a just and compassionate God, he can overcome fear of death and obsessive worry about his state of health. Reflecting on the loving presence of God the Healer brings hope to the sick person and can prevent feelings of isolation and loneliness from leading to depression and despair. Rather than dwelling on pain and loss, the invalid should see the time of sickness as an opportunity, a chance to learn spiritual truths that would otherwise be hidden from him.

By allowing the basic teachings of the Qur'an to shape one's attitudes and reactions to this most common of human hardships, Nursi offers a spirituality that is practical and suited to the needs of ordinary believers. With the advice he offers, he shows his followers how the unhappy condition of illness can be transformed by God's guidance into an opportunity and occasion for spiritual growth and deeper submission to God's will.

The God-centered Life:
an Antidote to a Culture of Violence

1. The God-centered life

What, according to the *Risale-i Nur*, is the goal of human life? Or, to put the question another way, what kind of life is Said Nursi trying to encourage his disciples to pursue? Can we find in the *Risale-i Nur* a text that brings together in summary fashion the fundamental ideas that Said Nursi was trying to convey?

I have been reading through the *Risale-i Nur* looking for an interpretative key that would help me understand the kind of person that Said Nursi was himself striving to be and the kind of believer that he hoped would result from his efforts to form disciples according to the *Risale-i Nur*. I propose that such a passage might be found in the Tenth Word. There Nursi is arguing for the reality of the Resurrection and holds that it is inconceivable that God would betray the hopes of those who have lived faithfully in accord with God's word. He says: "Is it at all possible that He should not prepare a realm of reward and eternal bliss for those believers who respond to the Merciful and Compassionate One's making Himself known by recognizing Him in faith; to His making Himself beloved by loving Him in worship; and to His mercy by offering thanks and veneration?"[204]

Here we find in summary form the kind of person that Nursi is trying to form, one whose hopes will surely be fulfilled by God. This is the believer who responds to the initiatives of grace that God makes to him: 1) God makes Himself known by teaching His word of *truth*,

---

[204] *The Words*, The Tenth Word, Second Truth, p. 76.

and the believer responds by recognizing God in faith; 2) God reveals Himself as *loveable* and the faithful servant responds by loving and worshiping Him; 3) God shows Himself as *merciful* and the grateful penitent responds with praise and thanksgiving. In other words, God manifests Himself to those who believe in terms of truth, love, and mercy and they respond to God with faith, worship, and thanksgiving.

I believe that here we find a succinct statement of Nursi's understanding of human existence. As humans, we exist in order to learn the truth of this world and the next from the Word of God, to worship the loving God who is himself eminently worthy of our love, and to thank and praise God continually for the great mercy that God has always shown to us. This goal, which marks Nursi's personal spiritual path to God as well as the aspiration he hoped to share with his disciples, we might call "a God-centered life."

A God-centered life is a life of faith that is more than simply adhering to a dogmatic list of beliefs or performing ritual actions of whose purpose the worshiper is ignorant. It is a way of going beyond perfunctory religiosity to put God at the heart of one's human consciousness and at the center of one's hopes and motivations. As a Christian student of the *Risale-i Nur*, I find that Said Nursi's vision of the God-centered life is one that resonates with my own understanding of the purpose of human existence. In the most basic Christian catechism we read that men and women were created "to know, love, and serve God." Thus, the ideal of the God-centered life is a point of convergence between the two faiths that should unite Muslims and Christians.

2. The culture of violence

The preamble of the Constitution of the United Nations Educational, Scientific, and Cultural Organization (UNESCO) states: "Since wars begin in the minds of men, it is in the minds of men that the defenses of peace must be constructed." Said Nursi's *Risale-i Nur* can be seen as an appeal to his disciples to build a culture of peace flows from a commitment to respond faithfully to the Prophetic message of God's guidance and strength.

A God-centered life in which God's will is paramount and where humans regard themselves as faithful servants of the Divine Master, as elaborated by Said Nursi in his *magnum opus*, is an antidote to the culture of violence that is so prevalent in the world. There are many possible definitions of what is meant by a "culture of violence," but that given by S. Batsanov of ISODARCO would seem to be as good as any. A culture of violence refers to "a mentality that presupposes that a human life is expendable in the name of some holy goal, or even without such a goal, and that any institution, group or individual, in a position to do so, can resort to coercion by force to deal with other institutions, groups or individuals that have different values or ways of life."[205] There are two key elements to this definition: 1) the expendability of human life in pursuit of a selfish or even commendable end, and 2) the willingness to resort to force to impose one's views, beliefs, and way of life on others.

According to Said Nursi, a person's actions proceed from the inclinations of one's heart and emotions and from the sensibilities and needs of his spirit. If those basic drives are left unchecked, one's emotions can easily lead him to either spontaneous or premeditated deeds of violence. However, according to Nursi, religious faith "places in the heart and mind a permanent 'prohibitor.' When sinful desires emerge from the soul, it repulses them and declares them forbidden."[206] In this way, he holds the violent impulses that arise from a person's emotions and sensitivities can be controlled and held in check by one's religious convictions before they lead to aggressive and destructive behavior; "Blinder emotions will not drive him down the wrong road and defeat him."

Faith brings together the light of the mind and the heart. In other words, an enlightened mind can control and heal the heart's emotions, at the same time that an enlightened heart can soften and mitigate the often harsh judgments of the mind. But, as Nursi warns, "So long as the lights of the mind and the heart are not combined, there

---

[205] S. Batsanov, "Culture of Violence," Rome, Italy: Tor Vergata University, International School on Disarmament and Research on Conflicts (ISODARCO).

[206] *The Damascus Sermon*, First Addendum, Second Part, p. 69.

is darkness, producing violence and ignorance."[207] When God is at the center of a person's life, the mind and the heart, one's thoughts and emotions, are in harmony because they are guided by God's word and strengthened by God's grace.

Moreover, religion teaches the inviolable dignity of each person. A sincere believer in God cannot consider another person's life expendable for any reason. He cannot even violate the dignity of other by forcing them to accept his ideas, beliefs, or behavior. Nursi notes, "Belief necessitates not humiliating others through violence and despotism and not degrading them."[208] In a God-centered approach to life one must not humiliate others by subjecting them to violence and threats.

3. Strength for the victims of violence

Similarly, true religion forbids one to humiliate one's own self by bowing down to anyone other than God alone. While it is not in keeping with God-given human dignity to degrade oneself, faith can help someone to respond with forbearance and perseverance to situations of injustice, rather than by lashing out, on the one hand, in vengeance, thus perpetuating the cycle of violence or, on the other hand, by finding one's self-esteem destroyed in despair and desolation.

In his "Treatise for the Elderly," Nursi reflects on his personal experience of prison: "Just when in those freezing conditions I was most in need of rest and not catching cold and not thinking of the world, I was overcome with anger and vexation at those who had sent me into this intolerable exile, isolation, imprisonment, and oppression, in a way that spelt out their hatred and ill-intentions, Divine grace came to my assistance."[209] Nursi was led to understand through his faith that Divine providence had a large role to play in his imprisonment. In God's mercy and wisdom, Nursi was given the opportunity to guide and console other prisoners, and he was granted time to repent

---

[207] *The Words*, "Gleams," p. 739.

[208] *The Damascus Sermon*, Sixth Word, p. 56.

[209] *The Flashes*, The Twenty-Sixth Flash, For the Elderly, p. 329.

and seek forgiveness for his own faults. He also had the possibility of acting magnanimously by forgiving those who were responsible for the injustice against him, thereby practicing the Qur'anic injunction *"Those who suppress their anger and forgive people, truly God loves those who do good"* (Qur'an 3:134).

Nursi came to realize that the injustice and violence he suffered could actually benefit him spiritually. "If this ill-treatment, distress, and oppression inflicted on me by 'the worldly' are for my faulty soul, I forgive it. Perhaps my soul will be reformed by means of it, and perhaps it will be atonement for its sins."[210] Rather than advising revenge and retribution against his enemies, Nursi leaves vengeance to God: "If the worldly oppress me because of my service to belief and the Qur'an, it is not up to me to defend it. I refer it to the Mighty and Compelling One."[211]

In a strong rejection of the principle that "the end justifies the means," Nursi refers to the Qur'anic injunction that one may not kill a single innocent person even in order to save all humanity. "The pure justice of the Qur'an does not permit spilling the life and blood of an innocent, even for the whole of humanity. The two are the same, both in the view of Divine Power, and in the view of justice. But through self-interest man becomes such that he will destroy everything that forms an obstacle to his ambition."[212] Thus, in the view of Said Nursi, a God-centered life is a strong deterrent to the use of violence, even to pursue praiseworthy ends, whereas for a person for whom God's will is irrelevant to the way he acts, such a person will be likely to lack the inner motivation necessary prevent him from inflicting violence in the pursuit of his self-interest.

Even for those for whom living in accord with God's will is not a sufficient motivation for avoiding violent behavior, religion can still be a powerful deterrent to violence and mayhem. Referring to the youths of his time, his judgment is applicable to people of all ages and cultures: "It is only the thought of Hell-fire that checks the turbulent emo-

---

[210] *The Letters*, The Sixteenth Letter, p. 87. Cf. *The Rays*, The Fourteenth Ray, p. 461.
[211] Ibid.
[212] *The Damascus Sermon*, "Seeds of Reality," no. 64, p. 106.

tions of youths, the most vigorous element in the life of society, and their violent excesses, restraining them from aggression, oppression, and destruction, and ensuring that the life of society continues tranquilly. If not for fear of Hell, those drunken youths would, in accordance with the rule 'might is right' in pursuing their desires, turn the worlds of the wretched, weak, and powerless into Hell."[213]

To Nursi, violence is an inevitable effect of rejecting God and God's promise of resurrection. He warns that when people give up such beliefs and hopes, human dignity suffers and along with it, civic values and social harmony. He states: "Towns are households for their inhabitants. If belief in the hereafter does not govern the members of that large family, vices like malice, self-interest, false pretenses, selfishness, artificiality, hypocrisy, bribery, and deception will dominate, displacing sincerity, cordiality, virtue, zeal, self-sacrifice, seeking God's pleasure and the reward of the hereafter, which are bases of good conduct and morality. Anarchy and savagery will govern under the superficial order and humanity, poisoning the life of the town. The children will become troublemakers, the youth will take to drink, the strong will embark on oppression, and the elderly start to weep."[214] Positing a direct link between godlessness and a culture of violence in society, Nursi holds that without God's guidance and help, people can become "monsters" who do harm to others even as they are destructive to themselves.[215]

4. Seeing as God sees

A God-centered life serves as an antidote to a culture of violence by putting injustices, oppression, and discouragement in perspective. As Nursi approached the end of his life, his health impaired by his many years in prison and exile, he was grieving the shortness of life and oppression he experienced. Nursi was only able to avoid recourse to

---

[213] *The Words*, The Tenth Word, First Part of Addendum, p. 110. Cf. also, *The Rays*, The Ninth Ray, p. 204.

[214] *The Rays*, "The Fruits of Belief," Eighth Topic, p. 246.

[215] *The Damascus Sermon*, Sixth Word, p. 58.

anger and resentment by bearing in mind the verse: *"For us God suffices, and He is the Best Disposer of Affairs!"*[216] This enabled Nursi to consider life, not from the point of view of his own experience of injustice and suffering, but from the perspective of God. Nursi realized that by dwelling upon his miseries was limiting his reflections to but one of the myriad aspects of the human condition of which God is aware.[217] In other words, life is much greater than what he thought and felt at any given time.

Nursi believes that the sufferings of the present time are insignificant compared to the reward that is awaiting those who persevere with patience. Near the end of his life, he wrote: "Because of the sacred solace for the pains and despair of the adventures of my old age arising from belief and the Qur'an, I would not exchange this most distressing year of my old age for ten of the happiest years of my youth. Especially since each hour in prison of those who repent and perform the obligatory prayers become like ten hours' worship, and with respect to merit, each transient day spent in illness and oppression gains ten days of perpetual life."[218] The suffering of an innocent person is itself a kind of worship of God,[219] so that the person whose sight is fixed on God can endure even the worst wrongs and injustices without responding in kind.

Perhaps the most powerful contribution that a God-centered life can make toward overcoming the universal human tendency to violence is the influence of God's loving nature. Since God is both most loving and most loveable, living daily in the conscious presence of this loving Creator should make the believer aware of the centrality of love in human life. When consciousness of God's love is the guiding principle of one's actions, violence is seen as the human perversity that it is, a distortion of what it means to be human. Nursi expresses it well in *The Damascus Sermon*: "The thing most worthy of love is love, and that most deserving of enmity is enmity. That is, love and loving,

---

[216] Qur'an, 3:173.

[217] *The Rays*, The Fourth Ray, p. 80.

[218] *The Flashes*, The Twenty-Six Flash, "For the Elderly," pp. 327–328.

[219] Ibid., p. 332.

which render man's social life secure and lead to happiness are most worthy of love and being loved. Enmity and hostility are ugly and damaging, have overturned man's social life, and more than anything deserve loathing and enmity and to be shunned."[220] Thus, when God is the focus of one's daily attention, since God's nature is the epitome of loving, the importance of love is impressed on the consciousness of the believer, and the aberrant nature of violence becomes evident.

Nursi teaches a God-centered vision of life in which faith, worship, and thanksgiving are the key elements in one's relationship to God and forgiveness, love, and patience are the fundamental basics of a person's relations with others in society. Such a program can be maintained over time only if one is focused sincerely on God and on doing everything to please God. In this way, the central Islamic virtue of sincerity (*ikhlas*) is of paramount importance. Nursi holds that especially those who have suffered violence and oppression are in need of sincerity if they are to persevere. He writes: "We are certainly compelled more than anyone to work with all our strength to gain sincerity. We are in utter need of instilling sincerity in ourselves. Otherwise what we have achieved so far in our sacred service will in part be lost, and will not persist.[221]

5. The *jihad* of the word

Many people will object that in the past religion has often been the cause of war and that even in our own time religion is an important factor in modern-day violence and war. If by "religious adherence" one means belonging by birth to a group of people who share a religious allegiance that is often reinforced by ethnic identity, there is undoubtedly some truth to this claim. In what sociologists call "identity conflicts," a person's religious affiliation is often an important factor determining which side of the conflict one is on. At the same time, such conflicts are almost never about theology or religious principles, and the way such wars are waged is but rarely influenced by the ethi-

---

[220] *The Damascus Sermon*, Fourth Word, pp. 49-50.
[221] *The Flashes*, The Twenty-First Flash, "On Sincerity," pp. 212–213.

cal tenets of the professed religions. The real dynamic is not determined by religious teaching but rather the atavistic need to make "our" group to overcome "their" group at all costs.

Said Nursi is not interested in shoring up attitudes of nationalistic or ethnic chauvinism, but wants to instill in his students, the students of the *Risale-i Nur*, a way of life that responds worthily to God as Teacher, Lover, and Pardoner. To him, faith, worship, and thanksgiving are the central issues; worldly affairs, such as who is winning and who is losing a military battle, are not worth his attention. For this reason, Nursi states that he takes refuge in God from partisan politics, and by the end of his life he refused to follow the progress of ongoing wars.

In *The Damascus Sermon*, Nursi takes up the question of violence in the name of religion and holds that *jihad* of the sword is passé. Nursi notes that in the past Muslims resorted to violence and war, but he suggests that such actions displayed their weakness and distance from the teachings of Islam rather than their strength of faith. He states: "History shows that the Muslims increased in civilization and progressed in relation to the power of the truths of Islam, that is, to the degree that they acted in accordance with that power. History also shows that they fell into savagery and decline, and disaster and defeat amidst utter confusion to the degree of their weakness in adhering to the truths of Islam."[222]

The true characteristics of Islamic civilization are, according to Nursi, opposed to enmity and violence, and it is only when Muslims depart from those innate characteristics of Islam that they turn to childish deeds of violence: "Love, brotherhood, and affection are the temperament of Islam, they bond it. The people of enmity resemble a spoilt child who wants to cry, and so looks for an excuse to do so... They resemble an unfair, pessimistic person who so long as it is possible to distrust, never thinks favorably."[223]

---

[222] *The Damascus Sermon*, First Word, p. 28.
[223] Ibid, p. 50.

Even if violent action might have been considered appropriate in the past, the world has changed and violence can no longer be justified. He writes: "In the Middle Ages, Islam was compelled to be bigoted and hostile in the face of the Europeans' savagery, but it nevertheless maintained its justice and moderation. It never instituted inquisitions and the like. In this time of modern civilization, the Europeans are civilized and powerful, and harmful hostility and bigotry have therefore disappeared. For in respect of religion, the civilized are to be conquered through persuasion, not through force, and through showing by conforming to its commands in actions and conduct that Islam is elevated and lovable. Force and enmity are only to combat the barbarity of savages."[224] Here Nursi is calling for "the jihad of the word" to replace that of the sword. In a civilized world, Muslims must seek to convince and persuade others; they do that by bearing witness to the elevated and noble beliefs of their religion. "In the future, in place of weapons, the immaterial, moral swords of true civilization, material progress, and truth and justice will defeat and scatter the enemies."[225]

Nursi states that if we have learned anything from the Twentieth Century's two World Wars, it is that the evil and destruction unleashed by war prove nothing about right and wrong. Reward and retribution should be left to God, not carried out by human hands. "The time for enmity and hostility has finished. Two world wars have shown how evil, destructive, and what an awesome wrong is enmity. It has become clear that there is no benefit in it at all. In which case, on condition they are not aggressive, do not let the evils of our enemies attract your enmity. Hell and Divine punishment are enough for them."[226]

6. The diabolic origin of violence

Nursi expects that as the Day of Judgment draws near, believers in God will face a twin challenge on the part of forces opposed to God's

---

[224] Ibid, p. 85.
[225] Ibid, p. 38.
[226] Ibid, p. 50.

will. These two forces are personified by the figures of Dajjal and Sufyan. Dajjal, the Antichrist, will work outside the Muslim community and will seek to turn people away from God. He will be opposed by the Prophet Jesus who, when he returns will defeat the Dajjal. In the Muslim community, Sufyan will work to spread corruption and dissention among Muslims, and he will be opposed and defeated by the Mahdi, the Rightly-guided One.

Nursi does not believe that these two figures of Dajjal and Sufyan need be understood ad individuals, but could represent the collective personality of unbelief. He is waiting for the day when the students of the *Risale-i Nur* will join hands with the true Christians who are following the path of Jesus, and together these two communities will overcome the forces of evil represented by Dajjal and Sufyan.

In this context we can understand Nursi's view that violence is a characteristic of the work of the Dajjals, who exercise an invasive despotism that violates even the most private matters of life. He writes: "Because both Dajjals employ the severest despotism, the greatest tyranny, and the maximum violence and terror, they appear to have vast power. Yes, theirs is a despotism so extraordinary that under the cloak of laws, they intervene in everyone's consciences and religious beliefs, and even their clothes."[227] The "lovers of freedom," as he refers to them, opposed the violent tyranny exercised by the agents of the Dajjals at the turn of the century but they erred in misdirecting their resistance. The historical reference to events in Turkish history is somewhat obscure:

> "It is my guess that with a premonition of the future the lovers of freedom at the end of the last century perceived this awesome despotism, and letting fly their arrows at it, attacked it. But they were sorely misled and attacked on the wrong front. It is tyranny and coercion so great that it wipes out a hundred villages because of one man, punishing hundreds of innocent people and ruining them by forced migrations.[228]

---

[227] *The Rays*, The Fifth Ray, Second Station, p. 115.
[228] Ibid.

7. Origins of class violence

While Nursi does not ascribe to a Marxist analysis of history that would posit inevitable conflict and warfare between social classes, he is aware from his own background that the common people have in the past and still experience violence and oppression on the part of the elite classes. In the God-centered life that Nursi is proposing, a keen sense of justice must be developed in order to defend the rights of the poor against the tyranny of the wealthy and powerful. In a telling passage, he relates:

> By birth and the way I have lived I am from the class of common people, and I am one of those who by temperament and intellectually have accepted the way of 'equality of rights.' Due to compassion and the justice proceeding from Islam, I have for a long time opposed and worked against the despotism and oppression of the elite class called the bourgeoisie. I therefore support total justice with all my strength, and oppose tyranny, oppression, arbitrary power, and despotism.[229]

Class conflict is not part of the inevitable march of history, but arises rather from human failings and a refusal to follow God's guidance. Instead of the modesty and humility that come from a God-centered life, those who have economic and political power follow their own inclinations to greed and arrogance. "While the virtues of those known by the world as the upper classes should be the cause of modesty and humility, they have led to oppression and arrogance. And while the poverty and powerlessness of the poor and common people should be the cause of compassion and bounty, they have resulted in captivity and condemnation."[230]

Too often, the upper classes show a disregard for the fate of those who do not share their prosperity. "So long as I'm full, what is it to me if others die of hunger?" summarizes the attitudes of neglect on the part society's elite that have produced oppression and lack of mercy.[231]

---

[229] *The Flashes*, The Twenty-Second Flash, p. 226.

[230] *The Letters*, Seeds of Reality, p. 546. Cf. also, *The Damascus Sermon*, p. 102.

[231] *The Words*, The Twenty-Fifth Word, First Light, Third Ray, p. 421.

To this the lower classes respond with hatred and envy and, when the circumstances present themselves, with violence. The kind of class violence that has upset the peace and equilibrium that should exist between rich and poor[232] is thus a direct result of the lack of social justice. Until both classes deepen their commitment to be guided by God in their social relations, Nursi does not foresee any serious improvement in the state of society.

8. Conclusion

Although one of the charges made against Said Nursi by his enemies was that he employed a certain "violence of expression," the implication being that he was mentally unbalanced,[233] Nursi firmly maintained until the end of his life that he never incited violence nor meddled in politics or affairs of state. In the period after he underwent his transformation into The New Said, he withdrew from worldly issues and arguments. He addresses his accusers: "I have not meddled in any way in your world, nor have I had anything to do with your principles, nor as is testified to by my life during these nine years of captivity, have I had any intention or desire to meddle in the world again."[234] During these final years, he devoted his time instead to showing his disciples how they could live in response to God's teachings, the signs of God's love, and the experience of God's mercy, and thus build a life that would serve as an effective antidote to his century's culture of violence.

---

[232] *The Letters*, The Twenty-Second Letter, Second Topic, p. 324.
[233] *The Rays*, The Thirteenth Ray, p. 367.
[234] *The Flashes*, The Twenty-Second Flash, p. 227.

Dialogue among Believers

1. Elements of goodness in other religions

In a sense, the title of my paper is somewhat anachronistic. One would look in vain through the *Risale-i Nur* for any reference to a "dialogue" among the followers of various religions. The term "dialogue of religions" did not come into current usage until after Said Nursi's death in 1960. So it is not the precise *term* that we need to look for in the *Risale-i Nur*; rather, we must try to discover whether Said Nursi believed that Jews, Christians, and Muslims had anything positive to say to one another and whether he felt that there was any basis for their cooperating in the world.

If Nursi's notion had been simply that Jews and Christians were irreconcilable enemies of Muslims, to be opposed by pen and sword, there of course could be no possibility of real dialogue among them. Similarly, if he believed that the teachings of the three "heavenly" religions, as he called them, were so different and contradictory that no meaningful encounter was possible, if he considered the earlier religions as being wholly corrupt and devoid of any holiness, truth, and goodness, he could not be said to advocate a dialogue of religions. However, as I hope to show in this paper, Nursi does regard the other religions as possessing elements of holiness, truth, and goodness, which are the bases for a real conversation and cooperation among the followers of all three religions.

In this paper I limit myself to Nursi's views about the possibility of dialogue with Christians and Jews. In the *Risale-i Nur*, Nursi was not writing a theoretical treatise on whether Muslims should be involved in dialogue with Buddhists, Hindus and the followers of other religions; the *Risale* is written as practical information and advice aimed at forming devout Muslims and answering the questions of the day. The non-Muslims encountered by the students of the *Risale-i Nur* were Jews and Christians, so it is the relationship of Muslims to these that is addressed.

2. The universality of worship of God

The followers of other religions worship God, each in their own way. The fact that not only the inanimate world worships the one God by performing its various natural functions, but the various religious groups seek to do God's will as they understand it, is an argument, according to Nursi, for the existence of the One God. If there is "a kind of" real worship among the religions, it follows that there is a kind of spirituality and holiness present in them. Nursi explains:

> The involvement of each group of men in a mode of worship dictated by their innate dispositions, the species of worship engaged in by other animate beings, as well as inanimate beings, through the performance of their essential functions, the way in which all material and immaterial bounties and gifts in the cosmos become means inciting men to worship and thanks, to praise and gratitude; the fashion in which all the manifestations of the unseen and epiphanies of the spirit, revelation and inspiration, unanimously proclaim the exclusive fitness of one God to receive worship—all of this in most evidential fashion, proves the reality and dominance of a single and absolute Divinity.[235]

Nursi's insights such as the following: "the fashion in which all the manifestations of the unseen and epiphanies of the spirit, revelation and inspiration unanimously proclaim the exclusive fitness of one God to receive worship"[236] invite Muslim scholars to explore the ways in which the One God might be active also in other religions. Such theological investigations could form the basis of an "Islamic theology of religions."

---

[235] *The Rays*, p. 172.
[236] Ibid. *"vahy ve ilhamlar gibi bütün tereşşuhat-ı gaybiye ve tezahürat-ı maneviyenin bir tek İlahın mabudiyetini ilan etmeleri…"*

3. The possibility of friendship

On the basis that there are genuine elements of holiness and goodness in the other religions, Nursi holds that it is proper for Muslims to befriend and love their neighbors of the People of the Book. Challenged that this was against the teaching of the Qur'an, Nursi showed that the Qur'an presumes that Muslims can love Christians and Jews, and gives the example of a Muslim man married to a woman from one of these communities. "Of course he should love her,"[237] states Nursi.

Nursi lived according to his word and admits that he had Christian friends, even in the most tragic of circumstances. When Nursi visited Van after the destruction of the city in the Russian invasion, he wept without distinction for both the Christian and Muslim victims, who had been his "friends and acquaintances." "Most of the people of those houses had been my friends and acquaintances. The majority of them had died in the migrations, may God have mercy on them, or had done into wretched exile. Apart from the Armenian quarter, all the Muslim houses of Van had been leveled."[238]

4. The two sides of Europe

Since Nursi accepts that there are elements of goodness and truth in the earlier heavenly religions, and that it is permissible for Muslims to have friends with those of the other communities, it is proper to ask whether there are any factors modern life that should drive Muslims and People of the Book into dialogue and cooperation. Nursi acknowledges that modern civilization is not all bad. He states that there are many good qualities to be found in modern Western civilization that derive "from the guidance of the Qur'an, especially, *and from the preceding revealed religions.*"[239]

---

[237] *Münazarat*, pp. 26–27.

[238] *The Flashes*, The Twenty-Sixth Flash, "For the Elderly," p. 315.

[239] *The Words*, The Twenty-Fifth Word, First Light, Third Ray, p. 421. *"İşte medeniyet-i hazıra, edyan-ı sabıka-i semaviyeden, bahusus Kur'anın irşadatından aldığı mehasinle beraber, Kur'ana karşı böyle hakikat nazarında mağlub düşmüştür." Sözler,* Envar Neşriyat, p. 408.

However, in Nursi's view, these positive virtues that are beneficial for humankind are outweighed by a number of negative values that modern civilization has adopted from non-religious and anti-religious philosophies. He says that European civilization has two sides. One current has worked to establish justice and to develop scientific thought for the benefit of society. In this it has been inspired by the teachings of true Christianity. The second current, rejecting Europe's Christian heritage, has pursued various atheistic and materialistic philosophies to produce a selfish, impoverished, self-destructive civilization.

Nursi states that he has no argument with the first, current of a Europe of faith. It is the second Europe that he considers a danger, not only to Islam, but to all the revealed religions.[240] In opposing themselves to "the bases of all heavenly laws," those promoting the atheistic current of European civilization produce more harm than good and actually give false guidance to humanity.[241]

Since the Divine and humane values beneficial to humanity are taught not only by the Qur'an, but also by "the preceding revealed religions," such values form the basis for dialogue and cooperation between the followers of the "revealed religions" of Judaism, Christianity, and Islam. Taking Nursi's lead in the *Risale-i Nur*, one can conclude that dialogue among Jews, Christians, and Muslims is both a legitimate activity and an important tool for the religions to carry out their reason for existence in today's world.

5. The religions confronting modern civilization

In proposing constructive relations between the followers of the revealed religions, Nursi is not content to state a general principle; instead, he gives concrete examples of societal values on which dialogue is needed. Noting that many of the standards taught by the heavenly religions challenge the assumptions of modern societies, he tries to point out specific contrasts between Divinely revealed values and those devised by human caprice. According to Nursi, there is a need for the various

---

[240] *Emirdağ Lahikası*, I / 270.
[241] *Emirdağ Lahikası*, II / 99–100.

adherents to religious faith today to share their views and insights on these and similar topics, so that together they can offer to secular society the wisdom contained in revealed truth.

In suggesting that there be a correspondence and cooperation among the followers of the "heavenly religions," Nursi was proposing, long before other religious leaders were speaking about interfaith dialogue, a platform on which interreligious encounter needs to take place. Dialogue among the true followers of the various religions should focus on questions of the values by which societies are guided.

Nursi holds that human philosophy proposes a set of values that should characterize modern societies, and to these he contrasts the "Divine values" learned from revelation and taught by the religions. He thus lays the groundwork for dialogue, not only among the religions, but also between religious believers and those whose value systems derive from human philosophy. The contrasts he suggests are:

- force – truth,
- self-interest – virtue, God's pleasure,
- conflict – mutual assistance,
- racism, nationalism – the bonds of unity created by religion, class and nation.

1. Force vs. truth. According to Nursi, there is an innate tendency in modern societies for people to resort to force to obtain what they want and to make their will prevail over their opponents. This willingness to regard human life as expendable and to consider it acceptable to force others to accept one's beliefs and preferences is what is often called a "culture of violence." A basic characteristic of such societies is aggression. One does not have to be a very acute observer of modern life to recognize that a culture of violence is an apt description of many of the attitudes that lie behind personal, national, and geopolitical decisions today.

To the endemic acceptance of the use of force to attain one's objectives, Nursi counters with the Qur'anic emphasis on "truth." According to Nursi, the Qur'an takes truth as its starting point. Rather than trying to force others to follow one's point of view, the Qur'an invites people to engage in a study of the truth. People are invited to "consider, reflect together" on the truth of reality, and the Qur'an specifically invites the Jews and Christians, "People of the Book," to "come together on a common word." Since this Divine value of truth over against the use of force is taught not only by the Qur'an but also by the "preceding revealed religions," it follows that alternatives to violence and the use of force would appear to be fruitful areas for dialogue among the spiritual children of Abraham.

Nursi is aware of the sad facts of history that the followers of Judaism, Christianity and Islam, while professing to worship and obey the God of love and compassion, have often resorted to violence and use of force to impose their will on others. What Nursi is calling for is, in light of the present tendency, both in international relations and in the microcosms of societal and family life, to accept and perpetuate a culture of violence, that the believers of all three revealed religions should engage in a dialogue of truth regarding the way that God wants people to live and act and together seek realistic alternatives to the use of force to achieve one's aims.

2. Self-interest vs. serving God. A second characteristic of modern societies is what Nursi describes as people using personal benefit or self-interest as the ultimate goal of their actions. This is what can be called a "what's in it for me?" mentality. Personal benefit dictates and directs what people do. "I can do what I want and no one has a right to stop me." In its most selfish expression it can lead to an individualistic social and political philosophy that holds: "If I want to amass wealth, to lead a wholly selfish existence, and to ignore the suffering of others, that is my inalienable right, which cannot be restricted or limited either by government legislation or by the moral teaching of the religions." In the business world, this attitude is expressed as a single-minded focus on "the bottom line," a concern with maximizing profit without attention to the human cost and environmental ruin.

Nursi is correct in understanding the characteristic of self-interest as a product of Enlightenment philosophy, particularly with its emphasis on self-fulfillment. From learned tomes to popular novels, songs, and films, self-fulfillment has been promoted and encouraged as both the goal of human striving and the measure of social achievement. This is succinctly expressed in the publisher's introduction to a work by Alan Gewirth. "Cultures around the world have regarded self-fulfillment as the ultimate goal of human striving and as the fundamental test of the goodness of a human life. The ideal has also been criticized, however, as egotistical or as so value-neutral that it fails to distinguish between, for example, self-fulfilled sinners and self-fulfilled saints."[242]

It is precisely this distinction between "self-fulfilled sinners" and "self-fulfilled saints" that, according to Nursi, needs to be addressed. In what does true self-fulfillment consist? What should humans be striving for? What should be the motivation that propels and directs one's activities? To self-interest or personal benefit Nursi opposes the attainment of virtue; as motivation for acts great or small, he proposes that everything be done for "God's pleasure."

This is a basic distinction and, depending on which set of values is accepted and followed in practice, will profoundly influence the shape and character of society. When a person studies, works, marries, and raises children, does he do this for purposes of fulfilling himself and making his life a satisfying whole, or because he wants to act according to God's will, to do something pleasing for God? So long as the activity in which a person is engaged continues to appear worthwhile and pleasing, there is no problem in regard to which set of motivations are being followed. However, when one's work or relationship or marriage becomes tedious or burdensome, the choices one makes concerning the future will be determined largely by how one regards the competing claims of self-fulfillment and moral obligation.

3. Conflict vs. solidarity. A third characteristic of modern societies is that of conflict as a natural and inevitable trait of social relations. Whether this is expressed as society being governed by "the law of the jungle," with a "dog eat dog" mentality of aggressive domination being accepted as unavoidable in commercial and political relations, or whether society is regarded as being inescapably subject to a recurrence of class warfare and alienation due to the conflict of inter-

---

[242] Princeton University Press, "Publisher's introduction to Alan Gewirth, *Self-Fulfillment*, Princeton UP, 2009, http://press.princeton.edu/titles/6413.html

est in a capitalist system, conflict is held by many to be normal and necessary element of human life. The late Samuel Huntington's thesis of a "clash of civilizations" was held up by many as a paradigm of international relations that provided an acceptable base for foreign policy decisions.

From the point of view of the Qur'an and "the earlier revelations," Nursi challenges this understanding of conflict as both inevitable and acceptable. To it he opposes the "principle of mutual assistance." The way that God intends that people live on earth is by supporting and helping one another, bearing one another's burdens, and lifting the yoke of oppression from the shoulders of those who are mistreated and oppressed. Certainly, anyone with even a passing knowledge of the teaching of the Jewish Prophets, of Jesus, and of Muhammad will find a consistent call for people to have an effective concern for others, particularly for the troubled and the vulnerable.

The religions do not teach that "man is enemy to man," but that God has created people as brothers and sisters whose lives will be judged on the way they obeyed God and treated one another. It is a sad fact of history that religious believers have not always acted in accord with the teaching of those sent to them by God, but Nursi's point remains valid that Judaism, Christianity, and Islam all teach that solidarity and mutual assistance are values by which society should be governed, rather than "aggression and thriving on devouring others."[243]

4. Nationalism vs. unity. Similarly, Nursi regards the type of racist and nationalist ideologies that caused such warfare and destruction in the 19th and 20th centuries as factors that divide humanity into competing and mutually aggressive adversaries. Judgments about others based solely on their race, ethnic group, religious adherence, or nationality may be a universal feature of modern societies, but Nursi holds that these tendencies need to be countered by the bonds of fellowship uniting people of various nations and backgrounds.

Near the end of his life, Nursi supported the Baghdad Pact on the grounds that by joining the Pact Turks would not only be united

---

[243] *The Words*, The Twenty-Fifth Word, First Light, Third Ray, p. 420.

with 400 million brothers and sisters among Muslim peoples, but that the international accord would also gain for Muslim Turks "the friendship of 800 million Christians"[244] and be a step toward a much-needed peace and general reconciliation between the two communities of faith. When Bayram Yüksel, one of Nursi's closest disciples, wanted to go to Korea to take part with the Turkish army as ally of the American forces during the Korean War, Nursi encouraged him, noting that the Americans were "*Ahl al-Kitab*" (the People of the Book).

The concern that society be marked by bonds of unity rather than torn asunder by racist attitudes and nationalist ideologies fits in with Nursi's priorities for modern societies. According to Nursi, the enemies of Muslims are not one or another non-Muslim community but rather the general obstacles to human happiness and solidarity that must be faced together by all religious communities. He identifies the most important of these enemies to human happiness as "ignorance, poverty, and disunity." That one of the marks of Islamic societies should be unity and fellowship, based on common human bonds, is a key to Nursi's understanding of the need for interreligious dialogue and cooperation.

6. The task of the religions: offer a transcendent perspective

Instead of fostering fellowship and mutual aid among nations, social values are too often oriented toward providing the populace with amusements, distractions, and opportunities for instant gratification. People easily become unfocussed regarding the needs and sufferings of others. The result, as Nursi notes, is "a superficial happiness for 20% of humankind, while casting 80% into distress and poverty."[245]

It is here that the teaching of Islam and the previous revelations, according to Nursi, must offer a transcendent perspective. The Sacred Books of Jews, Christians, and Muslims teach that rugged individual-

---

[244] *Emirdağ Lahikası*, II/24, 56, cited by Şükran Vahide, *Bediüzzaman Said Nursi*, p. 354.

[245] *The Words*, The Twenty-Fifth Word, p 420.

ism is not the way that God intended people to behave; God's will is that people must seek and establish bonds of unity and cooperation that go beyond those of strategic alliances and narrow self-interest.

In setting forth these dichotomies of force vs. truth, self-interest vs. service of God, conflict vs. solidarity, and nationalism vs. unity, Nursi is offering the followers of Judaism, Christianity, and Islam a platform for dialogue. These are, even today, the issues on which religious adherents must communicate with one another and confront together materialist value systems. In calling for this kind of encounter and cooperation, Nursi was ahead of his time, but his conviction of the importance of this interreligious dialogue is still valid a half-century after his death.

The Mystery of Human Responsibility

1. No compulsion in religion

In the *Risale-i Nur*, Said Nursi speaks of human responsibility as a *mystery*, that is, as something that is not fully understood by rational methods. A mystery is a reality that is perfectly understood by God and forms part of the content of Divine wisdom that God has revealed to humans through the Prophets. However, the mysteries of Divine wisdom are never fully understandable by human minds. Through faith that surpasses reason, people can come to know the mysteries revealed by God, but by rational processes they can only know some few particular elements of these Divine mysteries. How these particular realities hang together, how the seeming contradictions between known facts are to be resolved rationally, how one can accept and explain what appear to be logical absurdities—all this pertains to mystery and is material for religious faith.

Confronted with a mystery which seems to confound human reason, the believer acknowledges that he or she is standing before a revealed truth greater than what can be grasped by the human intellect and humbly submits to the Divine message which teaches what would otherwise be unknown by humans. Such is the case with the mystery of human responsibility, which reappears in various arguments in the *Risale-i Nur*.

On the one hand, for Said Nursi the mystery of human responsibility is evident in the fact that God leaves people free even in the crucial matter of being able to accept or refuse a Prophetic revelation. God does not use any form of compulsion, whether physical or logical, to *force* anyone to believe. The inviolate mystery of human responsibility that God does not preempt or violate is seen clearly in God's *inviting* people to faith through the use of reason and the exercise of their freedom to choose.

In speaking of the miracles of Muhammad, Nursi asks why God would not have made the miracles reported in the Qur'an and *hadith*, such as the splitting of the moon, so obvious and evident to all people on earth that everyone would have seen and known them and thus have been compelled to believe. As it was, such miracles were only shown to a certain number of people in a certain place, while most people on earth were unaware of them. Nursi's response is that if the evidence for Prophethood were so compelling that no reasonable person could possibly deny it, the mystery of human responsibility with which God had endowed humankind would not have been respected. In other words, faith that is either sensibly evident or logically compelled is not true faith, and the individual person who is responsible for responding without restraint to God's invitation would not be making a truly free response of faith. As Nursi puts it:

> If [the miracle of splitting the moon] had been shown to all and sundry, it would have been shown as a sign and miracle of Muhammad's (peace and blessings be upon him) Prophethood. His messengership would have been so manifest that everyone would have been compelled to affirm it. No choice would have remained for man's reason. But belief is attained through reason and the power of choice, and the mystery of human responsibility [italics mine] would have been lost.[246]

2. God's determination and human choice

With this example, the issue is joined of the greatest mystery of human responsibility, that is, the seemingly impossible, but religiously essential reality of human choice in the face of God's omnipotent nature. Human free choice would seem to be an illusion, impossible to reconcile with the Islamic doctrine of *taqdir* or *qadar*, which is the logical conclusion of belief in God's sovereign omnipotence. If God is the author of all potency and potentiality without exception, it follows

---

[246] *The Letters*, Miracles of Muhammad, Second Addendum, p. 250.

that everything is determined by God's will, including those actions that flow from human choice and decision. For this reason, it would seem impossible for a religious believer to hold that humans are truly free in choosing their acts and, in fact, the Divine determining, or *taqdir*, is a pillar of faith among Sunni Muslims.

On the other hand, if the essential choices to believe or disbelieve and to obey or disobey are mere illusions but have really already been determined by God, how can God be justified in rewarding or punishing those acts according to their moral quality? Unless humans in some way acquire responsibility for their actions or come to "own" their deeds, including the basic religious acts of belief and obedience, the ground is cut from any truly religious response to God's revelations. Were people to have no responsibility for their acts, they would become simply puppets, forced to act out, by the power of another, a pre-scribed scenario. But, as Said Nursi states in the above-mentioned citation, "belief is attained through reason *and the power of choice*" and, as the Qur'an states: "*Let there be no compulsion in religion*" (2: 256). God invites a person to choose freely to believe and obey His commands and on this basis God is just in rewarding those who believe and obey and in punishing those who choose to disbelieve and disobey.

For Said Nursi, this mystery of human responsibility is not first and foremost a philosophical conundrum to be solved through the use of logical methods. Rather, it is truly a mystery that touches upon some of the deepest levels of Islamic faith. As he states: "Divine determining and the power of choice are aspects of belief pertaining to state and conscience which show the final limits of Islam and belief; they are not theoretical and do not pertain to knowledge."[247] Thus, the believer's task is not to engage in a philosophical search for a rational "solution" to a logical puzzle, but rather to try to understand the Divine guidance and wisdom that can be found in this revealed message.

Nursi's way of approaching the question of human freedom and God's sovereign omnipotence from the point of view of Divine peda-gogy is a departure from the *kalam* tradition which sought to recon-

---

[247] *The Words*, The Twenty-Sixth Word, p. 477.

cile the apparent contradiction between the two concepts. However, Nursi's intent is different. He leaves aside the question of logical reconciliation and instead strives to see how adhering simultaneously to both these elements of Islamic faith can help one live responsibly before God.

One lesson taught by the twin concepts of Divine determining and human freedom is the need to use responsibly the gifts with which God has endowed each person. In other words, *taqdir* or the Divine determining is the source of the talents and scientific capacities which humans possess. Humans must recognize that these gifts do not arise from their own efforts, but have been determined by God. The same God who has determined human talents and capabilities has also determined that people will be able to freely execute these abilities. Denying either the Divinely determined gifts or the human responsibility to employ those gifts in a creative way will result in the misuse or dissipation of those gifts.

For example, God has endowed humans with scientific and intellectual abilities. Using these Divine gifts in a meaningful way in accord with God's will is for humans the source of energy and fullness of life. However, employing one's gifts wastefully in the pursuit of trivial whims and immediate gratification is tantamount to allowing these gifts to atrophy or to rot like spoiled fruit. Those who spend their lives wasting the Divine gifts with which they have been blessed tend to blame the limitations of their spirit for what is essentially their own failure to exploit their gifts properly. In other words, they are in practical denial of God's determining as well as ignorant of their own responsible freedom. At life's end, they wind up lamenting not only the time lost, but also the squandered talents and opportunities. In Nursi's words:

> Significant talents and valuable programs have been deposited in man's nature by Divine power and determining. If man uses those immaterial members on the desires of his soul and on minor pleasures under the soil of worldly life in the narrow confines of this earthly world, he will decay and decompose in the midst of difficulties in a brief life in a constricted place like the rotted seed, and

load the responsibility on his unfortunate spirit, then depart from this world.[248]

The religious value of *taqdir* is that the concept keeps one realistically humble. Rather than arrogantly believing that one's achievements have been accomplished by one's own power and therefore belong to oneself, belief in the Divine determining enables one to understand and appreciate one's own limitations and to be grateful for what one has been given by God. *Taqdir* is the recognition that all human achievements are in fact our acquisitions of what God has performed in and for us.

Thus, emphasis on awareness of God's determining is the "normal" way a believer proceeds through life until the moment of choice arrives. However, at that moment, one must acknowledge and become aware of the reality that God has left humans free to believe or disbelieve, to obey or disobey. Thus, recognition of free will is the basis of human responsibility for one's actions; acceptance of *taqdir* while denying freedom of choice would result in an evasion of the very responsibility with which God has endowed humans.

In short, a believer attributes everything to God, even all his personal actions. However, he has a real power to choose, and renouncing that power to choose would be an evasion of one's duty and responsibility. It is the power of choosing that underlines human responsibility for one's actions. In the words of the *Risale-i Nur*:

> A believer attributes everything to Almighty God, even his actions and self, till finally the power of choice confronts him, so he cannot evade his obligation and responsibility. It tells him: "You are responsible and under obligation." Then, so that he does not become proud at his good deeds and his achievements, Divine determining confronts him, saying: "Know your limits; the one who does them is not you." Yes, Divine determining and the power of choice are at the deepest levels of belief and Islam; the former has been included among the matters of belief to save the soul from pride, and the latter, to make it admit to its responsibility.[249]

---

[248] *The Words*, The Twenty-Third Word, Second Chapter, p. 331.
[249] *The Words*, The Twenty-Sixth Word, p. 477.

Those who do not want to follow God's guidance are quick to deny both *taqdir* and human responsibility. They want to take credit for their own deeds as though nothing had been determined by God and they come to think highly of themselves as a result of imagining their achievements to have been their own. Then, in situations of failure, they blame the Divine determining for their weaknesses of judgment and action and are unwilling to own their own limitations.[250] They claim that all has been determined by God; hence their shortcomings must be accepted as their fate or destiny. According to Nursi, the recourse to fate to provide an excuse for one's failings and disappointments is an irresponsible way of viewing both oneself and God. It shows a lack of respect for the true human freedom with which God has created humans as well as a lack of confidence in God's desire to treat with humans as creatures who have been taken up the responsibility of responding freely to God.

3. God's vicegerent on earth

According to Nursi, human dignity is bound up with the role God has given to the human person as God's vicegerent, or representative, on earth. Commenting on the Qur'anic verse *"We offered the Trust to the heavens and the earth and the mountains, but they, being afraid, refused to undertake it, but man undertook it"* (33:72), Nursi regards true human responsibility in light of this unique role as God's viceroy in the created world. Of all created animal and vegetable life, he states, "man is the most articulate and most responsible minister."[251] The human being is "the most important result of the universe, the most elevated of living creatures, possessing the most comprehensive capabilities,"[252] "a representation in miniature of God's cosmic processes."[253]

---

[250] Ibid., p. 480.

[251] *The Rays*, The Fruits of Belief, Seventh Topic, p. 238.

[252] *The Rays*, The Fifteenth Ray, the Shining Proof, First Station, p. 588.

[253] *The Words*, The Tenth Word, Eleventh Truth, p. 100. Cf. also, *The Words*, The Twentieth Word, p. 268 and The Twenty-Fifth Word, Second Light, Second Beam, p. 442.

The mysterious nature of the creation of the human person, which differs not only in degree but also in kind from the creation of the rest of animal and vegetable life, gives to the human person a level of responsibility which is neither possible nor expected from the rest of creation.

> It is because of this great mystery that Almighty God created mankind with a nature that would produce the shoots of thousands of species and display the levels of the thousands of other species of living creatures. No limit was placed on man's powers, subtle faculties, and senses like the other animals; since He left him free and gave him a capacity whereby they could roam through endless degrees, while being one species, mankind became like thousands of species.[254]

In fact, the vast responsibility which humankind has accepted over the created universe is the basis for much indulgence and compassion on the part of God. It is as though God were aware that the responsibility granted to humans is almost beyond their capabilities. Thus, God is neither surprised nor greatly displeased that people have failed to execute their Trust successfully. By exercising the scientific and artistic talents that God has placed in them, human beings show that they are the purpose, the masterpiece, and the ultimate fruit, of God's creative genius and thereby gain a measure of forgiveness for their shortcomings.

> There is man, who rules over the earth and has disposal over most creatures and subjects most living beings to himself. He so orders, displays, and gathers each remarkable species... that he attracts not only the attention and admiration of men and jinn, but of the dwellers of the heavens and the appreciative gaze of the universe's Owner, thus gaining great importance and high worth. He shows through his sciences and arts that he is the purpose of the universe's creation, its most important product, its most precious fruit, and the Divine viceroy on earth. Because has ordered and displayed excellently the miraculous arts of the world's Maker, he is left in this world despite his rebellion and disbelief, and his punishment is postponed...[255]

---

[254] *The Flashes*, The Twenty-Second Flash, p. 226.
[255] *The Rays*, The Ninth Ray, p. 209.

Nursi explains elsewhere[256] that it was the very human *disposition* to be taught, to learn, to express, and to organize knowledge logically and scientifically that was the basis for the human acceptance of the Divine Trust as ruler of the created universe. This ability to discover, recognize, and categorize the secrets of scientific knowledge amounts to an appreciative understanding of God's own attributes and qualities, and it is this ability to know God's creation scientifically and to express it artistically that affords humans a superiority not only over the cosmos but also over angelic beings.

4. True human fulfilment

Through reflection upon and contemplation of the wonders and effects of God's creative activity, an individual actually becomes the fully realized human person intended by God. "Through worship and contemplation of this kind [a person] becomes a true man."[257] In other words, scientific research and artistic expression are the primary methods by which the believer becomes aware of all that is involved in God's creative activity. By allowing oneself to grow in knowledge of the universe, one actually fulfils the purpose for which he or she was created and becomes God's vicegerent. In this way, Nursi underlines his conviction that science and art are not opposed to religious practice but, rather, are among its highest manifestations. Developing one's scientific and artistic talents, which are the products of God's determining (*taqdir*), thus amounts to the human acceptance of the primordial Trust offered by God and leads to true human fulfilment.

Because of the unique gifts and functions with which God has endowed the human person, a human being can exercise power of choice, thus assuming responsibility for his own actions and yet approaching God with the attitudes of worship and obedience which are owed by creatures to the Creator. Nursi's resolution of the "problem" of Divine determining and human choice is found in human dignity which places the two elements of faith in creative tension, opt-

---

[256] *The Words*, The Twentieth Word, First Station, p. 254.
[257] *The Words*, The Twenty-Third Word, Second Chapter, p. 339.

ing neither for the illusion of indiscriminate human freedom nor for a fatalistic determinism. Accepting Divine *taqdir* means gratefully recognizing God as the source of one's gifts and achievements and thereby one avoids arrogance and self-delusion. Accepting human choice permits one to overcome a desperate fatalism in the face of frustration at personal limitations.

> Since one knows himself and everything to be from Almighty God, he assumes the responsibility, basing it on his power of choice. He accepts that it is the source of evils and proclaims his Sustainer free of fault. He remains within the sphere of worship and undertakes the obligations with which he is charged by Almighty God. Moreover, he does not become proud because of his good deeds and achievements; he rather looks to Divine Determining and offers thanks. He sees Divine Determining in the calamities that befall him, and endures them in patience.[258]

A healthy rule of thumb offered by Said Nursi would be to consider the past and the various calamities that befall people from the point of view of *taqdir*, while the future and personal sins should be regarded from the aspect of one's responsibility before God.[259] In other words, God respects the human power of choice by allowing people to err and even to do what is against their own best interests. Divine determining does not mean that God prevents people from wrongdoing, nor that God wills and desires the evil that people do, but rather that God respects the power of free choice with which God has created humans.

Nursi uses the example of a child that insists on climbing a mountain in cold weather. A parent is ready to take the child, even though it means that the child might fall or catch cold. The parent may even punish the child for his obstinacy.[260] It is clear, however, that the responsibility for going up the mountain is the child's, who freely chose to climb the mountain when he could have decided on some other course of action, whereas the parent neither forced nor prevented the

---

[258] *The Words*, The Twenty-Sixth Word, p. 479.
[259] *The Damascus Sermon*, Seeds of Reality, p. 103. Cf. also, *The Letters*, p. 546.
[260] *The Words*, The Twenty-Sixth Word, p. 483.

child from his unwise course. On the other hand, the determining power came from the parent; the child would have been unable to climb the mountain alone.

One might criticize this example and suggest that Nursi could have found a better way to illustrate his point. On the one hand, the example demonstrates well how an all-determining God could leave an immature child free to choose an unwise action and then, despite his wise guidance to the contrary, employ his omnipotence to enable the child to perform that action and also to be justified in punishing the child's stubborn wilfulness. However, in real life a parent who would permit a child to carry out an unwise and dangerous action, rather than simply forbidding the deed and refusing to assist in facilitating the child's bad idea would be subject to the accusation of irresponsibility. A conscientious parent would never allow himself or herself to be drawn into and become part of the child's foolish project. Certainly, Nursi does not want to impute any irresponsibility to God in permitting humans to sin, but the reader must be aware of the limits of this imperfect analogy.

5. The illusion of absolute freedom

Affirming and holding together in tension the twin concepts of Divine determination and human choice is not only the proper response to Islamic teaching, but has practical benefits for the way in which a believer lives. A person who emphasizes *taqdir* while minimizing or denying the reality of human choice could easily fall into a type of passive fatalism in which he asks himself what is the use of exercising his innate talents, since everything has already been determined by God. In fact, certain schools of Islamic thought, such as that of the Ash'ariyya, have been often accused of fatalism by their opponents.

On the other hand, by over-emphasizing human choice to the detriment of God's determining power, as do the followers of the Mu'tazili school, one is led to a kind of scrupulosity. Confronted with a multiplicity of diverse and contradictory choices, on which someone's eternal destiny depends, the believer is faced with the dilemma of choosing the best course of action. In this scheme, there is no role for Divine determination, with the result that the burden of human responsibility becomes too great for a healthy religious life. How can a person make the best choice when he doesn't have all the necessary knowledge? What if he makes the wrong choice? How can he ever be sure that he has made the correct choice? Nursi regards the assertion of free human choice, with a corresponding disavowal of Divine determination, as imposing a crippling burden on the human psyche, one that places undue responsibility on the human person.

> There is a scruple arising from searching for the best form of an action. Supposing it to be fear of God, the more rigorous it becomes, the more severe becomes the person's condition. It even reaches the point that while searching for better forms of action, someone deviates into what is unlawful. Sometimes searching for a sunna makes him give up what is obligatory. He says: "I wonder if my act was correct?" and repeats it. This state continues until he falls into terrible despair... Scruples like this are typical of the Mu'tazila, because they say: "Actions and things for which a person is responsible are either, of themselves and in regard to the hereafter, good, and because of this good they were commanded, or they are bad, and because they are bad they were prohibited. That means, from the point of view of reality and the hereafter, the good and bad in things is dependent on the things themselves, and the Divine command and prohibition follows this." According to this school of thought, the following scruple arises in every action which a person performs: "I wonder if my action was performed in the good way that in essence it is?"[261]

According to Nursi, the Sunni affirmation, which acknowledges Divine determination, does not lead, unlike the Mu'tazili view, to paralyzing scrupulosity. Rather than positing an innate moral value to every human act, Sunni doctrine holds that the moral quality of human actions is dependent on the Divine decree. "Almighty God orders a thing, then it becomes good. He prohibits a thing, then it becomes bad."[262] Thus, the good or evil nature of an act is not determined by how an act appears in the light of worldly human judgment but rath-

---

[261] *The Words*, The Twenty-First Word, Second Station, p. 283.
[262] *Ibid*.

er how the act is judged and determined by God. Thus, someone need not agonize over the innate correctness or wrongness of an act and wonder whether what he has done was good or not, but can simply follow God's own teaching on the particular moral value of the deed.

6. Conclusion: the value of sincerity

Finally, what is the believer's responsibility to attain the spiritual attitudes and strengths necessary for the task which God gives? On the one hand, the believer needs to grant that the necessary strength and wisdom come from God, not from his own efforts but, on the other hand, the individual must work with all his strength to obtain those gifts of grace. A good example is sincerity, which Nursi sees as being at the heart of a religious believer's life in this world and essential to carrying out the task God appoints to each. If one does not do everything one can to respond to God's grace and the service expected of believers, that person will be held responsible for his failure. Thus, human responsibility means recognizing that both talents and capabilities stem from Divine initiative and that the ability to carry out one's mission of service is the result of God's grace, but at the same time, the believer must "work with all his strength" to respond with sincerity and honest effort to fulfil these physical and spiritual potentialities given by God.

> Since in sincerity lies much strength... and since at this dreadful time, despite our small number and our weak, impoverished, and powerless state, our being confronted by terrible enemies, and suffering severe oppression in the midst of aggressive innovations and misguidance, the extremely heavy, important, and sacred duty of serving belief and the Qur'an has been placed on our shoulders by Divine grace, we are certainly compelled more than anyone to work with all our strength to gain sincerity. We are in utter need of instilling sincerity in ourselves. Otherwise what we have achieved so far in our sacred service will in part be lost, and will not persist; and we shall be held responsible.[263]

---

[263] *The Flashes*, The Twenty-First Flash, "On Sincerity," p. 213.

Since "an ounce of deeds performed in sincerity is preferable to a ton performed without sincerity,"[264] one need not worry whether one has done enough, or has done the right action. The mystery of human responsibility suggests that a person fulfils one's duty by sincerely responding to Divine grace to the best of one's abilities. Decisions are the fruit of real human choices, yet they never fall outside the sphere of Divine determination.

---

[264] Ibid., p. 206.

The Resurrection of the
Dead and Final Judgment

One of the questions that most clearly distinguishes the followers of those religions that trace their origins back to their common ancestor Abraham from those who do not accept any Divine religion is their belief in the resurrection of the dead. In both Christianity and Islam, the resurrection of the dead, together with the Last Judgment, and the eternal reward or punishment granted on the basis of the individual's faith and deeds, is an essential element, a "pillar" of that faith. The two religions might differ on details concerning the eschatological fate that awaits humans, but on the key issues of the reality of resurrection, God's judgment of all humankind on the Last Day, and reward and punishment, there is broad agreement in the theology of Islamic and Christian faiths.

However, for a person thinking and operating in a positivistic frame of mind, the concept of resurrection is a religious myth that can be neither proven nor disproved, but must remain always a hypothesis whose validity depends on blind faith. Some of those who reject religious faith go farther to advance arguments that would attempt to disprove the possibility of resurrection, while for others the concept is simply an absurdity—"pie in the sky"—evidence of the fairy-tale wishful thinking of religious people.

This is not a new experience for believers in the Divine religions. In the Christian tradition, when St. Paul spoke at the Areopagus in Athens, the assembled scholars were interested in what he had to say until the moment Paul began speaking about the resurrection, at which point they sneered and turned away (Acts of the Apostles 17: 32). For Paul, God's raising Jesus from the dead is evidence of God's promise to raise all those who believe, and thus the resurrection becomes a key element in Christian faith. Paul says, "If there is no resurrection of the dead, then not even Christ has been raised, and if Christ has not been raised, our preaching is useless and so is your faith" (1 Corinthians 15: 13-14).

Many centuries later, the experience of Muhammad with the Quraysh was similar. When Muhammad spoke to the polytheist Arabs about God who causes death and resurrection, they answered, *"What, will we and our fathers be raised up, once we have turned into dust? We have been promised this, we and our forefathers, but these are merely legends of earlier peoples"* (Qur'an 27:67–68; cf. also, 23:82–83). The earlier peoples whom the Quraysh accused of perpetuating fanciful myths were evidently the Jews and Christians conveying the teaching of Moses and Jesus. Just as the polytheist Quraysh rejected the teaching of the earlier Prophets about the resurrection, so also they were rejecting Muhammad who was bringing the same message that the Divine judgment and eternal reward or punishment were awaiting every human person.

For Said Nursi, the resurrection and Final Judgment are central to the Qur'anic message. He goes so far as to say that a third of the Qur'an focuses on these eschatological elements with the intention of proving and demonstrating them to unbelievers. "All the miracles, truths, and proofs proving foremost the veracity of the Qur'an of miraculous exposition testify to and prove the realization and occurrence of resurrection. Almost a third of the Qur'an is about resurrection, and at the beginning of most of its short *surah*s are powerful verses about it. It expresses the same truth explicitly and implicitly, and in thousands of its verses it proves and demonstrates it."[265]

1. The resurrection and the demands of justice

Similarly, one could say that almost one-third of the content of *The Words*, the first part of the *Risale-i Nur*, focuses on questions of the resurrection, intent on demonstrating the reality of these elements of

---

[265] *The Rays*, The Ninth Ray, p. 205. Cf. The Fifteenth Ray, The Shining Proof, First Station, p. 578.

faith for modern unbelievers. In the Tenth Word Nursi strives to give systematic order to his argumentation in favor of the resurrection, and hence this portion of the *Risale-i Nur* can serve as a suitable starting place for our analysis of Nursi's view of this pillar of Islamic faith.

Nursi introduces the topic with a long allegory of two men journeying through an earthly Utopia. It is a well-ordered and prosperous place where no one locks their homes or shops, as there is no need to guard one's possessions. One of the travelers heedlessly wants to take and steal as much as he can carry, but his companion undertakes to show him, in twelve reasoned arguments, that in such a place, there must be a supreme tribunal where everyone will be judged according to their deeds.[266]

The underlying concept in these twelve arguments is that of justice. The manifest injustice of life on earth requires another world where wrongs will be corrected, victims will be avenged, and upright behavior will be rewarded. It is also in God's character to be just, and therefore any conception of the universe that would lead to the denial of God's justice and mercy is an attack on God's very nature. These principles are argued in the twelve arguments, which may be summarized as follows:

1) Even in the best-ordered earthly realm, there must be a mechanism for justice: for punishing misdeeds, defending the oppressed, and rewarding faithful service. Obviously, in the world in which we live, there is no manifest justice. Wrongdoers prosper while the innocent suffer; loyalty and honesty are not rewarded. The demands of cosmic justice demand a resurrection, for there is no reward and punishment in this world. There must be a resurrection to a next life where judgment, reward and punishment will correct earthly wrongs.

---

[266] This parable can be read on several levels. Nursi explains that the heedless companion indicates greedy, selfish human instinct, whereas the responsible friend corresponds to the human heart or conscience. At another level, the self-justifying rationalist indicates the student of human philosophy, while his upright companion is the student of the Qur'an; finally, the misguided individual stands for unbelievers, while the wise, thoughtful companion represents the community of faith. *The Tenth Word*, p. 70.

2) God's own just nature demands a resurrection. The One who so wisely ordered this universe could not fail, in his mercy, to provide justice for those who have remained upright and faithful. God's generosity and compassion demands justice towards the oppressed. But that justice is not found on this earth, so it must be found elsewhere, i.e., in the next life.

3) God would not be compassionate and merciful if He did not hear and respond to the cries of the oppressed. But those who are victims of wrongdoing do not find satisfaction on this earth, and the unjust operate freely and successfully in this world. Therefore, if one believes that God is compassionate and merciful, there must be a resurrection to judgment where the oppressed can finally obtain the redress they expect from such a compassionate and merciful God.

4) God's abundant gifts show God to be generous and loving. But if the gifts that God gives are all perishable, and all that awaits people is death, separation, and extinction, then these apparent gifts simply amount to a cruel joke. Moreover, God grants these gifts in order to be known and loved. But if there is no resurrection, those appreciating these gifts on earth would be only temporary admirers, and their appreciation would turn to resentment upon learning that the gifts were only fleeting hand-outs destined to be definitively snatched away in death.

5) All that God has granted humankind in this world is only meant to whet people's appetite for the more permanent, exalted gifts that God has yet in store for them. God would be a cruel charlatan to give and promise so much and then abandon people to eternal extinction without fulfilling His promises. Thus, God's integrity demands a resurrection and reward for faithful obedience.

6) This world is a constantly changing exhibition of God's gifts, both the ever-changing gifts of nature as well as man-made technological achievements. However, the very transient, fleeting nature of this worldly display requires that there be some eternal, stable world where the reality that shows itself here in an ephemeral way will reside permanently. Otherwise, God would be reduced to acting like a stage

magician who creates illusions with mirrors. None of the wonders of nature and human achievement would have any lasting meaning.

7) God's omniscience demands resurrection. If God is truly cognizant of all that occurs on earth, then it follows that God knows, notes, and remembers every human deed, whether good or evil, and that the record of these deeds will be the basis for Divine judgment. If misdeeds never went unpunished and the same end were foreseen for the virtuous and the evildoers, God would be no better than a negligent caretaker, which view is contrary to the dignity of God.

8) In all the revealed Scriptures God has consistently promised to reward the good and punish evil. If God is truthful and the Scriptures can be believed, there must be a resurrection. Can it be imagined that God will not fulfill God's promises?

9) All the Prophets and holy men have testified to God's promises and assure us that those promises will be fulfilled. Yet the Prophets are unanimous in affirming the resurrection and final judgment. Are we ready to disregard such unanimous testimony on the part of those sent by God?

10) The setting of this argument is Anatolian spring. All the varied and constantly burgeoning life that can be seen in springtime points to a wise order in the universe and indicates that this ordered universe cannot be an end in itself. If it all ends in total extinction, the world is absurd and without rhyme or reason. If there is truly a wise purpose in the universe, it must point to something real and permanent in another world. Nursi will return repeatedly to this argument, with different emphases, again and again in the Risale-i Nur.

11) Denying the resurrection and judgment would mean not only denying the wise order of the universe, but it would mean denying God's compassion, mercy, and justice. Nursi is saying that denying the resurrection is tantamount to denying the existence of God, as this God is known from the Scriptures. "We would also have to regard the One from whom all these wise measures proceed, all these generous acts, all these merciful gifts, as a vile gambler or treacherous tyrant

(God forbid!). This would be to turn truth on its head."[267] Moreover, denying the resurrection would mean not only denying God as God is known from Scriptural tradition, but it would also mean denying the evidence of our own senses.

12) Since the rewards for faithful service as well as punishments for evildoing are both deferred to the next life, denying the resurrection amounts to denying both reward and punishment. Good and evil become equivalent and have the same end. Thus, denying the resurrection reduces all religions, Scriptures, and claims to ultimate purpose to a relative value and condemns people to life in a pointless, superficial, ephemeral universe.

In his final argument, Nursi takes up what is most deeply at stake in the question of the resurrection and judgment. If this is the only world and life that exists, if there is no "Day of Reckoning" when accounts will be definitively settled, then religion and morality become human creations which point to no permanent reality. People are condemned to a shallow existence of validating their lives through a constant search for new and exciting pleasures and the acquisition of an unending stream of perishable consumer goods.

Nursi does not pretend that the twelve arguments which he produced for demonstrating the resurrection are exhaustive, or that no other proofs could be adduced.[268] In fact, the *Risale-i Nur* is replete with arguments in favor of the necessity of belief in the resurrection and Final Judgment. Nursi sees belief in God and the resurrection as a kind of double talisman which will protect and guide a person through the dangers of life.

In another allegory, he describes the situation of a wounded soldier on a battlefield, surrounded by dangers on all sides. In his hopeless plight, a stranger, "shining with light like Khidr,"[269] comes to teach him the twin talismans of "I believe in God and the Last Day," which will heal his wounds and protect him from the physical and spiritual

---

[267] *The Words*, The Tenth Word, p. 67.
[268] *The Words*, The Tenth Word, Tenth Truth, p. 102.
[269] *The Words*, The Seventh Word, p. 41.

dangers that surround him. In explaining the allegory, Nursi holds that the life of people in this world is like the situation of that soldier. The challenges and problems that beset us are greater than our strength can bear or our wisdom can comprehend. However, belief in God and the resurrection will overcome someone's weaknesses and enable that person to confront life's challenges with courage and persevere with patience in the face of adversity.

2. The miracle of springtime

Skeptics reacted to Nursi's teaching about the resurrection with the objection that it is scientifically impossible for dead bodies to come to life again. Irreversible processes of corruption, molecular changes, inter-ruption of brain waves, and the permanent malfunctioning of organs commence immediately after death. After some time in the grave, the human corpse itself reverts by inexorable biochemical processes to the substances from which it was composed. Not even God could reverse these changes. Perhaps one could speak, as did some of the philoso-phers, of the resurrection of the soul, while the body lies decomposed for eternity in the grave. On the Last Day, if there should be a Last Day, there would be nothing left for God to raise, all the body's elements and compounds, bones and tissues, having been dispersed and recy-cled elsewhere in nature.

This objection, posed repeatedly in modern times, is in fact not a new one. The polytheist Quraysh objected to Muhammad's preaching about the resurrection on the same grounds of impossibility. Not even God can bring life out of death. In response to this objection, the Qur'an appeals to the sense experience of the Quraysh and says that just as God has the power to bring the earth to new life at the begin-ning of each spring, so God has the power to revive the dead: *"Behold the marks of Allah's mercy, how He revives the earth after it was dead. He indeed is the one who revives the dead and He has power over everything"* (Qur'an 30:50).

One could say that Said Nursi's defense of God's ability to raise the dead is simply an elaboration or commentary on this Qur'anic verse. This is not a peripheral idea to his thought, as he uses over fifty times in the *Risale-i Nur* the image of new life in the spring as an illustration of God's power to resurrect the dead. For God, the one is as easy as the other. There is no doubt that Nursi must have personally found spiritual enrichment in the miracle of Anatolian springtime, with its "more than 300,000 species of plant and animal life"[270] appearing almost miraculously, but predictably at its appointed time every year at the end of the long, cold, grey winter.

I cannot hope to give all the references in the *Risale-i Nur* to this image, but a few citations must suffice to show Nursi's use of the figure of spring as a likeness of the resurrection.

> In exactly the same way, [God] creates the universe as easily as a city, and raises to life the springtime as easily as a garden, and raises to life all the dead at the resurrection as easily as creating the leaves, flowers, and fruits of the garden's trees in the spring.[271]

> The one who cannot create a spring cannot create a single apple either, for the apple is made at the same workbench. But the one who makes an apple can make the spring. Each apple is an example in miniature of a tree, even of a garden or a cosmos. The apple seed that carries within itself the life story of the huge tree is, from the point of view of artistry, such a miracle that the one who creates it is incapable of nothing. So too, the one that creates today is able also to create the day of resurrection, and it is only the One capable of creating the spring that is able to create resurrection.[272]

> In spring, the dead trees, roots and animals come to life again exactly as they were, thus providing hundreds of thousands of examples, specimens and proofs of the supreme resurrection. In the place of others, plants and animals resembling them exactly are brought into being and life, thus publishing the pages of the beings of the preceding spring, together with their deeds and functions.[273]

---

[270] *The Words*, The Tenth Word, Fifth Part of the Addendum, p. 131.

[271] *The Rays*, The Fifteenth Ray, The Shining Proof, Second Station, p. 627.

[272] *The Words*, The Tenth Word, Seventh Truth, p. 90.

[273] *The Rays*, The Supreme Sign, First Chapter, p. 164; cf. The Twenty-Sixth Flash, "For the Elderly," p. 291.

The raising to life of all animate beings at the resurrection of the dead can be no more difficult for Divine Power than restoring to life a fly in the spring, heavy with the death-stained sleep of winter.[274]

O you who deny resurrection! Look at the trees! One Who raises to life and makes green in spring numberless skeleton-like trees which have been dead throughout winter, and in every tree even demonstrates three examples of resurrection through the leaves, blossoms, and fruit—the power of such a One cannot be challenged through denial or by considering resurrection improbable.[275]

The raising to life of all animate beings at the resurrection of the dead can be no more difficult for Divine Power than restoring to life a fly in the spring, heavy with the death-stained sleep of winter. For Eternal Power is essential. It does not change; impotence cannot penetrate it; obstacles cannot intervene in it; there can be no degrees in it; everything is the same in relation to it.[276]

Now come back in the spring, the arena of the annual resurrection, and look! Note carefully the time in the spring when the Israfil-like angel of thunder calls out to the rain as though sounding his trumpet, giving the good news of the breath of life being breathed into the seeds buried beneath the ground. You will see that under the manifestation of the Divine Name of Preserver, those seeds that resemble each other and are all mixed up and confused, conform perfectly and without error to the creative commands proceeding from the All-Wise Creator.[277]

The administration and sustaining of the whole universe in relation to the power from all eternity of that All-Glorious One is as easy as that of the spring, indeed, of a tree. And the creation of the resurrection of the dead, the realm of the hereafter, and Paradise and Hell, is as easy as the resurrection in spring of a tree which had died the previous autumn.[278]

Nursi's point in this oft-repeated image is that it is no more difficult for God to raise the dead than it is for God to bring new life to

---

[274] *The Damascus Sermon*, The Seeds of Reality, p. 97.

[275] *The Words*, The Twenty-Fifth Word, First Light, Second Ray, p. 412.

[276] *The Letters*, Seeds of Reality, p. 542.

[277] *The Flashes*, The Seventeenth Flash, Fifteenth Note, p. 187.

[278] *The Letters*, The Twentieth Letter, Second Station, p. 297.

the dead earth or to bring about a single tree or flower from a dry, frozen bush. In other words, the resurrection of the dead is a part of God's creative power and energy. If God is able to create life once from nothingness or from dead matter, and to renew annually that miracle of rebirth, God is able to do that over and over, specifically, in the case of humans who die an earthly death.[279]

One must not think that Nursi is living in a pre-scientific world in which he thinks that vegetable and animal life actually dies in the winter. He is well aware of the botanical dormant period that plants undergo, of the hidden life that continues to pulsate in a winter landscape of forests and fields. This scientific awareness, however, makes the springtime miracle of regeneration—the formation of blossoms, leaves, and fruits—no less amazing, no less remarkable as the sign of an all-powerful Creator. He states:

> With what miraculous and elevated style [the Qur'an] describes the resurrection of the dead and the Great Gathering and points to the following convincing proof: one can observe that the seeds concealed as though dead in the darkness of the earth and drops of water hidden and dispersed, seemingly non-existent in the atmosphere are raised to life swiftly and with perfect order every spring, and they emerge into the field of trial and examination as perpetual examples of resurrection. At the supreme resurrection, beings will emerge with same ease. Since you observe the one here, you cannot deny the other.[280]

In fact, it is not only the miracle of spring that demonstrates the resurrection. An individual's own sense perception repeatedly gives evidence of resurrection. Waking from sleep can be seen as a type of resurrection, as does the physical process of replacing all the molecules in the body. Nursi states: "There are many varieties of resurrection that a person experiences during his lifetime. Just as one sees the signs of the resurrection in a sort of dying every night and rebirth every morning, so it is agreed that he undergoes what resembles a resurrection

---

[279] *The Rays*, The Fifteenth Ray, The Shining Proof, Second Station, p. 629.

[280] *The Letters*, The Twenty-Ninth Letter, First Section, p. 459; cf. also, *The Rays*, The Supreme Sign, First Chapter, p. 164.

every five or six years by changing all the particles in his body, and even undergoes a gradual resurrection twice a year."[281]

The phenomenon of springtime is not only a sign and symbol of the resurrection in demonstrating God's power to bring new life out of the seemingly dead, but it is also a demonstration, for those who are able to perceive it, of the transitory nature of life in this world. The wildflowers and blossoms that flourish in all their glory for a week or ten days and then vanish for another year are reminders that this world and all that pertains to it are not permanent. In world-weariness reminiscent of the great Sufi masters, Nursi expresses the sorrow he experienced at witnessing the transient nature of springtime beauty.

> One time when observing the season of spring, I saw that the successive caravans of beings, and especially living creatures and the small young ones, which followed on one after the other and in a flowing torrent displaying hundreds of thousands of samples of the resurrection of the dead and Great Gathering on the face of the earth, appeared only briefly then disappeared. The tableaux of death and transience amid that constant, awesome activity seemed to me excessively sad. I felt such pity it made me weep. The more I observed the deaths of those lovely small creatures, the more my heart ached. I cried at the pity of it and within me felt a deep spiritual turmoil. Life which met with such an end seemed to me to be torment worse than death.[282]

Clearly, the transient splendor of nature that flourishes today and tomorrow is dry stubble reminds people of the passing away in human life of youth, beauty and vitality. Today's beauty queen or Olympic athlete is tomorrow's toothless wheel-chair patient. For those who believe in no other life than this, this awareness can produce misery and despair, but for those who see the power of God at work in the fragile and transitory nature of created things, the cycle of youth, aging, and death is always followed by rebirth. This is the promise Nursi holds out for those who are able to proceed from a contemplation of the patterns of nature to an awareness of God the Resurrector (Al-Qa'im).

---

[281] *The Words*, The Twenty-Ninth Word, Second Aim, p. 539.
[282] *The Rays*, The Second Ray, First Station, p. 21.

3. The Great Gathering

Nursi's usual term for God's calling together all humankind from every stage of history in order to enact the final judgment according to their deeds is the Great Gathering. No doubt the figure is taken from the Qur'anic verse *"(And remember) the Day when He will gather you on the Day of Gathering. That will be the Day of mutual loss and gain. And whosoever believes in God and performs righteous good deeds, He will remit from him his sins, and will admit him to Gardens under which rivers flow to dwell therein forever"* **(64:9).** This imagery of calling all humankind together for judgment is common to both Islam and Christianity. In the Christian Bible, for example, the Epistle to the Hebrews sees "The Universal Gathering" as equivalent to "Mount Zion, the New Jerusalem" (Hebrews 12:23; cf. also, 2 Thessalonians 2:1), an appointment to which all are called.

The image depicts generations of dead arising from their graves all over the earth and brought together for the final Day of Judgment. Can God actually bring together every individual in the history of the human race to be judged each according to one's deeds? Surely this must be some fanciful imagery but is not meant to be taken literally? Nursi responds by citing again God's creative power in nature to affirm that such is well within God's capabilities. Nursi addresses the Creator as follows: "Through Your activity in the atmosphere, Your power, which continuously displays examples of the resurrection of the dead and Great Gathering and transforms the summer into winter and winter into summer and similar acts, gives the sign that it will transform this world into the hereafter and there display its everlasting acts."[283]

The Great Gathering may be seen as the final act and the wise climax of God's creation.[284] Nursi's point is that God accomplishes much greater things in the continuous exercise of his providential activity. The difficulty of producing the Gathering pales by comparison with the intricacy of the creative act and yet the ease of its execution. "That He will bring about a resurrection and Gathering is far easier for Him

---

[283] *The Rays*, The Third Ray, p. 56.
[284] *The Words*, The Twenty-Ninth Word, Second Aim, p. 543.

than the thousands of miraculous gatherings that occur every spring, each more wondrous than the Supreme Gathering."[285] Nursi explains: "The One Who performs these matters with infinitely fine art and perfect order and changes with infinite wisdom, bounty, and perfection of power and art the traveling worlds which follow on one after the other and are attached to the string of time, is certainly All-Powerful and All-Wise... in relation to His power the resurrection and Great Gathering are most easy and free of trouble. Since His creational command comprises power and will, and all things are entirely subjugated and obedient to His command, and He creates with no difficulty or hindrance.[286]

One might object that the Gathering staggers the mind. It seems preposterous to suppose the whole human race, from Adam onward, all summoned to the same place at the same moment. Moreover, how can one imagine God keeping track of every good action and misdeed over the course of millennia? Nursi agrees that the Gathering is not something that can be known by human reason. "A man of the night who has never seen the sun, but has only seen its shadow in the mirror of the Moon, cannot squeeze into his mind the resplendent light and awesome gravity particular to the Sun, and so submits to those who have seen it and imitates them; similarly, one who cannot attain to the maximum degrees of Names like All-Powerful and Giver of Life through the legacy of Muhammad (peace and blessings be upon him) must accept the resurrection of the dead and Great Gathering imitatively, and declare that it is not a matter which can be known by reason."[287]

Nursi is not claiming that the Gathering is irrational or even that it is beyond reason in all cases. He does state, however, that for most people, the Gathering is beyond their powers of reasoning. They must accept the Gathering "imitatively," that is, they should accept the word of those who have been given to know about this, that is, the Prophets and the message they bear from God.

---

[285] *The Rays*, The Supreme Sign, First Chapter, p. 193.
[286] *The Words*, The Sixteenth Word, pp. 212–213.
[287] *The Words*, The Twenty-Fourth Word, Second Branch, pp. 349–350.

This, however, is not an invitation to blind fideism, for even if the concept of the Gathering is too hard for most people to imagine, nevertheless there are many arguments in Scripture and indications in the natural world that point to the Gathering as a coming reality. "The Day of Judgment' (*Yawm ad-Din*)," affirms Nursi, "alludes to a vast and powerful proof of the resurrection of the dead... for various parts of the *Risale-i Nur* have proved with hundreds of powerful arguments that the morning and spring of the resurrection of the dead and Great Gathering will occur as certainly as day follows night and spring follows winter."[288]

One need not be a genius or philosopher in order to recognize and acknowledge these signs. They are evident to any sincere seeker of ordinary abilities, and the person who denies the evidence of his own common sense is either willfully blinded or deranged.

> You can, moreover, behold with your own eyes, the numerous designs made by God as signs, similes and indications of resurrection, designs placed by Him in every age and epoch of the world, in the alternation of day and night, even in the appearance and disappearance of clouds in the sky. If you imagine yourself to have been living a thousand years ago and then compare with each other the two wings of time that are the past and the future, you will behold similes of the Gathering and indications of resurrection as numerous as the centuries and days. If, then, after witnessing so many similes and indications, you still regard corporeal resurrection as improbable and rationally unacceptable, know your behavior to be pure lunacy.[289]

What will the command be like? Nursi prudently refrains from engaging in fanciful descriptive speculation, and instead relies on what can be known from sound Qur'anic revelation. The Qur'an teaches that the Gathering will be instantaneous, a concept very difficult to grasp. Thus, people are permitted to indulge in the imagery of the graves being opened, the corpses rising up and being transported immediately to the site of the Judgment. As Nursi states: "*The command of the Hour*

---

[288] *The Rays*, The Fifteenth Ray, "The Shining Proof," First Station, p. 584.

[289] *The Words*, The Tenth Word, Ninth Truth, p. 94. Cf. also, *The Words*, The Twenty-Fifth Word, Second Light, Second Beam, p. 438.

will be like the glance of the eye' (Qur'an 16:77) shows that the resurrection of the dead and the Great Gathering will occur instantaneously, in a flash. But man's narrow reason requires some tangible example so that it can conceive of this wondrous, extraordinary and unparalleled event and accept it."[290] In other words, people should focus on the essence of this teaching, that is, the reality of God's judgment, and the actuality of human responsibility for one's deeds on earth, rather than getting distracted by the images that are intended to help human reason to approach conceptually and visualize what is meant by the Gathering.

4. The Final Judgment and God's wise purpose in creation

It is not only the possibility of the resurrection and Gathering that is difficult to understand, but also the Judgment that follows. Nursi explains the "laying open" of humanity's deeds:

> At the resurrection, all the deeds of everyone will be produced, written on pages. Being very strange on its own, the mind cannot grasp this matter. But as the Sura indicates, the same way as in the resurrection of the spring, the things similar to this laying open of the pages are quite clear. For all fruit-bearing trees or flowering plants perform deeds, acts, and duties, and in whatever way they display the Divine Names and glorify God, they perform worship. All these deeds are written in their seeds together with their life histories, and emerge in another spring in another place. Just as they mention most eloquently the deeds of their mothers and lineage through the tongues of the shapes and forms they display, so they publish the pages of their deeds through their branches, leaves, flowers, and fruits.[291]

---

[290] *The Rays*, The Second Ray, Conclusion, p. 45. Cf. also, *The Rays*, The Supreme Sign, First Chapter, p. 183. "'The Hour shall be but a blinking of the eye, or even closer,' that is, the bringing about of resurrection and the Gathering that follows upon it shall take no longer than the opening and closing of an eye, or even less." Also, *The Words*, The Tenth Word, Third Part of the Addendum, p. 125.

[291] *The Words*, The Twenty-Fifth Word, Second Light, Second Beam, p. 439. Cf. also, *The Words*, The Tenth Word, Fourth Part of the Addendum, p. 129.

As he does on other occasions, Nursi looks to the natural world for his argument. Just as plant life bears within itself the hidden seeds of its own resurrection, so also humans bear within themselves the hidden seeds of their own eternal destiny, either the good deeds and faith that will bring them eternal reward, or the evil actions and faithlessness that will earn them eternal punishment. Even though in this world these seeds of destiny are hidden from view, like the latent promise of life secretly dormant within seeds, nevertheless to the same God who brings new life in fields and orchards, men and women are already determining their eternal fate by their good or evil deeds. Judgment Day will simply reveal what humans have already prepared for themselves.

Nursi insists strongly on the resurrection of the dead and the Day of Judgment because for him these are neither marginal elements of Islamic faith nor mythological representations of eschatological hope. They are expressions of Divine wisdom that validate the whole intention of God's creation. For if God has not created the world "in jest" or "purposelessly," as the Qur'an affirms (Qur'an 38:27; 23:115), but with a serious purpose in mind, then Divine wisdom must guide the whole of human history towards a climactic moment when God's justice, power and mercy, reward and punishment, promise and judgment will all become manifest.

The wisdom that is seen in the created world parallels that which guides human destiny. For Nursi, if creation were not governed, in matters small and great, by God's wisdom, human existence would be futile and absurd. The guarantee of this sovereign wisdom of God, who orders all things wisely, is the resurrection of the dead and the Great Gathering for the Final Judgment. I conclude with Nursi's own words:

> In just the same way, the All-Wise Maker attaches hundreds of instances of wisdom to each of the beings in the palace of the universe and equips them to perform hundreds of duties. To all trees He bestows instances of wisdom to the number of its fruits and gives duties to the number of its flowers. For Him not to bring about the resurrection of the dead and the Great Gathering, and for all those incalculable numbers of purposes and instances of wisdom

and infinite duties to be meaningless, futile, pointless, and without purpose or benefit, would impute impotence to that Absolutely Powerful One's perfect power, just as it would impute futility and purposelessness to that Absolutely Wise One's perfect wisdom, and utter ugliness to the beauty of that Absolutely Compassionate One's mercy, and boundless tyranny to that Absolutely Just One's perfect justice. It would be quite simply to deny the wisdom, mercy, and justice in the universe.[292]

---

[292] *The Flashes*, The Thirtieth Flash, p. 409.

Dialogue, Tolerance and Engagement with the Other

1. A methodological problem

The topic assigned to me is that of Said Nursi's view of tolerance, engagement with the other, and the future of dialogue. There is no doubt that Nursi had much to say on these points, which are of great relevance to our world today, but first I must begin by stating a methodological problem. Terms come into vogue at certain times in history and gradually take on accepted meanings which, as the exchange of views continues to progress, undergo their own evolution and take on greater clarity and precision.

Although a *term* comes into popular or academic usage at a certain given historical period, this does not mean that the *concept* itself is new. The idea may have been discussed in previous ages, but other terms were used to describe it. The above-mentioned terms of "tolerance," "engagement with the other," and "future of dialogue" are good examples of this. In the years when Said Nursi was writing the *Risale-i Nur*, terms such as "the other," and "future of dialogue" were not part of everyday speech. Since Said Nursi was writing his immense commentary on the Qur'an not as an academic treatise but as a practical guide for ordinary believing Muslims who were seeking to live their Islamic faith in the context of rapidly modernizing societies, it is not surprising that unfamiliar terms such as "dialogue" and "the other" appear but rarely in the *Risale-i Nur*. Hence, our task is to discover Nursi's views and advice on what today we call tolerance and dialogue, although Said Nursi may have couched his ideas in the popularly accepted terminology of the day.

2. God's dialogue with humankind according to the *Risale-i Nur*

On the few occasions when Nursi speaks explicitly of *dialogue*, he is first of all thinking of the way that God communicates His message to humankind. Dialogue is seen as an aspect or style of God's revelation and finds its most perfect expression in the Qur'an. When God reveals His word through the Prophets, God is engaging humans in a process of discovery whereby they learn necessary information which they would not otherwise know and God elicits a response on part of the person who studies the Qur'an. This dialogical nature of the Qur'an is, for Nursi, a sign of the miraculous nature of the Qur'an.

> The value, superiority, and eloquence of a speech or word are apparent through knowing, "from whom it has come and to whom, and for what purpose." The Qur'an then can have no like, and none can reach it. For the Qur'an is the speech and address of the Sustainer of all the worlds and Creator of the whole universe and a dialogue in no way hinting of imitation and artificiality.[293]

Thus, the concept of dialogue is primarily meant to form and shape the approach of Muslims to the Sacred Book. The Qur'an is not a dry, ancient text to be preserved and honored, nor a list of regulations to be blindly followed, but rather a living conversation initiated by the sovereign Creator who teaches people "what they did not know" about the works of his own creation. As Nursi says:

> The Qur'an is a dialogue with no imitation... It describes and explains the matters concerning happiness in this world and the next, the results of the creation of the universe, and the sovereign purposes within it. It expounds also the belief of the one it addresses, which was the highest and most extensive of belief and bore all the truths of Islam. It turns and shows every side of the huge universe like a map, a clock, or a house, and teaches and describes it in the manner of the craftsman who made them.[294]

---

[293] *The Words*, Twenty-Fifth Word, First Addendum, p. 463.
[294] *The Rays*, The Supreme Sign, First Chapter, p. 161.

The idea of God in ongoing dialogue with humankind is not limited to the nature of the Qur'an as revealed Scripture. For Nursi, dialogue is a constant aspect of God's creative activity, an idea he expresses in a beautiful passage written near the end of his life. In reflections inspired by his old age and the nearness of death,[295] he turns to the Light Verse in the Qur'an (24: 35) for guidance, and then catalogues the wonders of creation, which he sees as signs or manifestations of the loving and compassionate nature of God. He sees God as a skilled architect who designs a palatial structure to reflect his own admirable qualities and aesthetic sense.

> One who sees the exhibition of wonders and beauties of the magnificent palace of this world, that is, the universe, will realize that the palace is a mirror, decorated the way it is in order to show the beauties and perfections of another. Since there is nothing similar to the palace of the world from which its beauties could have been imitated and copied, certainly its Maker possesses the necessary beauties in himself and in his Names. It is from these that the universe is derived and according to them that it was made.[296]

The skill which the Divine architect employs in order to beautify the palace of the natural universe is surpassed only by what He has bestowed on His creatures who are able to possess a conscious awareness of the Creator. God has blessed human beings, men and women, with an ability to know God and has invited humans to respond freely to God's gifts. He has called people to relate to God as His friends and to establish a dialogue with the Creator. It is friendship and dialogue with God that should thus characterize the human religious experience. God speaks and teaches, but also listens and responds to prayers.

> In order to please conscious creatures [humankind] and make them happy and friends of Himself, He has bestowed every sort of delightful bounty from unexpected places in a way it is impossible to attribute to chance. Also to be observed are His generous treatment, a mutual acquaintance and friendly dialogue with the tongue of disposition, and a compassionate response to supplication which

---

[295] *The Rays*, p. 83.
[296] Ibid., p. 88.

make [God's] profound compassion and elevated mercy able to be perceived.[297]

3. Pope Paul VI on "the dialogue of salvation"

As a Christian, I would like to pause for a moment and reflect on Nursi's understanding of creation as a dialogue of God with human-kind, in the light of my Christian faith as enunciated by the late Pope Paul VI. Writing in 1964, only four years after the death of Said Nursi, hence less than a decade after Bediüzzaman wrote the above words, Pope Paul VI, in his encyclical *Ecclesiam Suam*, elaborated on the idea of human history as "a dialogue of salvation" initiated by God with men and women. Many of the phrases used by the Pope show the correspondence of thought between these two men.

> The noble origin of this dialogue is in the mind of God Himself. Religion of its very nature is a certain relationship between God and man. It finds its expression in prayer; and prayer is a dialogue. Revelation, too, that supernatural link which God has established with man, can likewise be looked upon as a dialogue... God tells us how He wishes to be known: as Love pure and simple; and how He wishes to be honored and served: His supreme commandment is love. Both child and mystic are called to take part in this unfail-ing, trustful dialogue, and the mystic finds there the fullest scope for his spiritual powers.[298]

"God Himself took the initiative in the dialogue of salvation. 'He hath first loved us.' We, therefore, must be the first to ask for a dia-logue with men, without waiting to be summoned to it by others."[299] Our dialogue should be as universal as we can make it,... relevant to everyone, excluding only those who utterly reject it or only pretend to be willing to accept it."[300] "Our dialogue must take cognizance of the slowness of human and historical development and wait for the hour when God may make it effective. We should not on that account post-

---

[297] Ibid., p. 89.
[298] Pope Paul VI, *Ecclesiam Suam*, Vatican City, 1964, par. 70.
[299] Ibid., par. 72.
[300] Ibid., par. 76.

pone until tomorrow what we can accomplish today. We should be eager for the opportune moment and sense the preciousness of time."[301]

4. Dialogue in Nursi's life and thought

Paul VI's view that, since God has invited humans to enter into a dialogue of salvation, religious believers must be the first to seek dialogue with others, "without waiting to be summoned to it by others," would provide a good description both of Said Nursi's life as well as the thought of the *Risale-i Nur*. Although a person by nature attracted to solitude and silent reflection, Nursi's life shows him in constant dialogue with Muslim scholars of various points of view, with secular authorities and ideologues, with ordinary people who posed questions to him on countless topics, even with his jailers, magistrates and others who oppressed him. Particularly toward the end of his life, he took the initiative to seek dialogue with committed Christians and Jews.

A glance at Said Nursi's biography gives evidence of a life characterized by repeated dialogue. His early education grew out of a fascination with intellectual interchange. "Whenever the opportunity arose, and especially in the long winter evenings, Said would go and listen to any discussions being held by students and teachers of the *madrasahs*, that is, the religious schools, or by religious figures. These discussions, often about the famous scholars, saints, and spiritual leaders of the past, usually took the form of contest and debate"[302] (p. 4). His discussions were not limited to religious topics, but included philosophy and the natural sciences. On one occasion a debate with a teacher led him to memorize a geography book, and on a second occasion, he is said to have mastered the principles of inorganic chemistry in five days (p. 24).

It was, however, questions of religion that most stimulated his desire for dialogue with men of differing points of view, first at the Van residence of the Governor, Tahir Pasha (p. 28), later at the Fatih Madrasah (p. 40), then with schoolteachers on the train to Skopje (p. 107),

---

[301] Ibid., par. 77.
[302] Şükran Vahide, *Bediüzzaman Said Nursi: The Author of the Risale-i Nur*, p. 4.

and much later with court officials in Afyon (p. 285). As Mardin points out, Said Nursi's dissatisfaction with the *madrasah* system, with its emphasis on rote memorization and its discouragement of intellectual speculation, led him to develop his thought in ongoing interaction and disputation with a wide variety of religious and political viewpoints.[303]

As much as his *life* gives evidence of an approach to knowledge based on the give-and-take of intellectual interchange, it is the *thoughts* on dialogue enunciated in the *Risale-i Nur* that are of primary interest today. For Nursi, dialogue is to be a typical mark that characterizes Islamic society. For Muslims who are convinced of the revealed message received from the Creator, all elements of social intercourse are to be employed in the pursuit of truth. This was the case even in the earliest period of Islamic history. He states:

> At the time of the first generations of Islam and in the market of that age, deducing from the Word of the Creator of the Heavens and the Earth His wishes and what He wants of us were the most sought-after goods, and obtaining the means to gain through the light of Prophethood and the Qur'an eternal happiness in the world of the hereafter... At that time, since people's minds, hearts and spirits were directed with all their strength towards understanding the wishes of the Sustainer of the Heavens and the Earth, the discussions, conversations, events, and circumstances of social life all looked to that. Since they occurred in accordance with those wishes, in a person of high ability, his heart and nature unconsciously received instruction in knowledge of God from everything. He received knowledge from the circumstances, events, and discussions which took place at that time. As though everything became a teacher for such a person, and inculcated in his nature and disposition the preparatory knowledge for independent judgments.[304]

Nursi laments, however, that in modern times, dialogue, while no less necessary, has become a greater challenge. Modern people are too often cut off from the life of the spirit and their attentions scattered in

---

[303] Şerif Mardin, *Religion and Social Change in Modern Turkey: the Case of Bediüzzaman Said Nursi*, Albany: SUNY, 1989, pp. 68–69.

[304] *The Words*, The Twenty-Seventh Word, pp. 495–496.

many directions. Interreligious dialogue presumes that all those involved are serious in their desire to understand the will and commands of the Creator, yet modern people are frequently alienated from the Source of true knowledge. Nursi observes: "At this time, due to the domination of European civilization and the supremacy of natural philosophy and the preponderance of the conditions of worldly life, minds and hearts have become scattered, and endeavor and favor divided. Minds have become strangers to non-material matters."[305]

The concerns of dialogue in the form of good communication determine Nursi's approach to theological discourse. He is impatient and critical with those whose goal in discussion is simply to impress others with their cleverness and erudition or to claim for themselves positions of pre-eminence.[306] Sincere dialogue should follow the pattern of Divine revelation, which takes into account the knowledge, background and presuppositions of the hearer. God "knows and regulates the thoughts of the heart, and through an exposition of this sort, transforms that simple and unlettered level and particular discussion which takes into account the minds of ordinary people into an elevated, attractive, and general conversation for the purpose of guidance."[307] Thus, in elaborating the ideas of the *Risale-i Nur*, Nursi adopts a "simple and common language in a straightforward style,"[308] rather than an erudite style meant to impress the reader.

This concern to adapt one's discourse to the needs of the partner in dialogue Nursi sees as the model followed by Muhammad preaching as reported in the Qur'an.

> As for the Madinan Suras and verses, since the first line of those they were addressing, those who opposed them, were the People of the Book, such as the Jews and Christians who affirmed God's existence, what was required by eloquence and guidance and for the discussion to correspond to the situation, was not explanation

---

[305] *The Words*, p. 496.

[306] *The Words*, Twenty-Seventh Word, Addendum, p. 511.

[307] *The Rays*, The Fruits of Belief, p. 268; cf. also, *The Words*, "A Flower of Emirdağ," p. 470.

[308] *The Words*, The Tenth Word, p. 59.

of the high principles of religion and pillars of belief in a simple, clear, and detailed style, but the explanation of particular matters of the shari'a and its injunctions, which were the cause of dispute, and the origins and causes of secondary matters and general laws. Thus, in the Madinan Suras and verses, through explanations in a detailed, clear, simple style, in the matchless manner of exposition peculiar to the Qur'an, it mostly mentions within those particular secondary matters, a powerful and elevated summary; a conclusion and proof, a sentence relating to Divine unity, belief, or the hereafter which makes the particular matter of the shari'a universal and ensures that it conforms to belief in God.[309]

Nursi has something important to say on the limits of dialogue. In dialogue, one cannot prove matters of faith to one who does not believe. One can strive to explain clearly what faith teaches and to show how that faith is a blessing from God, but it is not possible to demonstrate aspects of religious teaching to one who does not profess any religious faith. Speaking in the context of the Night Journey and Ascension of Muhammad, Said Nursi has this to say:

> The Ascension is a question that results from the essentials and pillars of belief and follows upon them... The Ascension cannot be proved independently to irreligious atheists who do not accept the pillars of belief, because it cannot be discussed with those who neither know God, nor recognize the Prophet, nor accept the angels, and who deny the existence of the heavens. Firstly those pillars must be proved. Since this is the case, we shall address the discussion to a believer who, since he considers it unlikely, has misgivings about the Ascension... However, from time to time we shall take into account the atheist who is the position of listener and shall set forth the matter to him.[310]

Said Nursi mentions a second important limit to dialogue. One must not dispute about questions of belief. Since religious faith comes from God, the elements of faith held by each believer are holy. They are matters that touch directly upon the believer's relationship with God and, as such, should not be submitted to the same kind of dispu-

---

[309] *The Words*, "A Flower of Emirdağ," p. 469.
[310] *The Words*, p. 583.

tation that is common in political or economic affairs. It is permissible to discuss questions of faith with the proper respect and reverence, but people should not get into arguments about them as they would over worldly matters. At one point, some disciples asked Said Nursi questions in an argumentative fashion and sought to draw him into a dispute. Nursi refused to get involved in the dispute, but some days later, when tempers died down, he prepared a thoughtful response to the questions submitted to him and advised his hearers to consider his views, not as they would read a newspaper article, but as the sharing of one humble servant of God to another.

> You asked me a question that night and I did not reply, for it is not permissible to argue over questions of belief. Your discussion of them was in the form of a dispute. Now I am writing very brief replies to your questions that were the basis of your dispute. You will find the details in The Words... It did not occur to me to mention the Twenty-Sixth Word, about Divine determining and man's faculty of will. Look at that too, but do not read it like a newspaper.[311]

5. Dialogue between Muslims and Christians

At the Fourth International Symposium on Bediüzzaman Said Nursi, held in İstanbul in September, 1988, I gave a paper entitled "Muslim–Christian Dialogue and Cooperation in the Thought of Bediüzzaman Said Nursi,"[312] which treated this topic. I will not repeat what I said in that paper, but would like to note several points that I believe to be relevant to the need for interreligious dialogue in the world situation at the present time.

Very early on in his career, Nursi stressed the need to distinguish between sincere, believing Christians, on the one hand, and Western civilization, which Nursi saw as "Christian" in name, but non-religious

---

[311] *The Letters*, The Twelfth Letter, p. 61.

[312] Thomas Michel, "Muslim–Christian Dialogue and Cooperation in the Thought of Bediüzzaman Said Nursi," in *Three Papers from the Fourth International Symposium on Bediüzzaman Said Nursi*, İstanbul, 1998. In this volume, a revised version of the paper is entitled "Be United with the Truly Pious and Spiritual Christians," pages 11-33.

and materialist in reality, on the other. Time and again in the *Risale-i Nur*, Nursi affirmed that the enemy of the Muslims was not all Christians; rather, true Muslims and true Christians must see one another as allies in confronting the true danger to human society, that is, the refusal to believe in God and to respond to God in faith. If Muslims and Christians are together to work to uphold the principles of faith in the modern world, they must move beyond ancient polemical debates and inimical attitudes toward each other and put aside, least for the time being, discussion of issues that divide the followers of the two religions. Nursi emphasizes that this is not simply his own opinion, but part of the Islamic heritage rooted in the sound *hadith*s from the Prophet. He states:

> It is recorded in authentic traditions of the Prophet that at the end of time, the truly pious among the Christians will unite with the People of the Qur'an and fight their common enemy, irreligion. At this time, the people of religion and truth need to unite sincerely not only with their own brothers and fellow believers, but also with the truly pious and spiritual Christians, [and refrain] temporarily from the discussion and debate of points of difference, in order to combat their joint enemy—aggressive atheism.[313]

It is interesting that this passage was added by Nursi as a footnote to his Nine Rules for acting with sincerity. Because of the relevance of these rules for understanding Nursi's view of dialogue, I include them here:

1. Act positively with love for one's own point of view but avoid enmity for other views; do not criticize the views of others nor interfere in their beliefs and practices.
2. Build unity within the fold of Islam by recalling the numerous bonds of unity that evoke love, brotherhood, and harmony.
3. Adopt as a rule of conduct that the follower of any sound position has the right to say, "My outlook is true, or very good," but not "My outlook alone is true," or "My outlook alone is good," implying the falsity or repugnance of other views.

---

[313] *The Flashes*, The Twentieth Flash, "On Sincerity," p. 203.

4. Consider that union with pious friends brings Divine aid and supports one's faith.

5. Realize that error and falsehood will be defeated through unity among pious believers; this depends upon their ability to create a united and collective force to preserve justice and right.

6. Defend truth from the attacks of falsehood.

7. Abandon self-centered egoism.

8. Give up the mistaken notion of self-pride.

9. Cease from all trivial feelings aroused by rivalry.[314]

In these nine rules, Nursi is primarily concerned with showing how through the practice of sincerity, the unity of the Islamic *umma* can be built and preserved. Differing points of view need not cause division, factions, and enmity within the community. If each Muslim is willing to admit that others also have part of the truth, even when they disagree with one's personal view, unity can be maintained despite differences of opinion. One might say that Nursi's understanding of a positive tolerance towards others and differing views is summed up in these nine rules of sincerity. By adding the above-mentioned *hadith* at the end of the nine rules, he notes that these principles indicate not only the way that Muslims should relate to one another but also imply how Muslims should act towards sincere and pious Christians—and, I might add, to the way that Christians should act towards sincere and pious Muslims and, for that matter, towards their fellow Christians.

A point that needs to be clarified is Said Nursi's view of "aggressive unbelief" as the most dangerous enemy of modern man. Nursi is not trying to turn back the clock, to return to some traditional way of life based on nostalgia for the past. He recognized that there is much good in modern civilization, whose origins he locates in the Prophetic tradition which has influenced the development of society.

However, there is also a negative current in modern life that, if followed, will alienate modern people from their roots in the teachings of the Prophets, will alienate them, in fact, from their own true nature. This negative tendency can be called a radical secularism that either

---

[314] Ibid.

denies God directly or, more often, simply ignores God's Prophetic message and pushes religion to the margins of social life.[315] Against this destructive ideology, which can reduce modern people to becoming pleasure-seeking consumers, pious, believing Muslims and Christians, "the people of truth," must make common cause.

I would like to draw a final point out of Nursi's view of Muslims, Christians, and Jews in modern pluralist societies. Dialogue must characterize the way that religious groups live together in every place, and it makes no difference who is governing and who is governed. Said Nursi is not in favor of religiously segregated societies, but advocates societies in which each individual and religious community has an inalienable right to their proper freedom. This right is one which must be respected by governments and is limited only by people's willingness to abide by and contribute to societal harmony. He adds that those who study the *Risale-i Nur* are restrained thereby from causing trouble and dissension in society.

> There were Muslims under Zoroastrian rule and Jews and Christians under the Islamic government of the Caliph 'Umar. All those who do not cause trouble to the government or disturb public order have personal freedom, and this may not be curtailed. Governments look to the hand and not to the heart. Without doubt, no one can attack me and my brothers [students of the Risale-i Nur] on grounds of governmental wisdom, the laws of politics, and principles of justice. If they do, it is due to misunderstanding or out of hatred or obduracy.[316]

6. Conclusion: The true meaning of tolerance

It should be obvious from the above that what Nursi is advocating is *tolerance* in human relations, not only towards students of the *Risale-i Nur* and other Muslims, but towards Christians and other believers whose outlook is different. Tolerance is an ambiguous term, and because of this ambiguity, some prefer to avoid it. Tolerance can mean putting up with someone even though one would wish to be rid of them.

---

[315] *The Flashes*, The Seventeenth Flash, Fifth Note, p. 160.
[316] *The Rays*, The Fourteenth Ray, p. 380; cf. also, p. 398, 444.

This kind of tolerance, of gritting one's teeth and suppressing one's anger, is no virtue and can be psychologically counter-productive.

This is not what Nursi means by tolerance. He sees tolerance as a loving acceptance of the other despite that person's failings and differences. In this sense, tolerance means letting the other be himself and not trying to make him like one's own self. It means recognizing that it is in the nature of persons to err and fail and that we should not judge other's failures more harshly that the merciful and compassionate God would do. In the *Risale-i Nur*, Nursi frequently asks his brothers to "look fairly and with tolerance" at any of his faults, mistakes, or shortcomings.[317] He asks them to "correct him when they are able and to pray for his forgiveness."[318] He is not asking them merely to put up with him, but to accept him as a brother who, like them, is not perfect. This kind of tolerance is much needed in our world today.

In conclusion, I want to point out how much Nursi's advice resonates with me as a Christian. I believe that his meditations on God's Word in the Qur'an lead Nursi to offer guidance for establishing the bond of unity among believers which is very similar to the counsel that St. Paul gave to the Christians of Ephesus, when he wrote: "Walk in a manner worthy of your calling, with all humility and gentleness, with patience, showing tolerance for one another in love, preserving diligently the unity of the Spirit in a bond of peace" (Ephesians 4: 1-3). I believe that Muslims and Christians have much to share with each other regarding the value of tolerance and love in growing more deeply united in their worship of the Creator.

---

[317] *The Words*, The Twenty-Fifth Word, p. 375;
[318] *The Words*, The Thirty-Third Word, p. 723.

Sincerity and Wisdom in the Fully Human Person

1. Building unity through the practice of sincerity

S ome years ago, I gave a paper at a *Risale-i Nur* symposium held in Bonn, Germany. The paper was entitled "Nursi's View of Tolerance, Engagement with the Other, and the Future of Dialogue." In that paper, I tried to draw out the implications of Said Nursi's "rules for sincerity." In these nine counsels, found in The Twentieth Flash of the Risale-i Nur, Nursi's main concern is to affirm that the way to preserve and build unity within the Islamic *umma* is through the practice of sincerity. In The Twenty-First Flash, Nursi elaborates his teaching on sincerity; it is Nursi's advice to his disciples on sincerity in The Twenty-First Flash on which I will try to focus in this paper.

Nursi sometimes noted among his disciples a sense of rivalry and competition. This troubled him because such rivalry could easily lead, if left unattended and unchecked, to hard-feelings, resentment, and even divisive factions in the community. Moreover, Nursi saw that if this tendency can be found among the students of the *Risale-i Nur*, it is even more evident in the broader Islamic *umma*. These divisive inclinations must be taken seriously for, in Nursi's view, disunity personifies—along with ignorance and poverty—the most serious enemy of modern men; combating this triple enemy presents pious Muslims with their greatest social challenges.

The basis of Nursi's advice to his students is that the way to combat tendencies to factionalism and rivalry is through the practice of sincerity. Because of the importance of these "rules of conduct," I will summarize them briefly once again (cf. p. 168 above).

1. Act positively with love for one's own point of view but avoid
    enmity for other views; do not criticize the views of others
    nor interfere in their beliefs and practices.
2. Build unity within the fold of Islam by recalling the numerous
    bonds of unity that evoke love, brotherhood, and harmony.
3. Adopt the rule of conduct that the follower of any sound posi-
    tion has the right to say, "My outlook is true, or very good,"
    but not "My outlook alone is true," or "My outlook alone is
    good," implying the falsity or repugnance of other views.
4. Consider that union with pious friends brings Divine aid and
    supports one's faith.
5. Realize that error and falsehood will be defeated through unity
    among pious believers, which depends upon their ability to cre-
    ate a united and collective force to preserve justice and right.
6. Defend truth from the attacks of falsehood.
7. Abandon self-centered egoism.
8. Give up the mistaken notion of self-pride.
9. Cease from all trivial feelings aroused by rivalry.[319]

Nursi's point is that differing points of view need not cause division, factions, and enmity within the community. If every Muslim is
willing to admit that others also have part of the truth, even when
they disagree with one's personal view, unity can be maintained despite
differences of opinion. However, this can only be done if the believer
is truly worshiping God with sincere intention. To this end Nursi cites
the Qur'anic verse *"Truly We sent the Book down to you in truth, so worship
God in sincerity, for God's is sincerely practiced religion"* (Qur'an 39:2).

As a Christian, I find the advice contained in these nine rules valuable for several reasons. In its narrowest application, Nursi is guiding
his disciples to avoid the kinds of self-aggrandizement and competition that can cause rancor and splits among the students of the *Risale-i
Nur*. His advice has a broader application in calling Muslims to heal
the wounds of disunity and enmity within the worldwide Islamic community. However, the value of Nursi's advice is not limited, in my

---

[319] *The Flashes*, The Twentieth Flash, "On Sincerity," p. 203.

opinion, to the followers of Islam, for it is the same tendencies toward the egoistic defense of one's views, an intolerance of differences, and the judgmental criticism of others' views that has caused and exacerbated so many of the historical divisions and so much enmity among Christians. Thus, his advice is also useful for building and maintaining unity in various Christian communities, as well as for preserving purity of intention of any believer desiring to serve God.

The disunity brought about by a lack of sincerity has characterized relations between Christians and Muslims down through the centuries, and I feel that Muslim–Christian relations at the present time could benefit from taking seriously and following Nursi's rules of sincerity. Rather than recognizing one another as two communities of believers who seek only to worship and love God sincerely, Christians and Muslims have too often regarded one another as enemies and rivals, making exclusive claims to truth and condemning the other's beliefs as false and repugnant. How much healthier would relations between the two communities be if both were to follow Nursi's Third Rule: "The follower of any sound position has the right to say, "My outlook is true, or very good," but not "My outlook *alone* is true," or "My outlook *alone* is good," implying that the views of others are wrong, foolish, or worthless.

It is significant that Nursi himself appended to his nine rules of sincerity a surprising footnote. It reads as follows:

> "It is even recorded in authentic traditions of the Prophet that at the end of time the truly pious among the Christians will unite with the People of the Qur'an and fight their common enemy, irreligion. And in our day, too, the people of religion and truth need to unite sincerely not only with their own brothers and fellow believers, but also with the truly pious and spiritual among the Christians, temporarily from the discussion and debate of points of difference in order to combat their joint enemy, aggressive atheism."[320]

By linking his rules for sincerity with the Prophetic expectation of Muslim–Christian unity, Nursi is implying that the way to build unity

---

[320] Ibid., footnote 7, p. 203.

between the two communities in our day is by promoting and following "sincerely practiced religion." Nursi is pointing out that the principles of sincerity indicate not only the way that Muslims should relate to one another, but also imply how Muslims should act towards sincere and pious Christians (and, I might add, to the way that Christians should act towards Muslims).

2. Sincerity as purity of intention

One might ask what Nursi means by *sincerity*. Everyone knows the common dictionary definition of sincerity as indicating "an honesty of mind, freedom from dissimulation or hypocrisy." More to the point, perhaps, is the data of personal experience, by which sincerity is universally recognized as being an affective and intellectual honesty, a lack of pretence to be other than what one is, a faithful correspondence between one's inner thoughts and emotions and their outer expression in word and action. A sincere person is not self-promoting, hypocritical, pretentious, two-faced, or devious. He is neither a flatterer nor a manipulator. In the words of Jesus in his Sermon on the Mount, the sincere person says "yes" when he means yes, "no" when he means no (Matthew 5: 37).

Nursi's use of the term goes much deeper than that derived from everyday parlance. When he writes of sincerity he is referring to the Qur'anic concept of *ikhlas*. This notion, which brings together the notion of "purity" with that of "dedicating, devoting or consecrating oneself" to something, is a key virtue in Islamic practice.[321] *Ikhlas* is an eminently interior disposition by which the faithful Muslim performs all external actions a spirit of service and directed solely toward pleasing the Divine Lord. In fact, the perfection of one's witness to faith can be gauged by the double standard of *ikhlas* (purity of intention) and *ihsan* (goodness).

It is noteworthy that the brief expression of the Islamic creed found in the Qur'anic Surah 116: *"Say: He, Allah, is One. Allah is He on Whom all depend. He begets not, nor is He begotten. And none is like Him."* This

---

[321] L. Gardet, *Encyclopaedia of Islam*, Leiden: 2006, III: 1059.

has been known in Islamic tradition as the Surah al-Ikhlas, that is, "The Chapter of Sincerity" or "The Chapter of Pure Religion."

The importance of *ikhlas* has been commented upon down the centuries by Muslim scholars, exegetes, and spiritual guides in every generation. The Sufi masters have been particularly fond of elaborating on this virtue, to the extent that in the minds of many Muslims, *ikhlas* is considered a "Sufi concept." In commenting on *ikhlas*, Nursi must repeatedly distinguish his own advice from that of the teaching of the Sufis. While acknowledging the beneficial value of the instruction of the Sufi masters, he notes that "I am not a Sufi, but these principles of theirs make a good rule for our path."[322] Nursi's approach differs from that of the Sufis because of his praxis-oriented approach, what he calls the "way of reality," in which he eschews contemplative speculation in favor of practical guidance for his disciples' life together. He states: "However, since our way is not the Sufi path but the way of reality, we are not compelled to perform this contemplation [of death] in an imaginary and hypothetical form like the Sufis."[323]

Because of its roots in the Qur'an and in the tradition of Islamic spiritual writing, Nursi's use of *ikhlas* can perhaps be more adequately conveyed in English by "purity of intention" or "pure religion" than simply by "sincerity." *Ikhlas* is when one practices all the acts of religion solely for God's pleasure rather than for any personal benefit that may accrue to them, whether that be prestige, pride, or the admiration of others. When one "worships God with sincerity" one's intention is pure and undefiled by base or irrelevant motives. As the Qur'an states, *"And there is the type of man who gives his life to earn the pleasure of Allah: And Allah is full of kindness to (His) devotees"* (Qur'an 2:207).

3. Correspondence between purity of intention and Divine wisdom

In The Twentieth Flash, Said Nursi instructs his disciples on the necessity of sincerity to overcome divisive tendencies and build fraternal unity

---

[322] *The Flashes*, The Twenty-First Flash, p. 216.
[323] Ibid., p. 217.

in their community. If one accepts the principle that fraternal love and unity demands sincerity, some questions inevitably arises, such as: "Why is sincerity so important? How does one acquire this purity of intention? And, what obstacles might a person encounter in seeking a pure intention in religious acts?" These are the topics treated in The Twenty-First Flash. So much importance does Nursi place on a purity of intention in religious observance that he instructs his disciples to read The Twenty-First Flash once every two weeks.

According to Nursi, a pure intention is "the most important principle in works pertaining to the Hereafter." In his praise of the value of sincerity he resorts to the rhetorical device of personification. Purity of intention is like a spiritual mentor: the source of a believer's greatest strength, the firmest supporter of one's faith, and the believer's most welcome intercessor before God. Sincerity enables the most acceptable prayer one can make to God, the most effective means of achieving one's goal, and the shortest path to reality. One might compare Nursi's paean in praise of Sincerity with the evocative description of Wisdom in the prayer of Solomon in the Bible.

Nursi in Praise of Sincerity

And O my companions in the service of the Qur'an! You should know that in this world sincerity is the most important principle in works pertaining to the Hereafter. It is the greatest strength, and the most acceptable intercessor, and the firmest point of support, and the shortest way to reality, and the most acceptable prayer, and the most wondrous means of achieving one's goal, and the highest quality, and the purest worship.

Since in sincerity lies much strength and many lights, and since at this dreadful time, despite our small number and weak, impoverished, and powerless state and our being confronted by terrible enemies and suffering severe oppression in the midst of aggressive innovations and misguidance, an extremely heavy, important, and sacred duty of serving belief and the Qur'an has been placed on our shoulders by Divine grace, we are compelled more than anyone to work with all our strength to gain sincerity. We are in utter need of instilling sincerity in ourselves. Otherwise what we have achieved so far in our sacred service will in part be lost, and will not persist; and we shall be held responsible.[324]

---

[324] *The Flashes*, The Twenty-First Flash, pp. 212–213.

Solomon's Prayer for Wisdom

God of my fathers, LORD of mercy! You who have made all things by your word and in your wisdom have established man to rule the creatures produced by you, to govern the world in holiness and justice, and to render judgment in integrity of heart:

Give me Wisdom, the attendant at your throne, and reject me not from among your children, for I am your servant, the son of your handmaid, a man weak and short-lived and lacking in comprehension of judgment and of laws.

Though one be perfect among the sons of men, if Wisdom, who comes from you, be not with him, he shall be held in no esteem.

With you is Wisdom, who knows your works and was present when you made the world, who understands what is pleasing to you and what conforms to your commands.

Send her forth from your holy heavens and from your glorious throne dispatch her that she may be with me and work with me, that I may know what your pleasure is. For she will guide me discreetly in my affairs and safeguard me. Thus my deeds will be acceptable, and I shall judge your people justly and be worthy of my father's throne.[325]

---

[325] The Book of Wisdom 9: 1–18.

The correspondence between Nursi's understanding of purity of intention and the Biblical concept of wisdom as found in the "Wisdom Books" of Proverbs, Wisdom, Sirach, and Ecclesiastes can be explained as follows. For Nursi, it is the purity of one's intention that guards the Muslim from performing his religious duties for any reason other than that of seeking God's pleasure. To be seen and admired by others, to try to show oneself more faithful or more assiduous than others, to take selfish satisfaction or pride in the praise given by others, and to denigrate the intellectual or spiritual achievements of others are all common temptations of religious people, even as they are destructive of community life.

Nursi honestly and humbly admits that it was the sincerity of his students that saved him from such temptations in the past: "I have also to confess that through your heartfelt sincerity, you have saved me to an extent from the hypocrisy which used to flatter my soul under the veil of fame and renown."[326] He cites the Prophet Yusuf (Joseph) in the Qur'an to show that no one is exempt from this universal tendency: *"Nor do I absolve my own self [of blame]; the soul is certainly prone to evil, unless my Sustainer do bestow His mercy"* (Qur'an 12:53).[327]

Similarly, in his prayer recorded in the book of Wisdom, King Solomon acknowledges his human weakness and his constant need for the guidance and support that comes from God. It is true wisdom, of exclusively Divine origin, that teaches Solomon how he can serve God for God's sake alone. Solomon affirms that, unlike worldly and even devilish human cunning, true wisdom will guide him discreetly in his affairs and will safeguard his faith. Eternal wisdom that comes from God will enable him to render judgment "in integrity of heart." Solomon declares that even if one were perfectly endowed with intelligence, beauty, power, and wealth, without wisdom that person would not be worthy of esteem. Wisdom that cannot be acquired through human effort, but will be freely granted by God to His servants who ask, will enable that servant to act with a pure intention and to judge with integrity.

---

[326] *The Flashes*, The Twenty-First Flash, p. 215.
[327] *The Flashes*, The Thirteenth Flash, p. 124.

4. Rules to obtain purity of intention

The awareness in faith that a pure intention can only be obtained with God's grace does not mean that human effort is useless or irrelevant. God gives gifts to those who actively seek them through right conduct. In this context, Nursi offers to his disciples some rules of conduct which they should follow in order to acquire sincerity.

1) The first rule is to do everything only to seek God's pleasure. Whether or not others approve of what one does or whether one is successful in attaining one's worldly goal, if that deed is performed out of desire to please God, then someone need not worry about human approval. "Once His pleasure has been gained and He has accepted an action, even if you do not ask it of Him, should He wish it and His wisdom require it, He will make others accept it. He will make them consent to it too."[328] In short, performing ones actions purely in order to give due worship to God will free a person from temptations to pride in achievement, desire for adulation, or rivalry with fellow worshipers.

2) The second principle for obtaining purity of intention is not to criticize others. Nursi is aware that nothing is more likely to destroy unity among fellow believers than carping criticism. He holds that the students of the *Risale-i Nur* should regard one another as members of one body, who need and complement one another to achieve their common goal. "Each of the members completes the deficiencies of the others, veils their faults, assists their needs, and helps them out in their duties. Otherwise man's life would be extinguished, his spirit flee, and his body be dispersed."[329] In addition to the image of the human body, Nursi also employs the metaphor of a complex piece of machinery whose smooth functioning demands the constant synergy of all parts.

Nursi envisions the students of the *Risale-i Nur* as forming a collective personality who together make up "the Perfect Man." The Perfect Man, or *al-Insan al-Kamil*—although the words do not appear in the Qur'an—had a long tradition of study and speculation in Muslim

---

[328] *The Flashes*, The Twenty-First Flash, p. 213.
[329] Ibid., p. 214.

scholarship. The Sufi authors, and especially Ibn 'Arabi, gave key importance to the concept for understanding the spiritual nature of the Prophets and *awliya'* (God's special friends). Derived from the idea that in
all creation, humankind has a special status and is given uniquely the
task of manifesting God's qualities in one's life and behavior, the Perfect Man is recognized primarily in Prophet Muhammad, but also to
be sought in those who have received the light of Muhammad.

For Nursi, the term has a special sense in that it is his disciples,
the students of the *Risale-i Nur*, who collectively are called to live as
the Perfect Man, displaying God's qualities in all they say and do.
Since the personal transformation that is brought about through the
study of the *Risale-i Nur* is a grace given not only for the individual but
is oriented toward renewing the whole Islamic *umma*, the duty of the
Risale-i Nur students demands unity and fraternal love among themselves. The complaining, fault-finding, and nit-picking that springs from
lack of a pure intention thus becomes an obstacle to the Divine qualities of compassion and love that should be manifested by the collective Perfect Man.

3) The third rule of conduct is to give preference to others, over
against one's own inclinations, desires, and penchant for honors. One
must not be self-centered, even in spiritual matters, but must be constantly more concerned about the state of soul of one's companions
than about one's own condition. Nursi writes: "Choose your brothers' souls to your own soul in honor, rank, acclaim, in the things your
soul enjoys like material benefits."[330] In preferring the other person to
oneself, the student of the *Risale-i Nur* will find much strength and
will gain the blessing and support of God's friends like Ali ibn Abu Talib
and Ghawth al-A'zam ('Abd al-Qadir al-Jilani), who will "honor you
with their miraculous wonder-working and wondrous vision of the
Unseen because of this mystery of sincerity. They will offer you consolation in protection and applaud your service. You should have no
doubt that this attention of theirs is because of sincerity."[331]

---

[330] *The Flashes*, The Twenty-First Flash, p. 216.
[331] Ibid., p. 215.

4) The fourth and final rule of conduct that Nursi offers is to imagine the achievements, the virtues, and the aspirations of fellow disciples to be one's own. In this way, one can glory in the triumphs of others, share in their hopes, and enjoy their good qualities and virtues, without succumbing to envy and a sense of competition. This fellow-feeling Nursi sees as the characteristic path of those who study the *Risale-i Nur*. He writes:

> Forget the feelings of one's own carnal self and live in one's mind with one's brothers' virtues and feelings. The basis of our way is brotherhood, not the way between father and son or shaykh and follower. Our way is the closest friendship, which necessitates being the closest friend, the most sacrificing companion, the most appreciative comrade, the noblest brother. The essence of this friendship is true sincerity."[332]

In short, the way to build a deep friendship among the students of the *Risale-i Nur* is through the practice of sincerity. He goes so far as to say that purity of intention is the essence of the friendship he wants to exist among his disciples.

Nursi concludes his treatment with two suggestions for attaining a pure intention. The first way to achieve sincerity is through a contemplation of death. Since it is worldly ambition which militates against a pure intention, the contemplation of death helps the believer put things in perspective. The world is transitory, the believer is a transient on this earth, yet people find themselves caught up in a web of petty rivalries, self-aggrandizement, and hypocrisy. By contemplating death, one can become aware that it is only God, who is imperishable, who is deserving of service and devotion.

The second way is to reflect on God's omnipresence and omniscience. Living consciously in the presence of the Compassionate Creator should make the believer aware that to be acting for others' approval is an unworthy attitude before God who sees and knows all. To have one's attentions and emotions dominated by oneself or another companion when the Creator is present is actually a hidden form

---

[332] Ibid., p. 216.

of *shirk*, the sin of associating others in the worship due to God alone. "This is to flatter the ego and give high status to one's lower nature through attracting attention to oneself and public acclaim, driven by the desire for fame, renown, and position. This is a serious spiritual sickness which opens the door to the hypocrisy and self-centeredness. It may be called a *hidden association of partners with God* and damages sincerity."[333]

The main themes of this chapter—sincerity and purity of intention and their relation to true wisdom, and the dangers of factionalism, hypocrisy, pride, and criticism arising from pride and carping criticism—come together in a remarkable passage in the Bible. I will conclude my paper with a quotation of that passage, taken from the Letter of James, to show how the spiritual advice given by the spiritual masters of Christianity and Islam so often coincide and complement one another. Clearly, James was dealing with the same dangers to the unity of the community as was Said Nursi, over a space of 20 centuries, and his advice is significantly similar to that found in the *Risale-i Nur*.

> Who among you is wise and understanding? Let him show his works by a good life in the humility that comes from wisdom. But if you have bitter jealousy and selfish ambition in your hearts, do not boast and be false to the truth. Such 'wisdom' does not come down from heaven but is earthly, unspiritual, demonic. For where jealousy and selfish ambition exist, there is disorder and every foul practice. But the wisdom from above is first of all pure, then peaceable, gentle, compliant, full of mercy and good fruits, impartial and sincere. Peacemakers who sow in peace raise a harvest of righteousness (James 3: 13-18).

---

[333] Ibid., p. 220.

The Prophets:
a Blessing for Humankind

The purpose of this paper is simple. First I want to explain the concept of prophecy according to the beliefs of Christian faith and to see how Christians understand prophecy as a blessing for humankind. Secondly, I would like to take some points raised in the *Risale-i Nur* to show how, according to this commentary on the Holy Qur'an, God has blessed humankind through the Prophets. Thus, I hope that the points of convergence and divergence will become clear.

1. Christian concept of Prophethood

The Christian view of prophecy has been summarized by the prominent Catholic theologian, Karl Rahner in his article on "Prophetism" in the theological compendium *Sacramentum Mundi*.[334] As I list the characteristics of the Prophet according to Christian faith, I invite Muslim readers to reflect on whether and how these elements are found in the life and mission of Muhammad as reported in the Qur'an and *hadith*. Similarly, the Christian reader can reflect on Gospel passages to see how these points are exemplified in the life and teaching of Jesus.

1) The Prophet always comes with a new message
2) and has to produce his own credentials.
3) The uniqueness of his vocation is essential to the Prophet.
4) He is the religious revolutionary,
5) the critic of society,

---

[334] Karl Rahner, "Prophetism," *Encyclopedia of Theology: The Concise Sacramentum Mundi*, New York: Crossroad, 1986, pp. 1286–1289.

6) and does not confine himself to truths which are already evident his hearers.

7) He sees himself as the instrument of the personal, living God.

8) He brings a message not meant for himself alone, but primarily for others.

9) The "word" is constitutive of the Prophet and his mission.

10) In his criticism of religion and society and interpretation of historical events,

11) the Prophet exerts an influence upon events

12) by making known their real depth and truth

13) and by offering a new and forward-looking situation in his criticism of society.

14) In seeking to transform the status quo,

15) the Prophet is the organizer of religious and social changes

16) and thus institutionalizes his message.

It is worth taking a closer look at these points. Writing as a Christian I will note some ways in which for me Jesus exemplifies these characteristics, and at the same time I invite Muslims to reflect on the extent to which these same characteristics apply as well to Muhammad.

The Prophet brings a new message (1). He is not simply a teacher of old truths, but is bringing a message that his hearers perceive as new. In the Gospels, Jesus' hearers are constantly saying, "This is something new." New doesn't necessarily mean different from what the earlier Prophets taught. Often the Prophet repeats and confirms what the earlier Prophets taught, but he does it in a new way and—this is important—with new authority. He has been directly authorized by God to bring people a fresh, unexpected message that calls them to a new commitment.

The Prophet produces his own credentials (2). The Jewish leaders were always challenging Jesus to say by what right he was teaching, healing and casting out demons. Did he have permission from the Jewish High Priest, or was he doing this on his own? Jesus' answers imply that he was acting on authority given by God. Similarly, Muslims will remember how the polytheists of Mecca used to challenge Muhammad to produce evidence that his message was really from God.

Each Prophet is unique (3). In the Bible, some of the Prophets, like Elijah and Elisha, were miracle-workers. Ezekiel and Isaiah had ecstatic experiences and used to deliver their messages through symbolic acts and gestures. Amos delivered angry denunciations of society, whereas Hosea reflected on his unhappy family life. Jeremiah never wanted to be a Prophet, but God called him to do so against his will. Elijah and Nathan had dealings with kings, while John the Baptist left city-life to live and preach in the desert. The Prophet never did what was expected and didn't fit into the usual patterns or traditional religious bureaucracies.

The Prophet is a religious revolutionary (4), a critic of society (5). Jesus broke the Jewish law to eat with sinners, to heal people on the Sabbath (Saturday). He foresaw a day in which people would no longer need to worship God in the Jerusalem Temple. He drove the money-changers out of the Temple and criticized the religious leaders of his time who "laid heavy burdens on people and wouldn't lift a finger to remove them." Similarly, Muslims recall how Muhammad criticized the polytheist Arabs for killing their infant daughters, for stealing the property of widows and orphans, for charging heavy interest on loans, for wastefully spending their money on frivolous things, for oppressing their slaves.

The Prophet doesn't simply state the obvious or repeat platitudes (6). His message comes from God and teaches people what they cannot know by use of reason and science. He insists that he is not speaking on his own, but is delivering a message that comes directly from God. In John's Gospel, Jesus says that he speaks only what he has heard from God. The Prophet is thus God's instrument, spokesman, and mouthpiece (7). The Prophet's message is mainly meant for others (8). It is not for self-improvement, but rather God's way to communicate His will to humankind. We think of John the Baptist preaching to the Jews who came out into the desert to listen, of Jesus' preaching to the simple people in Galilee about the need to repent and allow God to rule over their lives, and his telling the religious scholars that they too need to repent. We remember also how Muhammad delivered his message to the polytheists of Mecca, telling them to repent, to believe in God and the Last Day and to do good works.

The Prophet is the messenger of the Word of God (9). He is distinguished from other religious figures such as the priest, the mystic, the shaman, and the teacher of wisdom, precisely by his claim to be "bearer of revelation." He does not restate traditional teaching in the manner of a preacher nor offer his own insight into what has been previously revealed, as does the theologian. What he brings is a new revelation which he received from God. Without credentials beyond his own claim to bear a Divine message, the Prophet is the charismatic outsider both separate from and critical of the political and religious establishment.

The Prophet criticizes religious practices (10) of his time and interprets historical events (11). We think of Jesus' criticizing the religious scholars and of Muhammad condemning the polytheistic practices associated with the Ka'ba. Jesus interpreted the events leading up to the destruction of Jerusalem and showed how these were connected with the people's unwillingness to accept him whom God had sent (12). Similarly, Muhammad spoke about the people of Noah, of the tribes of 'Ad and Thamud, who rejected their Prophets, of Pharaoh who rejected the message of Moses, and interpreted the history, showing how those peoples were destroyed because of their refusal to believe. Thus, the Prophets are saying, it is no accident that these things are happening. God is at work in human history (12).

When the Prophet criticizes the unbelief and immorality of his people, he is always looking to the future (13). Jesus envisions a day when it won't matter if people worship God on this mountain or that, but they will worship God "in spirit and in truth." Jesus looks forward to the day when the Holy Spirit will come and guide people according to the fullness of truth. He began to call disciples and form them into a community that would live in a new way, one characterized by love and faith (14). Similarly, in Mecca, Muhammad began to form a community that would live according to the message of Islam and in Medina he taught the ways that communal life would be regulated (15). Thus, after Jesus' death, his disciples believed that in and through Jesus, God had brought about a dramatic change in people's relation to God, expressed in the life of the new community of Christians (16). By the time of Muhammad's death, the Islamic community that would live according to the Qur'anic teaching and the example of Muhammad was formed.

2. The uniqueness of each religion

When we look at these characteristics of prophecy according to Christian belief and when we reflect on the ways that these qualities were expressed in the lives of the Prophets, we find many similarities between the Christian and the Islamic understanding of prophecy. By this, I do not mean to imply that Christian faith and Islamic faith are saying the same thing. The differences between religions are just as important as the points of convergence.

It is the differences that make each religious community unique, distinguished from all others. We each regard the uniqueness of our faith, our community as God's special blessing to us. For us Christians, Jesus is the great Prophet, who not only taught God's message and perfectly embodied it in the way he lived, but we believe that Jesus had a special, unequaled relationship to God which resulted in his life and death as having a unique power to save us and reconcile us to God. This is what distinguishes Christian faith from that of Jews or Muslims.

Similarly, for Muslims it is the belief that Muhammad is the final Prophet who brought the complete and perfect message of the Qur'an, so that by following the Qur'an and the sunna of Muhammad Muslims live according to the *shari'a* or Islamic way of life. It is this second phrase of the *shahada*, *Muhammadun Rasulullah* (Muhammad is the Messenger of God), which distinguishes Muslims from other monotheists, such as Jews and Christians, who with Muslims affirm *La ilaha illa'Allah* (There is no deity but God).

So, while Muslims and Christians have much in their faith that they hold in common, each community also has those elements of faith that distinguish them and make them unique. I believe that Christians and Muslims can rejoice and celebrate not only what we have in common, our points of convergence, but also we can glorify God because of what is unique in the faith of each. I thank God for what makes me a Christian, and I also thank God for what makes Muslims to be the community trodding the path of Muhammad their Prophet. We need not belabor the points where we differ, because we are all returning to God and at that time God will inform us about the points where we disagreed.

This is the greatest benefit to humankind that God has bestowed in the Prophets, our faith. Through what we have received by way of the Prophets, we come to know God, to serve God, and to love God. We receive the promise of our eternal life with God. What greater benefit could we imagine as the result of God's goodness through the Prophets?

3. The Prophets, a blessing for humankind, according to Said Nursi

In the Islamic tradition, so many Muslims down through the centuries have reflected and commented on the benefits to humankind of God's sending Prophets, I cannot hope to address all that has been written on the subject but will limit myself to a few remarks on what Said Nursi has had to say in the *Risale-i Nur*.

1. The Prophetic and the philosophical. Said Nursi understands the spiritual and intellectual history of humankind, of whatever nation, religion or culture, as following simultaneously two currents. He describes it with the image of a tree whose trunk divides into two main branches, which themselves continue dividing into numerous smaller branches. One current is that of Prophethood and religion and the other is the human philosophical tradition.[335] When these two currents interact and cooperate, teaching and learning from each other, the result is prosperity and social harmony for humankind. When the two currents proceed separately or run counter to one another, the result is disorder, war, confusion and moral degradation.

---

[335] *The Words*, The Thirtieth Word, First Aim, p. 561.

The reason for this is that the Prophets bring to mankind God's teaching on people's duties toward God, toward their neighbor, and towards themselves. In other words, the Prophets offer God's guidance on how people should behave and how society should be structured. Thus, the Prophets teach that people should approach God humbly, recognizing each one's limitations of knowledge, strength, and goodness, and serve God as a faithful servant. This is what the Qur'an means by saying that believers should be "guided by God-given morals."

The philosophical tradition, or what today might be called the scientific approach, is not totally in error. Science and philosophy discover real truths and can offer a measure of guidance for ordering society and bettering the human condition. Philosophy can even arrive at some understanding about God. What philosophical reflection cannot perceive by itself is human frailty and neediness and the infinite distance that separates humanity from divinity. A true understanding of a person's place in the world can be attained only when the philosophical current is willing to learn from the Prophetic. As Said Nursi says,

> The self-seeking rule of philosophy, "Try to imitate the Necessarily Existent One," is mankind's aim for perfection. No indeed, the essence of humanity has been kneaded with impotence, weakness, poverty, and need, while the essence of the Necessarily Existent One is infinitely omnipotent, powerful, self-sufficient, and without need.[336]

It is not only in coming to recognize one's proper place before God that the insights of the Prophetic tradition are essential. Also, for a correct understanding of social life, the teachings of the Prophets are a sure guide. The Prophets show the interrelatedness of all things and teach mutual interdependence. The importance of referring to Prophetic teaching for a balanced relationship to nature and the responsible use of the benefits of the natural world, which today we call ecology, was foreseen by Said Nursi.

A religious approach to nature recognizes the unity of creation and that all that exists in nature is a blessing from God to be used by

---

[336] Ibid., p. 564.

people with moderation and gratitude. However, an approach to nature that is divorced from the Prophetic guidance reduces creation to a mass of raw material—oil, forests, water, animal life etc.—which is there to be selfishly exploited, fought over, and taken by the most powerful. Life then follows the "law of the jungle" and conflict is seen as essential to social life. Said Nursi puts it as follows:

> Among the principles of the line of Prophethood concerning social life are those of mutual assistance, magnanimity, and generosity. These have been harnessed for the help and assistance of all things from the sun and moon down to even plants. For the assistance of animals, for example, and the benefit of animals for human beings, and even that of particles of food for the cells of the body. Whereas, one of the principles of the line of philosophy concerning social life is conflict, which springs from the misuse of their inborn dispositions by tyrants, brutish men, and savage beasts. Indeed, they have accepted this principle at so fundamental and general a level that they declare: "Life is conflict."[337]

This perception of Said Nursi has broad implications. It has relevance for the ecological crisis which the world is facing at the present time, but it is equally important to understand the moral crisis facing humanity at this moment. Once again, in recent years the world has been plunged into bloody, destructive wars. In Iraq, a wealthy, powerful nation has attacked and, not surprisingly, defeated a small country of limited means to defend itself. As a result, a tyrant has been deposed, but in the process many innocent people have lost their lives, families have lost their breadwinners, and many others must go through life maimed or with terrible burns covering their bodies.

If one accepts conflict as a fundamental principle, according to what Said Nursi calls the philosophical current, one might regard this as a victory, but if people view human society according to the Prophetic current, which takes human solidarity, mutual assistance, and generosity as basic axioms of human interaction, this recourse to overwhelming force and use of violence must be seen as a defeat and setback for humanity. If the billions of dollars spent on this destructive

---

[337] Ibid.

war had been used for education, health care, and ecological preservation, the present generation would be handing on a far better world to future generations. The recent war in Iraq, in my opinion, thus exemplifies well what happens when the philosophical current becomes divorced from the line of Prophetic teaching.

2. Speaking to the heart. A second blessing of the Prophets for humankind, according to the *Risale-i Nur*, is that Prophetic teaching is not limited to offering information to the mind about religious subjects, but goes beyond that to teach the human heart about God. Of itself, the acquisition of information or cognitive knowledge cannot change attitudes, cannot transform people, and cannot provide people with the courage and strength to change their lives.

This can only come about by a change of heart, and this is what Prophetic teaching is all about. In the view of Said Nursi, of all the teachings of the Prophets, the most exalted is that of God's oneness. Although through philosophy the mind might arrive at a concept of monotheism, such knowledge is able to reside in the heart only among those who follow Prophetic guidance. He states:

> It is because Divine beauty and perfection are to be seen with the heart in the affirmation of Divine unity and perceived by the spirit that all the saints and holy people have found their sweetest illumination and most delectable spiritual sustenance in repeated recitation of 'There is no god but God,' the profession of Divine unity. Because Divine grandeur, magnificence, and glory, and the absolute sovereignty of the Eternal One are realized in the profession of Divine unity that God's Noble Messenger (Peace and blessings be upon him) declared: "The best thing I and the Prophets before me have said is: "There is no god but God."[338]

3. Revealing the mystery of life. A third way in which the Prophets have benefitted humankind is by revealing the mystery of life itself, as a gift flowing from the eternal life of God. According to Nursi: "The essential nature of life also looks to the pillar of 'belief in the Prophets,' and proves it indirectly. The universe was created for life, and life is the greatest manifestation of the Pre-Eternal Self-Subsistent

---

[338] *The Rays*, The Second Ray, First Station, p. 17.

One, His perfect inscription, His most beautiful work of art. Eternal Life shows Itself through the sending of Prophets and revealing of scriptures, for if there were no Books or Prophets, that Pre-Eternal Life would not be known."[339]

He goes on to say that just as we know someone is alive by their speech, so also we know that God exists and is alive through the Word that God speaks through the Prophets. One could say that the Prophetic revelations manifest the self-communication of God's own life[340] to humanity or, as Said Nursi puts, it the Scriptures are "the rays, manifestations, and communications of that pre-eternal Life."[341]

> Yes, the infinite miracles bestowed by God on the Prophets (Peace be upon them) each one being like a confirmation of their mission; the heavenly blows dealt to their opponents, each being like a proof of their truthfulness; their individual perfections, each one being like an indication of their righteousness; their veracious teachings; the strength of their faith, a witness to their honesty; their supreme seriousness and readiness to self-sacrifice; the sacred books and pages held by their hands; their countless pupils who through following their paths attain truth, perfection and light, thus proving again the truthfulness of the teachings; the unanimous agreement of the Prophets—those most earnest warners—and their followers in all positive matters; their concord, mutual support and affinity—all of this constitutes so powerful a proof that no power on earth can confront it, and no doubt or hesitation can survive it.[342]

In other words, God has confirmed the mission of the Prophets in many ways, through miracles, by defending them against their opponents, by the Sacred Books which they delivered, and by generations of pious believers who have followed the Prophets' teaching and example. God has confirmed the truthfulness of their message, their moral uprightness, their seriousness of purpose and, in their innumerable followers, the process whereby God makes use of the mission of the Proph-

---

[339] *The Flashes*, The Thirtieth Flash, The Divine Name of Ever-Living, p. 434. Cf. also, *The Words*, The Tenth Word, Second Part of the Addendum, p.122.

[340] *The Words*, The Tenth Word, Introduction, p. 72.

[341] *The Flashes*, The Thirtieth Flash, The Divine Name of Ever-Living, p. 434.

[342] *The Rays*, The Supreme Sign, First Chapter, p. 142.

ets to change human hearts and open paths to truth, goodness, and genuine happiness. In this way, the eternal mystery of life which had always resided in God comes to be communicated to humankind, so that by following the Prophetic message men and women can live in a way that produces benefits for themselves and work for the welfare of others.

Belief in the Prophets, according to Said Nursi, is a pillar of faith because it is through the Prophets that life's deepest mystery has been revealed.

> The cosmos was created for the sake of life, and life is in turn one of the supreme manifestations of the Living, Self-Subsistent and Eternal One. It is one of His most perfect designs, one of His most beautiful arts. The eternal life of God shows itself only through the sending of messengers and the revelation of books. If there were no books or Prophets, then eternal life would remain unknown. When a man speaks, he is recognized to be alive. Similarly, it is the Prophets and revealed books that make manifest the words and decrees of the Being Who, from behind the world of the unseen that is veiled by the cosmos, speaks, talks, and emits His commands and prohibitions.[343]

This must be considered the greatest blessing for humankind that has come through the Prophets. Through Prophetic revelation, ordinary men and women can come to know something of God's own eternal life. If it were not for the Prophets, the cosmos would act as a veil to conceal God's reality and His beautiful Names and Qualities. However, through the Prophets, the veil is lifted and the cosmos itself is revealed to be God's masterpiece of creative art, a path by which humans can be guided to praise and proclaim the magnificence of the Creator. What greater benefit could the Prophets be imagined to provide for the happiness of humankind than their being bearers of the revelation of God's eternal life?

---

[343] *The Words*, The Tenth Word, Second Part of the Addendum, "What one can learn from the Prophets," p. 122.

Democracy and Societal Values:
an Evaluation of Social Ethics

S aid Nursi was not a political scientist, nor was he interested in carrying out a theoretical analysis of the nature of democracy, a term which hardly ever appears in the *Risale-i Nur*. His famous statement "I take refuge in God from the Satan and politics"[344] is an indication of the extreme skepticism with which he viewed political developments.

More than politics, what Nursi was interested in was society. Specifically, he was concerned with the values by which human societies are governed and the way that the prevailing political, economic, and social structures reflect and sustain those values. For Nursi, these are key questions that have to be answered by every nation, if their society is not to become a vehicle hurtling forward without direction or brakes.

Nursi recognizes that societal values are founded on the philosophical standards that people adopt. From their philosophical understanding of life in common they derive the values that are then instilled into society. Where do people look to find that philosophy of life? Is its source the postulates of human reason, or does it come from revealed information whose origin is outside and beyond human experience?

Nursi roots the divergent ethical systems in the recourse to what might be called a "materialist" or "spiritual" philosophy of life. This is an issue that goes beyond any specific religion. On the one hand, for example, a Muslim or Christian could follow a deeply religious way of life and adopt spiritual values which would inspire and direct that person's involvement in society. The pious Muslim studies and learns

---

[344] *The Letters*, p. 317.

guidance from the Qur'an; the Christian seeks to apply what he has
found in the Bible. Through the study and meditation on God's revealed
message, a religious believer can compile a truly spiritual set of values
by which he or she can live in the public sphere.

On the other hand, another person might identify himself as
Muslim or Christian, but his societal values might derive entirely from
a materialist understanding of the world. Despite that person's claim
to religious adherence, the way he lives in the world is actually determined by his adoption of a materialist philosophy. This is precisely
what Nursi judges to have occurred in the course of European history. People who claimed to be Christians were in fact trying to create a
social and political system on the basis of incompatible principles.

In many places in the *Risale-i Nur*, Nursi notes the divergence
between the societal values proposed by modern civilization and the
vision of society presented by the Qur'an. To Nursi the Qur'anic vision
offers a set of values which should characterize a humane, just, and
dignified society. This Qur'anic ethic differs only in details from what
had been proposed by all the Prophets before Muhammad, hence it is
a vision that Muslims share with "true Christians" who are followers
of the Prophet Jesus. Jesus' Christian followers sought to build European society on these Prophetic values, but this effort was sabotaged
from the beginning by their reliance on an alien philosophy, that of
Greco-Roman thought.[345]

In the 18th and 19th Centuries, by way of the naturalist and materialist philosophical systems proposed by the scholars of the Enlightenment, even the vestiges of Prophetic teaching which remained in
European civilization were attacked and abandoned. Thus, the Enlightenment philosophers set themselves the task of building "modern
Europe" on principles of their own making. Modern Western civilization, according to Nursi, is the fruit of their labors. Since the principles on which they based the new civilization were the result of their
human rational speculations which rejected the teaching of the Proph-

---

[345] *The Words*, pp. 119–120, 379–382, 664–666.

ets, modern civilization offers a very different set of values which should characterize social relations.

When Nursi looked at Turkish society of his day, he saw that the same process which had previously occurred in Europe was taking place in his own country. Adopting the notion that religion was an obstacle to progress, many in the Turkish Republic were attempting to replace religious values and way of life with ways of acting derived from modern Europe. Often these changes were justified in the name of democracy. Consequently, the proponents of this "democratic" revolution opposed the dissemination and study of the *Risale-i Nur* as well as other value systems based on revealed teaching.

In his defense in the Afyon court, Nursi pointed out the futility of the campaign to replace a religious outlook with one of secular modernity. "No sort of progress or civilization can take the place of religion, or righteousness, or the learning of the truths of belief in particular, which are the innate need of the people of this country, who for a thousand years have enlightened the world with their religion and heroically preserved their firmness of faith in the face of the assaults of the whole world."[346] Nursi appealed to democratic and patriotic principles to defend himself against the treatment he and the students of the *Risale-i Nur* had received at the hands of state authorities.

> Although the patriotic service they have performed for this country and its government has been greater than a police force of thousands, and is worthy of recognition and appreciation, it has been misinterpreted and we have been arrested, as though deliberately on behalf of some foreign power. Our work and businesses have gone to ruin and our wretched families and children have been left weeping and destitute. Which laws of democracy does this conform to? Which just decisions of which just judges?[347]

Those who promote modern values claim that they are simply interested in providing a good life for the majority of the people. However, when this concept of "the good life" is examined carefully, it

---

[346] *The Rays*, The Fourteenth Ray, p. 379.
[347] Ibid., p. 562.

becomes clear that it is a "deceptive fantasy."[348] The concept is usually limited to providing for bodily needs, based on the supposition that if people have food in their bellies, a roof over their heads, and access to medical treatment, they have achieved "the good life."

To Nursi, this is a short-sighted understanding of the true needs of humankind. A person also has spiritual needs, which cannot be met by modern facilities. Concentrating on the limited goals of the good life ultimately reduces man to a tame animal, a well-fed, well-cared for pampered pet, but an animal nevertheless. Nursi writes:

> O foolish friend! Do you suppose your life's duty is restricted to following the good life according to the requisites of civilization and to gratifying the physical appetites? Do you suppose the sole aim of the delicate and subtle senses, the sensitive faculties and members, the well-ordered limbs, the inquisitive feelings and senses that make up your life is restricted to satisfying the low desires of the base soul in this fleeting life?[349]

The basic problem, according to Nursi, is that modern civilization has clouded people's minds so that they are unable to see the value of the life of the spirit. Modern societies focus on the immediate, temporal, and ephemeral, and find it difficult to see beyond immediate gratifications to questions of eternal importance. "At this time, due to the domination of European civilization and the supremacy of natural philosophy and the preponderance of the conditions of worldly life, minds and hearts have become scattered, and endeavor and favor divided. People's minds have become strangers to non-material matters."[350] Instead of seeking the truly good life intended by God for people, men and women are caught up in a rat race of seeking wealth, prestige, and political power in the mistaken fantasy that these things will bring them happiness.

The psychological toll of modernity is high, and people can become frozen into inactivity. Modern man, "since his thought is submerged in philosophy, his mind plunged in politics, and his heart is giddy at

---

[348] *The Words*, The Thirteenth Word, p. 167.
[349] *The Words*, The Eleventh Word, p. 139.
[350] *The Words*, Twenty-Seventh Word, p. 496.

the life of this world," is unable to evaluate seriously questions of eternal weight. He becomes dulled to reality and unable to take serious decisions and exercise his creativity in a positive direction. "Through philosophical investigation and natural science, and the seductive amusements of dissolute civilization and its intoxicated passions, sick philosophy has both increased the world's frozen state and inaction, and made denser heedlessness, and increased its opaqueness and turbidity, and caused the Maker and the hereafter to be forgotten."[351]

By contrast, Nursi holds that the teaching of the Qur'an "gives the world a transparency and removes its turbidity." Nursi insists on drawing the contrast between the values of materialist societies and those based on Divine guidance. He points to five characteristics of "modernity" which are destructive of human relations, rather than enhancing them, as do religious values. Firstly, modern civilization relies on force rather than reasoning or persuasion, and it is thus characterized by aggression. Secondly, modern values are oriented toward self-interest and characterized by selfish competition. Thirdly, modernity is based on the principle of conflict and characterized by constant strife. In modern life, what links people one to another are ethnic and nationalist bonds, which are marked by judging others to be enemies. Finally, the immediate motivation for action is immediate gratification.[352]

These five principles, which have an immediate bearing upon Nursi's evaluation of democracy, can be summarized as follows: 1) might makes right, 2) self-interest and competitive edge, 3) the law of the jungle, every man for himself, 4) ethnic and nationalistic chauvinism, 5) I can do what I want and keep what I have. Nursi regards these principles as both destructive of human relations and self-destructive of the individual human person. To these "modern" values Nursi contrasts the teaching of the Qur'an, which is based on truth rather than force, goodness rather than greed, service rather than self-

---

[351] *The Words*, Twenty-Fifth Word, p. 451.
[352] *The Letters*, Seeds of Reality, aphorism 61.

ishness, unity rather than racism and nationalism, sound guidance rather than hedonism.

What does all this have to do with democracy? As I mentioned at the beginning, Nursi did not write a treatise on the principles of democracy. No one could claim that Nursi was opposed to the notion of democracy and in the early years of his life, before he turned away from public issues, he was much involved in the life of the early years of the Republic.

However, the principles by which he judged democracy were those elucidated in the *Risale-i Nur*. If democracy can be seen to be compatible with the values found in Divine guidance, it can be an effective way to provide for people's material needs. But when democracy gets manipulated by materialist principles to become an instrument for forcing the will of some on others, when it becomes an instrument for pursuing self-interest, promoting competition, justifying greed, and establishing racial or national superiority over others, Nursi is the first to criticize and condemn.

Theology of Hope and the State of Societies Today

The beginning of change is hope

More than one hundred years ago, in 1911, Said Nursi delivered the Friday sermon at the Umayyad Mosque in Damascus. At that time, Nursi's fame had already spread to Damascus, one of the cultural capitals of the Ottoman Empire, and an estimated 10,000 worshipers attended the sermon. In the sermon, Nursi took a self-critical approach to the problems of the international Islamic community, outlining six basic societal illnesses and prescribing a Qur'an-based solution for each.

In Nursi's view, Muslim societies were beset by defects that prevented Muslims from making material progress and developing effective social organization. He saw Muslims as stagnating vis-à-vis Europeans. He put it: "I recognize that what has allowed foreigners, Europeans, to make progress and fly toward the future while we are arrested and kept, in terms of material development, in the Middle Ages, are six dire sicknesses."[353] In *The Damascus Sermon*, he names the illnesses afflicting Muslim societies and prescribes the remedy for each.

The six illnesses are: 1) despair, and the remedy is hope; 2) deceit, with honesty as the remedy; 3) enmity, for which the remedy is love; 4) disunity, whose cure is fraternal unity; 5) despotism, for which the remedy is Islamic dignity; 6) selfish individualism, whose remedy is consultation.

Of these diseases of society, the one to which Nursi devotes the most time is the first, that of despair or hopelessness. The sense of

---

[353] *The Damascus Sermon*, p. 26.

despair is enunciated by both scholar and the person in the street in phrases like: "There's nothing we can do"; "Nothing ever changes"; "What can I do? I'm just one person"; "The problems are too deep-rooted and long-standing to fix"; "It's all a hopeless mess." Nursi's view is that when people are sunk in such attitudes of despair, there is no point in looking more deeply into the basic problems of social life, for they will not be motivated to try to do anything to improve matters. Before people can commit themselves to work for change, they have to have hope that things can be made better, that their hard work has a chance of succeeding, that they can actually make a difference, that their efforts are not destined for failure because of some adverse hand of fate.

If the economic, political, and social condition of people is ever going to improve, according to Nursi, they have to begin by having hope: hope that with God's assistance they can actually change the present situation. For Nursi, hope is the basis of a positive attitude toward life, whereas giving way to despair is already a form of death.[354] Nursi holds that hope is what motivates people to change, grow, and develop, while despair results in stagnation and the triumph of status quo. He states: "In life, hope and thinking favorably of things are life itself. While to think the worst is despair, the destroyer of happiness and slayer of life."[355] In this light, I propose to examine Nursi's theology of hope and by applying it to his words in *The Damascus Sermon* I will try to see the relevance that Nursi's insights on hope might have for the situation of the world in which people find themselves today.

To the modern reader, two questions will inevitably come to mind. Firstly, after the dramatic political, demographic, and technological changes that have occurred in the world in the past 100 years, is Nursi's analysis of Muslim society, dating from 1911, still relevant for our time? Secondly, remembering that *The Damascus Sermon* was delivered in the context of an Islamic worship service, can the content of the sermon be said to have any relevance to non-Muslims and to non-Mus-

---

[354] *The Letters*, Seeds of Reality, p. 547.
[355] *The Words*, "Gleams," p. 744.

lim societies? I hope to explore both these questions in the course of this paper.

Facing "the mountains of the future"

For Nursi, human desires are without limit,[356] and because of this, human hopes are equally unlimited. Peoples' hopes are not restricted to what they have, for the more they have the more extensive and ambitious are their desires for having more.[357] The irony of human life, according to Nursi, is that man is cursed with a "short lifespan and dull mind, in the face of infinite pains and hopes"[358] which he vainly strives to attain. Most of these hopes come to nothing, and it can seem that the only element of human longing that persists is the pain.[359]

It is here that belief in the resurrection of the dead and eternal life plays a key role even in the pursuit of happiness here on earth. For the believer, human hopes are not an absurdity leading only to frustration and disappointment, for such hopes are destined to be ultimately validated in eternal life. Hope of eternal life transforms absolute despair into absolute hope[360] and gives the believer the psychological and spiritual tools by which calamity and failure can be faced with equanimity.

When persons who are not fortified with religious faith meet setbacks and disasters, they have nothing to fall back on and are likely to get discouraged and eventually admit defeat. However, those who face life's vicissitudes with religious hope can see God's hand even in failed plans and accept it as part of the human condition. Nursi says: "We may hope from Divine mercy that each minute of the calamity is equivalent to a day's worship."[361] One can see the application of Nursi's views

---

[356] *The Words*, The Twenty-Ninth Word, Second Aim, p. 540.

[357] "Man's hopes, desires, pains, and tribulations reach as far as the eye and the imagination can stretch." *The Words*, The Third Word, p. 30.

[358] *The Words*, The Thirty-Second Word, Third Stopping-Place, p. 662.

[359] *The Words*, The Seventeenth Word, Second Station, p. 227.

[360] *The Rays*, The Fourteenth Ray, p. 436. Cf. *The Words*, The Tenth Word, First Part of the Addendum, p. 110.

[361] *The Flashes*, The Tenth Flash, p. 72.

to the struggle for social change for, if God accepts the good intention of a people's efforts to change their lot for the better as a form of worship, such people will be encouraged that they ought to keep striving after their worthwhile goal, even when they do not see the visible results.

When they rely on themselves instead of depending upon God's strength, people are led by the frustration of their hopes to fall into despair, which is a kind of half-life or living death. In one of his characteristic parables, Nursi contrasts the believer and unbeliever as two brothers journeying in a strange land. At a crossroads, one placed his trust in God and followed the corresponding path, while the other did not. "The miserable one is suffering torments of desolation, despair, and loneliness, while the fortunate one [who placed his trust in God] is enjoying himself, full of hope, longing, and a sense of belonging. Moreover, the unfortunate one sees himself as a prisoner subject to the attacks of wild beasts, while the fortunate one is an honoured guest who is on friendly terms and enjoying himself with the strange servants of his generous host."[362] Nursi's point is that when one approaches the challenges of life with the hope that there is something beyond this "vale of tears," that person will be better prepared to operate joyfully and successfully in this world.

Nursi opines that God in His wisdom teaches that people should live their earthly existence in a perpetual balance between hope and fear.[363] If people were to act solely upon their hopes, they would be dreamers, heedless of the problems of life around them, complacently ignoring whatever they find uncomfortable or annoying, and basically achieving nothing. On the other hand, a man driven solely by fears would be frozen into inaction, anxious about uncertainties and imagining dangers everywhere, afraid to take any action for fear it could make matters worse, worried about what might happen if the status quo equilibrium were upset. So that humans would be led to spend their days in a healthy balance between hope and fear, God has left

---

[362] *The Words*, The Eighth Word, p. 48.
[363] *The Words*, The Twenty-Fourth Word, Third Branch, p. 352.

people uninformed about some key issues, most obviously the hour of one's death.[364]

Fear has a role to play in human life, but people need hope if they are to move forward, make progress, and prosper. This is the basis of one of Nursi's most severe criticisms of members of the secular elite in his country. He states that by trying to cut people off from their religious roots, the nation's leaders have been depriving the people of the basis of their hopes, and in doing so have prevented them from taking the necessary steps toward achieving their heart-felt desires. In an eloquent passage he states:

> Are the benefits of the disaster-stricken, the sick, and those who have despaired of life... to be found in the way of a European-type, irreligious civilization? For those unfortunates want a light, solace. They want a reward in return for the calamities they have suffered. They want to take their revenge on those who have oppressed them. They want to repulse the terrors at the door of the grave, which they are approaching. Through false patriotism, people like you plunge a needle into the hearts of those unhappy victims of disaster who are much in need of compassion, soothing, and healing, and worthy of them. ... You mercilessly destroy all their hopes! You cast them into despair! ... Is that how you provide benefits for the nation?[365]

On the other hand, when people are rooted in hope they are able to achieve much both at a personal level and for society in general. Living with the hope that one's life has meaning and is directed toward an imperishable goal, a person is motivated to strive for the good of all. Nursi calls this hope a "powerful point of support in the face of calamities and harmful things" and notes how his hope has led him to strive, as a Kurd, for the good of all Turks: "Yes, according to race, I am not counted as a Turk, but I have worked with all my strength, with complete eagerness, in compassionate and brotherly

---

[364] *The Flashes*, The Twenty-Fifth Flash, "Message for the Sick," p. 274.
[365] *The Letters*, The Twenty-Ninth Letter, Sixth Section, p. 493.

fashion, for the God-fearing, and the disaster-stricken, the elderly, the children, the weak, and the poor among the Turks."[366]

Any discussion of Nursi's theology of hope must include his "Treatise for the Elderly." In this extraordinary essay, the already-aged Nursi writes to others facing the rigors of old age in order to build up their hopes. In the introduction, he writes: "Respected brothers and sisters who have reached the age of maturity! Like you, I am elderly. I am going to write the 'hopes' I have found in my old age and some of the things that have befallen me, out of a desire to share with you the lights of consolation they contain. ... God willing, your pure and sincere dispositions will make the lights I have seen shine more brightly and strengthen the hopes I have found."[367]

In the "Treatise for the Elderly," Nursi outlines sixteen "hopes" that can sustain people in their senior years. More precisely, the treatise consists of sixteen faith-based reflections upon aspects of hope that can give strength and consolation to those beset not only by the physical aches and pains that seem to multiply as one ages, but even more by "spiritual afflictions": a sense of diminished capabilities, feelings of being "washed up" or "over the hill," loneliness, and anxieties concerning the inexorable approach of the moment of death. This Treatise is one of Nursi's most original—I know of nothing like it in Islamic literature—and deserves its own comprehensive study devoted to an exposition of its themes. Here, however, I am more interested in making the link to Nursi's societal concerns in *The Damascus Sermon*.

In this context, there is a fascinating passage in the "Seventh Hope" taken up by Nursi in the Treatise. In an autobiographical passage, Nursi recalls a meditation he had years before at the "Kale" or citadel of Ankara. In a level of honesty and humility that is not commonly met in spiritual writings, Nursi admits that in the course of his meditation he was led almost to the point of despair before he ultimately found a basis for hope. He writes:

---

[366] Ibid., p. 495.
[367] *The Flashes*, Twenty-Sixth Flash, "For the Elderly," p. 287.

> One time at the start of my old age I went to Ankara invited by some worldly people there. At the close of autumn I climbed to the top of the citadel, which was far more aged, dilapidated, and worn out than me. It seemed to me to be formed of petrified historical events. The old age of the season of the year together with my old age, the citadel's old age, mankind's old age, the old age of the glorious Ottoman Empire, the death of the Caliphate's rule, and the world's old age all caused me to look in the most grieved, piteous and melancholy state in that lofty citadel at the valleys of the past and the mountains of the future. As I experienced an utterly black state of mind in Ankara encompassed by four or five layers of the darkness of old age one within the other, I sought a light, a solace, a hope.[368]

I can personally relate to the setting of this passage. Having spent the past three years (2009–2011) living in Ankara a short ten-minute walk from the citadel, and having gone there often at sunset to read Vespers from my daily prayer book overlooking the city, I can testify that, yes, the Ankara citadel is truly aged, dilapidated, and worn out, even more so than I. It inevitably conjures up visions of the Seljuk and Ottoman rulers who built and maintained the citadel in good order, just as today's citadel in ruins is a stark reminder that those days of history are over and finished. Ankara has found new life as capital of the Turkish Republic, but the new buildings that house the government ministries are miles away on the lowland plain. The citadel exists as a reminder of past glories and days never to return, just as in my case the angina and shortness of breath that accompanied my walk to the top were a constant reminder that my days of trekking and recreational climbing were past.

Nursi's point is that the old age of each one of us and its symptoms are but a reflection of what is happening in history. Nations, cultures, governments, economic systems, renewal movements, political parties, labor unions, ethnic associations, and religious institutions all age, get tired, and eventually begin to break down. The Second Law of Thermodynamics in physics that predicts irreversible entropy in physical systems has a certain counterpart in the social order.

---

[368] Ibid., p. 293.

Practically speaking, this means that just as the aging individual must look outside himself or herself to overcome despair and find light, solace, and hope, so also must societies and societal institutions. When Nursi looked toward the past and the future without the light of faith, he found only empty graves on all sides. "Nothing ever changes." "What is the use of it all?" However, when his Islamic faith and the teaching of the Qur'an gave him new eyes he could find the strength he needed to continue his struggle, to face "the mountains of the future," to carry on his mission in life. He says:

> Through the light of the Qur'an, belief showed that the grave that would open its eyes and look at me in the future was not the mouth of a well, but rather the door to a world of light, and that the highway which stretched to eternity beyond it led not to nothingness and non-existence, but to existence, a realm of light, and eternal bliss. Since faith demonstrated this to a degree that afforded utter conviction, it was both a remedy and a salve for my afflictions.[369]

Nursi is affirming that true strength, whether it be for achieving material progress or fighting injustice and oppression, comes from the guidance and determination that God grants to those who believe in His Word. In *The Damascus Sermon* he notes five types of strength that Muslims can derive from Islamic faith. 1) The Qur'an, the Sacred Scripture of Islam, urges material, moral, and spiritual progress and shows itself to be a universal teacher and master. 2) The intense need and back-breaking poverty of many Muslims can be the source and raw material of development and industry. 3) The freedom that comes from living in accord with the *shari'a* encourages striving for good things, promotes competition, inspires enthusiasm, overcomes jealousy, and refuses to tolerate despotism. 4) Islamic faith teaches that both the oppression of others and servile submission to oppression are forbidden to Muslims; 5) The dignity of Islam in upholding the Word of God is attained by achieving material progress and true civilization.[370]

---

[369] Ibid., p. 294.
[370] *The Damascus Sermon*, pp. 36–37.

Armed with these faith-based elements of strength, Nursi holds that Muslims have sound reason to hope that they can make the needed changes that will bring about material progress and good government, as well as peaceful and just societies. In *The Damascus Sermon* Nursi is speaking not as a political scientist but as a preacher and encourages his hearers to respond faithfully to the message of the Qur'an.

He is aware of the defects in Muslim societies and he seeks to offer Qur'an-based remedies. He states that the struggle for change should be non-violent. If it is a case of opposing the universal enemies of humanity—poverty, ignorance, and disunity—this must be done by promoting education and knowledge. If it is a question of confronting the Muslim community's external enemies, such must be faced with persuasion and love. Nursi writes in an addendum to *The Damascus Sermon* which he added shortly after World War II:

> We shall therefore wage jihad with the weapons of science and industry on ignorance, poverty, and disunity, the worst enemies of upholding the Word of God. As for external jihad, we shall refer it to the decisive proofs of the Illustrious Shari'a. For conquering the civilized is through persuasion, not through force as though they were savages who understand nothing. We are devotees of love, we do not have time for enmity.[371]

A second conclusion that Nursi draws is that change must not come about by aping Western or European institutions. He holds that history shows that when Muslims faithfully followed the teachings of their religion, they were blessed also with material prosperity and national sovereignty, but when they departed from the straight path of their religion and accepted ideas and mores incompatible with Islamic teaching, they became weak. Nursi felt that something similar happened in European history. At first, Europeans lived according to the teachings inherited from the Prophet Jesus and his faithful followers, but then they abandoned those teachings for the human speculations of philosophers. He writes: "European civilization is not founded on virtue and guidance, but on lust and passion, rivalry and oppres-

---

[371] *The Damascus Sermon*, First Addendum, Third Part, p. 78.

sion; up to the present, the evils of civilization have predominated over its virtues."[372] If Muslim societies simply imitate what they see done in Europe and adopt its practices, they will not achieve healthy change; they will look ridiculous, like a man dressed in woman's clothes.[373]

Nursi's objection to the uncritical adoption of European ways is not only that they are not compatible with Islamic teaching and traditional Muslim practices, but also that Western civilization is not a good model to be imitated in terms of hard work and diligence. He believes that modern values rooted in Western societies can ultimately lead to laziness and self-destructive behavior. In a severe yet still apposite critique, Nursi states:

> Western civilization has both impoverished man and increased his needs. It has destroyed the principle of frugality and contentment and increased wastefulness, greed, and acquisitiveness ... By encouraging people to take advantage of the means of dissipation, it has cast unfortunate needy people into total laziness. It has destroyed the desire for effort and work. It has encouraged depravity and dissipation, and wasted their lives on useless things. It was made those needy and lazy people ill. Through abuse and promiscuity, it has been the means of spreading a hundred kinds of diseases.[374]

The Damascus Sermon and Today's Hopes

Nursi delivered the Damascus sermon one hundred years ago. In the past century, the world has witnessed dramatic political, demographic, and technological changes; many of the everyday items that people around the world use today were unknown to Nursi and his contemporaries. What relevance can Nursi's analysis of societies have to events that make up today's headlines?

Specifically, the so-called Arab Spring of 2011, with popular uprisings in favor of democratic government occurring in Tunisia, Egypt, Yemen, Bahrain, Syria, Libya and elsewhere appears as evidence that ordinary people in many Muslim societies are taking to the streets and

---

[372] *The Damascus Sermon*, First Word, p. 38.
[373] *The Damascus Sermon*, First Addendum, Third Part, p. 86.
[374] *The Damascus Sermon*, A Letter, p. 130.

risking their comfort, well-being, and even their lives to protest unjust, unrepresentative, and despotic governments. It is tempting to imagine what advice Nursi would give to such people were he still alive. From his writings we can extrapolate the values he proposes on which social change should take place, and on this basis we can presume that he would have approved of much of what has been happening in these various uprisings.

Firstly, the protests are a sign of courage and an expression of dignity. One imagines that Nursi would have viewed the largely non-violent protests in favor of democratic rule as a sign of hope, a sign that people would no longer be willing to accept the inevitability of tyranny. Nursi held that to accept tyranny or to bow down before despots was a violation of Islamic dignity, a form of collaboration with oppressors and wrongdoers. He held that despair in the face of oppression was a great sin. "Despair is a most grievous sickness of communities and nations, a cancer. It is an obstacle to success and opposed to the truth of the Sacred *Hadith*, 'I am with my bondsman who thinks favorably of Me.' Despair is the quality and pretext of cowards, the base and the impotent, and it does not exhibit Islamic courage."[375]

Secondly, the protests express the triumph of truth. Nursi, both in his life and in his writings advocated telling truth to power, for which he paid a high price by frequent imprisonment, house arrest, and even consignment to a mental institution. In *The Damascus Sermon* he challenged government leaders with the following words: "Rulers of this land! If you want success, conform to the Divine laws! Otherwise you will fail."[376] Thus, one can envision Nursi approving the chants and placards in the streets, the truth commissions, and the court cases to prosecute instances of violence and corruption.

It seems to me that he would insist that the purpose of such commissions and efforts must be a truthful acknowledgement of what happened in the past and the establishment of mechanisms of monitoring and control to insure that truth be served in the future. One

---

[375] *The Damascus Sermon*, Second Word, p. 44.
[376] *The Damascus Sermon*, First Addendum, Third Part, p. 75.

cannot imagine Nursi approving of truth commissions motivated solely by revenge or aimed at settling scores. Not all that is true, he writes, need be stated publicly.

> "Either truthfulness or silence." Everything you say must be true, but it is not right to say everything that is true. If on occasion it is damaging, then be silent. There is no fatwa for lying. Everything you say must be the truth, but you do not have the right to say everything that is true, because if it is not sincere, it will have a detrimental effect and truth will be spent on wrong.[377]

Thirdly, and most important, Nursi would approve of the Arab Spring Protests because they were faith-based and exhibited many Islamic values. He would have rejoiced to see the protesters line up for Prayer in Cairo's Tahrir Square and to hear Friday sermons expound the Islamic values by which Muslims should be governed. The fact that the protests were overwhelmingly non-violent, Nursi would have seen as a witness to Islam as a religion of peace. The ongoing discussions of citizens meeting to explore reasonably the path to true democracy Nursi would have seen as an exhibition of Islamic consultation; the fact that the democratic movements have not, at least up to now, been hijacked by some new strongman gives hope that the new governments to be established will be just and representative.

Nursi would not have been surprised that in several nations, the government authorities have responded to the pro-democracy demonstrations with repressive force. Nursi was not naïve about political realities, and he had personal experience of oppression by self-serving government officials. He would encourage today's abused protesters to respond with the same weapons that Nursi himself used: those of courage, forgiveness, and patient endurance.

Nursi always advocated the cooperation of true Muslims and Christians to renounce disunity and to work together to defend the values that come from God's Word. He would thus have approved the reports of Egyptian Muslims and Christians joining hands Midan at-Tahrir to form protective barriers around those who bowed down

---

[377] *The Damascus Sermon*, Fourth Word, p. 49.

or knelt to pray. In contrast to a secular model of revolution that would simply replace one ruling group with another, or a Marxist model that would pit social groups and ethnic groups one against the other, Nursi would have supported those faith-based uprisings that are rooted in the values of truth, dignity, love, consultation, and non-violence.

All this is possible if people have real hope that the future can be better than the past. Nursi is convinced that God has promised to Muslims that they will prevail in their thirst for good government, honesty, material progress, and effective social institutions. But the danger of despair is always present; after every temporary setback, people are tempted to give up the struggle. For this reason, he holds, it is important that Muslims encourage one another and be agents of hope to one another. He writes: "The most effective remedy for the ghastly troubles and hopelessness of the world, especially at this time, especially for those smitten by disaster and the *Risale-i Nur* students in particular, is to console and hearten one another and to strengthen one another's morale, and like true, devoted brothers to pour balm on one another's sorrows and afflictions and with true compassion, soothe one another's troubled hearts."[378]

In conclusion, I think that it is obvious that Said Nursi still has much to say to us all, even a century after he delivered his *Damascus Sermon*. His advice is still sound, his insights concerning the future shows his spiritual intellect. Not only can Muslims learn much that can improve the lot of the societies, but Christians and all persons of good will can find hope and inspiration and consolation in the teaching of the *Risale-i Nur*.

---

[378] *The Rays*, The Fourteenth Ray, p. 495.

The Supreme Sign:
an Invitation to Wonder

1. Coming before God in prayer

One of the themes that Muslims and Christians can fruitfully study together is that of the variety of ways in which we each come before God in prayer. On the one hand, there is the ritual prayer, which is best done in community. For Muslims, this is the five times Daily Prayers (*salah*); for most Christians, the preeminent act of communitarian worship is the Eucharist, with its various names in English. The Orthodox call this central act of worship "The Divine Liturgy"; Catholics usually refer to the sacred service as "The Mass"; Protestants most often refer to this commemoration of Jesus' last meal with his disciples as "The Lord's Supper."

In addition, both Muslims and Christians know a variety of forms of private prayer, all of which are aimed at helping the believer come close to God, to learn from God's Word, and to be guided and strengthened by God's grace. Islam and Christianity have various terms to denote specific forms of private prayer, and various Islamic and Christian spiritual traditions have placed their own emphasis on certain types of communication with God.

To take one example from the many that could be chosen in the Christian tradition, the "Benedictine" distinction of four stages of prayer is typical. As taught and practiced by the monks of St. Benedict, the "ladder of prayer" begins with 1) *lectio* (slow and attentive reading of the Bible), 2) *meditatio* (thinking about, pondering the Scripture text), 3) *oratio* (responding to God in prayer with mind and heart), and 4) *contemplatio* (remaining in quiet stillness in the presence of God.) Other great spiritual masters like John of the Cross, Teresa of Avila,

Francis of Assisi, and Ignatius of Loyola have offered their own variations and emphases on the basic forms of Christian prayer; a comparable history of spiritual instruction and practice characterizes the Orthodox and Protestant traditions of Christianity.

The Muslim community has an equally rich history of private prayers. Above all, there is the Qur'an, which not only contains many prayers but also teaches Muslims the best way to pray. Beyond its Qur'anic foundation, the Islamic tradition offers still more prayers, ranging from the *Jawshan al-Kabir*, which is said to have been taught to Prophet Muhammad by Jibril (Gabriel), to the medieval collections of prayers composed by saints like 'Abd al-Qadir al-Jilani and Ash-Shadhili which are still very popular among Muslims. Other Muslims enrich their prayer life with Sufi poetry like that of Mawlana Jalal al-Din Rumi's *Mathnawi* or the diwans of Yunus Emre, Hafiz and Sa'di.

2. *Tefekkür*

The Qur'an repeatedly calls people to reflect on their lives, on the ways that God has blessed them, on the world around them, and on the myriad signs of God's power and love. The term most often used for this type of reflective observation is *tefekkür* (*tafakkur* in Arabic); 17 times the Qur'an praises those who do *tefekkür*. God affirms the wisdom of those who take the time to reflect on God's many gifts. They should reflect on the mercy of God's sending Prophets (Qur'an 16:44), on God's power over death (Qur'an 39:42), on the exalted nature of the Qur'an (Qur'an 59:21), on the impermanence of worldly wealth (Qur'an 2:266 and 10:24), on the blessing that is married life (Qur'an 30:12), on the evils of wine and gambling and on the prudent use of worldly goods (Qur'an 2:219).

Above all, the Qur'an encourages reflection on the signs of creation that will lead individuals to knowledge of God and God's qualities. A believer who reflects on the specific blessings of creation should arrive at an awareness of God's mercy and power and respond by giving glory to God. It is taught in the Qur'an: "*Those who reflect (yatafakkaruna) upon the creation of the heavens and the earth (saying): 'Our Lord, You did not create this in vain. Glory be to You!'*" (3: 191). *"It is*

He who spread out the earth and placed therein firm mountains and rivers; *and of each kind of fruit He created two pairs. He causes the night to cover* *the day. Surely in that are signs for people who reflect (yatafakkaruna)"* (13: 3). *"From it he brings forth for you vegetation, olives, plants, vines* *and all kinds of fruit. In that, surely, there is a sign for people who reflect"* *(yatafakkaruna)* (16:11). *"From [bees'] bellies comes out a syrup of differ-* *ent hues, wherein is healing for mankind. Surely in that there is a sign for* *those who reflect" (yatafakkaruna)* (16:69).

Humans are invited to reflect on the serious purpose for which God created the heavens and earth, on the value of rivers and mountains as landmarks, on the wondrous variety of fruits, on the amazing origins of honey and its astonishing healing powers, and on the alternation of night and day. Since most people take such things for granted and fail to see evidence of the hand of a loving, purposeful Creator, the Qur'an challenges people to look more deeply at the world around them to discover the signs (*ayat*) of One who has created a universe filled with blessings for humankind.

3. The Supreme Sign

In the *Risale-i Nur*, Said Nursi takes up the Qur'an's exhortation and undertakes a thoughtful reflection on the message contained in the signs of God's Names and Attributes in the natural world. This is the central focus of the portion of the *Risale-i Nur* entitled "The Supreme Sign." Nursi introduces the treatise with the Qur'anic verse: *"The seven heavens and the earth and all that is in them extol and glorify Him, and there is nothing that does not celebrate His praise, but you do not understand their praise"* (17:44).[379] In this verse God teaches that God is glorified by: 1) the heavens, 2) the earth, and 3) all that is in them. Then God states the sad reality that we humans do not understand this constant glorification that all creation is giving to its Maker.

Nursi takes up the challenge to understand how the heavens, the earth, and all that is in them glorify God. He begins with the heavens. To establish the narrative of his reflections on creation as the supreme

---

[379] *The Rays*, The Seventh Ray, The Supreme Sign, First Chapter, p. 130.

sign of God's Names and Attributes, Nursi employs the literary device of a traveler who happens upon and wanders through an extremely beautiful kingdom.

4. The marvels of creation

Nursi directs the readers' attention firstly to the heavens, to God's supporting the hundreds of thousands of heavenly bodies, many of which are larger than the earth. These objects travel in paths on which they do not collide. The light of the stars burns continually without any visible fuel. The huge planets and even greater stars are obedient to the will of the Creator; their movements maintain a balance and continually sweep space clean.

Given the dramatic advances in science and astronomy in the past half-century since Nursi's death in 1960, we have much more information about the universe than was known in his day, and the sciences of astronomy and theoretical cosmology have taken opened up new avenues for speculation. Low frequency radio telescopes and gamma-ray observations permit scientists to examine distant galaxies, and theorize about spinning pulsars, supernova remnants, nonthermal filaments, black holes, cosmic strings, and other features of the universe that were unknown at Nursi's time. Quantum physics, most recently with the discovery of the Higgs Boson, has revolutionized the way we understand the movements and interrelationships of sub-atomic particles.

As the complexity and immensity of our universe become more and more apparent to us, our appreciation of God's creative power and wisdom is not diminished but enhanced. We know now that God's ongoing act of creation goes far beyond anything that humankind had ever previously imagined. How great, how powerful, how intelligent must be the God who has done and continues to do all this! Every new advance in astronomy and theoretical physics invites us to engage in deeper reflection about the Creator of this amazing universe.

Moving from the distant cosmos, Nursi finds much material in the atmosphere of our planet for his prayerful contemplation. The first object of contemplation is the aggregation of clouds that God in His wisdom has placed in the heavens in order to water the earth and to moderate the temperature of life on the planet. Nursi's *tefekkür* leads him to poetic heights in contemplating the appearance and disappearance of clouds as being similar to an army that, under orders to a commander, alternately makes its presence known and then hides itself again.

Nursi's contemplation turns to the wind, which he sees as a servant of the Creator bringing heat, light, electricity, and breath to all beings on earth, as well as transmitting sound, enabling sailing ships, and helping in the pollination of plants. One of the gifts brought by the wind is rain, with its concomitants thunder and lightning, so essential for plant and animal life on earth that it can be called "the very embodiment of Divine mercy."

Nursi is not personifying or romanticizing natural elements like clouds, wind, and rain; rather, it is the very unconscious and inanimate nature of these creatures that demands the agency of a wise Creator who has set them on the path of serving humanity. Nursi writes:

> The inanimate, lifeless cloud that resembles carded cotton has of course no knowledge of us; when it comes to our aid, it is not because it takes pity on us. It cannot appear and disappear without receiving orders. Rather it acts in accordance with the orders of a most powerful and compassionate commander.[380]

Nursi's *tefekkür* next leads him to contemplate thunder and lightning. Instead of being a frightening threat as they are for dumb animals, lightning and thunder are, for the believer, harbingers of good news. They announce the coming of rain, giving glad tidings not only to farmers and to their fields and livestock, but to all who satisfy their hunger by eating the fruits of the earth. Thunder and lightning also challenge self-absorbed individuals who are turned in on themselves and consumed by their own problems and shortcomings to look up and discover the world as a beautiful and purposeful act of creation. The thunder and lightning invite the self-centered person:

> Lift up your head. Look at the miraculous deeds of the most active and powerful being who wishes to make himself known. In the same way that you are not left to your own devices, so too, these

---

[380] Ibid., p. 132.

phenomena and events have a master and a purpose. Each of them is made to fulfill a particular task, and each is employed by a Most Wise Disposer.[381]

5. The riches of the earth

Turning his attention to the earth, Nursi's sense of wonder does not permit him to settle for one metaphor, but in his amazement he produces a variety of images. In its desirability as a place to reside, the earth is like a luxurious palace or hotel. In the variety of its delights, it is like a lavish banquet filled to abundance with many kinds of food. In its discipline and sense of order it is like the most modern and advanced of military instillations. In its wealth of opportunities for relaxation and enjoyment, it is like a Luna Park, recreation area, or picnic grounds. In offering immense possibilities for teaching, the earth is like a classroom or laboratory of an august university.

The movement of the earth around the sun catches Nursi's attention, and he thinks of the double movement of the Mawlawi dervishes as they whirl about their own center and simultaneously propel themselves forward in motion around the *semahane*. As it travels on its circuit, the earth resembles a great ocean liner loaded with food and equipment moving purposefully on its assigned path and carrying its passengers safely through the days, months, seasons, and years.

In his reflection, Nursi looks at the seeds of plants growing on the earth and he notes how they are transported from one place to another by the winds. In this way they take root and propagate, producing a wide variety of grains, fruits, and vegetables. The miracle of springtime when hundreds of thousands of tiny seeds, virtually identical to the human eye, burst forth from their winter "death" to a wide variety of abundant new life is for Nursi one of the strongest arguments in favor of the "Supreme Harvest," the resurrection and life after human death. The same Creator who produces new life annually in the natural world can just as easily resurrect those humans who have died. Moreover, the generosity and care of the Creator who pro-

---

[381] Ibid., p. 134.

vides sustenance for his creatures with the tender mercy of a mother nursing her child is evidence of the "solicitousness, mercy, and wisdom of the All-Merciful and the All-Compassionate."

When Nursi turns his thoughts to the unruly and ferocious movement of the seas, he sees it as a sign of God's sovereign mercy that the seas are kept within their bounds and not allowed to overrun the earth. As he casts his gaze reflectively into the depths of the ocean, Nursi observes the spectacular underwater world of fish, shells, coral, and marine gardens. He marvels that this world of astonishing variety and beauty, which is virtually inaccessible and almost unknown to man, is maintained in a medium of salt water and microscopic life forms.

When he turns from the seas to reflect on fresh-water bodies like rivers, streams, and lakes, his meditation focuses on the wealth of mercy of "the Compassionate One, the Lord of Glory and Generosity." So great are the blessings for humanity of rivers and fresh-water channels that they seem to flow into our world from Paradise itself. Commenting on the saying that "Four rivers flow forth from Paradise," Nursi says that the magnitude and benefits of the great river systems like the Nile so far surpass their apparent earthly sources that they seem to be flowing from Paradise itself.

Nursi's meditation in The Supreme Sign turns to the mountains and plains. In an observation that presages our knowledge about tectonic plates, he notes that the mountains arise from seismic forces and movements and form an escape valve for relieving underground pressures. In this he sees the wisdom of an intelligent Creator who maintains the earth in equilibrium by building into its structure a release for internal tensions.

> The mountains emerge from the earth by the command of their Sustainer, thereby alleviating the turmoil, anger, and rancor that arise from disturbances within the earth. As the mountains surge upward, the earth begins to breathe; it is delivered from harmful tremors and upheavals, and its tranquility as it pursues its duty of rotation is no longer disturbed.[382]

---

[382] Ibid., p. 138.

Mountains also serve as storerooms for water, minerals, and other substances useful for human well-being. Mountains also serve as landmarks to guide the weary traveler, as the Qur'an itself affirms: *"And He set up on the earth firm mountains, lest it shake under you; as well as rivers and pathways, so that you may be guided. And landmarks, and by the stars they are guided"* (Qur'an 16:15–16). Just as the mountains' grandiose panorama inspires men to reflect on the sovereign majesty of the One who produced them, so also the utility of mountains for human life reminds people of God's tender, compassionate care.

When Nursi turns his attention to the plant kingdom, he sees that from the mightiest tree to the tiniest seed, the vegetative world proclaims the glory of its Creator. This eloquent praise, found both in individual plants and in the totality of plant life, points to an intelligent Creator. The vast range of genus and species, their great variety in appearance, and the wide scope of beneficial usage for humankind all point to a Maker with genuine concern for His creatures. The various uses by which God provides for humans are evidence that the Creator has prepared this world for humankind. Whether it be plants whose existence is essential for human life in the form of food, wood, or medicine, or plants like flowers whose only purpose is to delight the eye and nose, they all proclaim the Creator's glory by their nature.

As is the case with flora, so also with fauna. When Nursi looks at the animal kingdom, he observes that the immense variety of animal life is all giving glory to God, indicating God's mercy, and proclaiming, "There is no god but He." The animal world teaches three great truths. Firstly, it shows that creation cannot be conceived as occurring by chance or random selection; the life of animals must come from One capable of wisdom and purpose. Secondly, symmetry and proportionality of innumerable species demands the existence of one who is all-Powerful who can accomplish this feat. Finally, the production of such an exhaustive variety of animal life from the mingling of virtually identical eggs and sperm shows the infinite capacity of the Producer.

Advances in biology and DNA mapping have in no way invalidated Nursi's arguments. Rather, science has shown the way that the life of animate beings has developed. The more that humans discover the workings of nature, the more deeply are they able to appreciate the fruits of creation and to understand the song of praise that all creation gives to its Maker.

6. The wonders of humankind

Finally, Nursi's reflection turns to humanity itself. The first sign of God's providential care is His sending the Prophets. Nursi considers the line of Prophets as essential to guiding the transition of men from the animal to angelic state. As humans learn to think and act less like animals and live more like angels, they are in need of guidance. God did not abandon humankind in their need and in order to bring them to the fullness of their true humanity, God sent the Prophets with His message of light. Through the Divine guidance found in the Prophetic word, people became able to transcend their lower natures and attain their Divinely granted lofty status.

The Prophets are the strongest manifestations of God's power, mercy, and blessings for humankind. As the most perfect of representations of humankind, the Prophets have been models for human emulation. Through them God was able to warn and correct those who were going astray and lead them on the Straight Path. Belief in all the Prophets has become a great source of strength for humans down through the centuries and a sign of God's loving providence. Beyond all else, the unanimity of the Prophets' teaching provides humankind with a sure sign of the truth of the message God has communicated.

After the Prophets, the next great proof of God's power and mercy are the saints, those remarkable individuals who have been formed by the Prophetic message. He is speaking of the "profound, original, exacting scholars who affirm the claims of the Prophets," whose lives, attitudes, and accomplishments have been shaped by their reflections on "affirmative matters connected with faith." Nursi is referring to the theologians, the legal scholars, the mystics, and the wise teachers whose faith-based lessons have applied God's Prophetic word to generations of believers.

The moral force of this great assembly of intelligent, conscientious thinkers and teachers down through the centuries gives the ordinary believer a powerful strength that he or she would not otherwise have. Nursi asserts that "the belief and firm conviction concerning the Divine unity that all luminous intellects possessed, despite their varying capacities and differing, even opposing, methods and outlooks, was the same, and that their steadfast and confident certainty and assurance was one."[383]

Their united voice in affirming and praising the one Creator enables the believer to rely not only on his own abilities and insights, but to be able to draw upon generations of accumulated and transmitted wisdom. Nursi is speaking not only of the intellectual heritage handed on by generations of scholars, but also the spiritual heritage transmitted by "thousands or millions of spiritual guides who were striving toward the truth and attaining the vision of certainty in the shade of the highway of Muhammad (peace and blessings be upon him)."[384]

Enriched and emboldened by this long history of belief in God and His Prophets and Books, the believer can confidently affirm "the necessary existence, the unity, and the sacred attributes of the Creator of this cosmos." Finally, in his meditation, Nursi turns beyond the phenomenal world to that of the Unseen. What can he learn of God's attributes from a reflection on those things that humans would have no way of knowing had they not been revealed through the Prophets?

> There comes with the truths of revelation and inspiration proceeding from the One All-Knowing of the Unseen, a testimony to His existence and unity far stronger than testimony of the universe and created beings. He does not leave Himself, His existence and His unity, only to the testimony of His creatures. Rather, He speaks with a pre-eternal Speech consonant with His own being.[385]

So, finally, his meditations on the One God manifested in creation lead Nursi to the truths revealed through the Prophets. From the Seen he proceeds to the Unseen. He has learned much on his mental voyage through the realms of creation, and is now prepared to listen

---

[383] Ibid., p. 145.

[384] Ibid., p. 143.

[385] Ibid., p. 147.

directly to the words of the Creator. *Tefekkür* focused on the creation will always lead back to the Author of that creation. He began the spiritual exercise of *tefekkür* in response to the Divine command to "reflect," and his reflections conduct him through the phenomenal world and back to the Unseen Commander. In the process, Nursi has affirmed the purposeful nature of creation and moved to give glory to the Creator. In the words of the Qur'an: *"Those who reflect upon the creation of the heavens and the earth (and say): 'Our Lord, You did not create this in vain. Glory be to You!'"* (Qur'an 3:191).

For Nursi, there are two great vehicles by which God has communicated His message to humankind; the message of revelation, found in the Qur'an, and the message of creation, found in the universe. As a Christian, I find Nursi's insight compatible with my own understanding of God's communicating His word to humans. Ilia Delio, a colleague of mine who specializes on the relationship between science and religion, has seen a similar approach in the 13th Century Christian theologian Bonaventure[386]: "Creation, Bonaventure wrote, is like a book from which we can gather insights about the Creator. The natural world bears the footprints of God, and the human person is created to read this book and know God."[387] I feel that this is an insight with which Said Nursi would have agreed, and it shows, once again, another of the commonalities between those for whom the One God is at the center of their consciousness.

* * *

As I noted at the beginning of this book, I don't consider myself an expert on the thought of Said Nursi. I have many friends who have devoted their lives—for 20, 30, 40 years and more—to the study of the *Risale-i Nur* in its original, somewhat archaic Turkish. They study the work alone at home, in student residences, in weekly *sohbetler* (conversations). These are people from all walks of life—professionals, laborers, housewives, civil servants, students. Some of these men and women I consider to be true experts in the thought of Said Nursi. At least

---

[386] St. Bonaventure (1221–1274), Christian philosopher and theologian
[387] Ilia Delio, *The Emergent Christ*, Maryknoll, NY: Orbis Books, 2011, p. 13.

they have always been able to give convincing and inspiring answers to any questions that I put to them.

But it may be the very lack of expertise that I bring, that of a guest at the *sohbet* who arrives from a different land and culture, formed in and professing a different religious path from the Islam shared by Said Nursi and his students that may give some of my insights their value. I have learned a lot from Nursi and am grateful to him for his ideas and his example of constancy and devotion to God. I feel that my life—including my faith life—has been greatly enriched by my encounter with the *Risale-i Nur*.

Thomas Michel, Washington,
D.C., 14 August 2012

INDEX

A

Abraham, children of, 144
Abu Bakr, 101
Abu Jahl, 101
Ad, 102
Afyon, 55, 109, 186, 221
Ahl al-Kitab, 147
Ali, Caliph, 204
alms, 101
Ankara, 230
anxiety, 120
Arab Spring, 234, 236
Armenians, 4, 28
Ash'ariyya, 158
Asian religions, 12, 139
Atatürk, 3

B

Baghdad Pact, 33
Batsanov, S., 127
Bible
   textual change, 18
blindness, 120
body
   divine possession of, 118
Bonaventure, St., 249

C

caregiving, 122
causality, 18
change, social, 228

choice, human, 156
Christianity, 146
   Christian history, 18
   purified, 22
   true and false, 19
Christians, 147
   freedom of, 28
   martyrs of a sort, 29
   pious, obedient, 21
civilization
   and decline, 133
   clash of, 146
   European, 57, 222, 229, 233
   future, 68
   Islamic, 69, 79, 133
   materialist, 59
   modern, 52, 54, 61, 66, 67, 141, 191
   Qur'anic, 57, 59
   values, 147
   withdrawal from, 72
class divisions, 136
class struggle, 38
colonialism, 92
compassion, 121
conflict, 145
consultation, 93, 95
consumerism, 63, 64
creation, 68, 242
   Book of, 249
culture of violence, 143

D

Dajjal, 23, 26, 135
Damascus Sermon, 3, 41, 92, 131, 225, 232
  relevance, 226, 234
  society sicknesses, 94
Day of Judgment, 100, 134, 172, 174
death, 116, 124
deceit, 90
Delio, Ilia, 249
democracy, 224, 236
Denizli Court, 65
depression, 113
despair, 88, 98, 113, 225, 235
despotism, 92
dialogue, 189
  of religions, 12, 143, 147
  of salvation, 184
disunity, 92
Divine determining, 101, 151, 152, 153, 154, 157, 189
DNA, 246

E

earthquake, 98
Elderly, Treatise for, 60, 71, 128, 230
Emirdağ, 44
enmity, 91
environment, 144
Epistle to the Hebrews, 174
Erzincan, 98
eternal life
  object of human yearning, 77
ethics, 79
Europe, 3, 52, 53, 62, 107, 134
  two sides, 14, 141

F

Fatih Madrasah, 185

fatwa, 90
Final Judgment, 179
forgiveness, 47
  for enemies, 48
  for Jews, Christians, 49
freedom, 192
  human, 151
French Revolution, 59
fulfillment, human, 156

G

Gandhi, 46
Gewirth, Alan, 145
Ghawth al-A'zam *See* Jilani, 'Abd al-Qadir
globalization, 53
God
  as Disposer of Affairs, 131
  as Teacher, Lover, and Pardoner, 133
  -consciousness, 79
  nature of, 132
Gog and Magog, 59
Great Gathering, The, 177

H

hadith, 235
health
  and monotony, 121
  versus fatalism, 122
heavenly religions, 143
Hell, 91, 102, 129, 134
  The Fire, 171
Higgs Boson, 242
Holy Spirit, 210
honesty, 90
hope, 89, 237
  eternal life, 227
  Treatise for the Elderly, 230
human dignity, 93
human rights, 65, 136

Huntington, Samuel, 146
hypochondria, 121

I

Ibn 'Arabi, 204
ignorance, poverty, disunity, 4, 28
ikhlas (sincerity), 9, 132, 160
Imam-i Rabbani, 71
individualism, 93
Insan al-Kamil (The Perfect Man), 203
interreligious marriage, 141
Islam, 146
    religion of peace, 236
Islamic identity, 92
Israiliyyat, 19

J

James, Letter of, 206
Jawshan al-Kabir, 240
Jesus, 54, 146, 164
    already come, 27
    Christians' love for, 16
    collective personality, 23
    return in the future, 25
Jews, 12
jihad, 2, 11, 132
    and violence, 133
    of the word, 134
Jilani, 'Abd al-Qadir, 204, 240
John the Baptist, 209
Judaism, 146
justice, 38, 165

K

Kastamonu, 44
Khidr, 168
Korean War, 147

L

Lailat al-Qadar, 76

Light Verse, The, 183
loneliness
    of the sick, 122
love, 3, 39, 91, 233

M

Madrasah az-Zahra, 4, 66
Mahdi, 135
Mardin, Şerif, 186
Martin Luther King, 46
martyrdom, 120
Marxism, 136
Masihiyyat, 19
meaning of human existence, 126
meditation, reflection *See tefekkür*
Medresetü'z-Zehra *See* Madrasah az-Zahra
Message for the Sick, 117
Misri, 114
modernity, 51, 52, 222, 223
    demonic influence, 61
    psychological toll, 56
    virtues, 64
morals, 213
Moses, 164
Muhammad, 146, 150, 187, 211
    Night Journey, Ascension, 188
    Prophet, 164, 169, 204, 248
murid, 110
Muslims and Christians, 26
    cooperation, 24, 62
    friendship, 33, 141
    shared values, 80, 94
    solidarity, 236
    unity, 2, 8, 11, 31, 126
Mu'tazila, 158, 159
mystery, 149

N

Noah, 102

Nursi
  accusations against, 45
  commander of militia forces, 73
  early education, 185
  New Said, 74
  Old Said, 73
  pacifism, 43
  passive resistance, 45
  prisoner in Russia, 74
  social ethics, 38
  spiritual crisis, 60

O

old age, 113
other religions
  spirituality, holiness, 13

P

Paradise, 119, 171
  rivers, 245
Patriarch Athenagoras, 33
peace, 49, 80, 82
  eternal, 40
  inner transformation, 44
  interior, 41
  two pillars
  justice, forgiveness, 36
  universal, 41
People of the Book
  friendship with *See Ahl al-Kitab*
Pharaoh, 102
philosophy
  contrast to Prophecy, 212
  Enlightenment, 144
  of life, 219
  political, 220
politicians, 76, 133
Pope John Paul II, 8, 35, 42, 79
Pope Paul VI, 8, 184

Pope Pius XII, 5, 33
poverty, 136
Prophet
  blessing for humankind, 217
  characteristics, 207
  Christian concept, 211
  Jewish, 146

Q

qabd, 110
qadar, 150
Qarun, 102
Qur'an
  Madinan suras, 188
Quraysh, 169

R

racism, 110
Rahner, Karl, 207
reconciliation, 46, 83
responsibility, 149
resurrection
  argument from springtime, 173
  arguments for, 169
  objections, 168
Risale-i Nur students
  and earthquake, 104
  collective personality, 40
Russian Revolution, 4

S

saints, 18, 247
Sarıyer retreat, 71
School of Joseph, 74
Second Vatican Council *See* Vatican II
Selahaddin Çelebi, 32
self-fulfillment, 144
Shari'a, 77, 233
Shi'a, 16

sickness
  of society *See* Damascus Sermon
  of the heart, 111
  remedy, 122
signs (of God's qualities), 241
sincerity, 30
  rules for, 30, 190
Sincerity
  Treatise on, 9, 32
social complacency, 38
social sin, 100
Solomon (Sulayman), 200, 202
Soviet Communism, 59
spiritual remedies, 117
spiritual sickness, 109, 110
splitting of the moon, 150
springtime, 167, 169
St. Paul, 163, 193
Straight Path, 247
Sufi, 173
Sufyan, 23, 135
Supreme Sign, 236, 248

T

tafakkur See tefekkür
Tahir Pasha, 185
tahrif See Bible
Tahrir Square, 236
taqdir, 150, 158
Tasbihat, 111
tefekkür, 240, 241, 249
Thamud, 102
tolerance, 192
truth, 143, 235
tsunami, 97
Turkish Republic, 3, 221

U

Ubeyd (Nursi's nephew), 75
Umar, Caliph, 192
Umayyad mosque, 92
Umma, 92
UNESCO, 126
unity, 92
Urfa, 5
USA, iv

V

values, divine, 143
Van, 141, 185
Vatican II, 2
Vengeance, 129
vicegerent, God's, 154, 156
violence, 130
  and youth, 130
  antidote to, 130
  class-based, 136
  culture of, 126
  strength for the victims of, 128

W

wisdom, 8, 112, 200
World Wars, 134
worship of God
  and caring for the sick, 121
  in other religions, 140
  natural world, 12

Y

Yüksel, Bayram, 147
Yusuf (Joseph), Prophet, 202

Z

Zoroastrian, 192